LAMESTAINS

LAMESTAINS

GRUNGE, SUB POP AND
THE MUSIC OF THE LOSER

NICHOLAS ATTFIELD

REAKTION BOOKS

For my little group

Published by
Reaktion Books Ltd
Unit 32, Waterside
44–48 Wharf Road
London N1 7UX, UK

www.reaktionbooks.co.uk

First published 2023
Copyright © Nicholas Attfield 2023

Printed and bound in Great Britain by TJ Books, Padstow, Cornwall

A catalogue record for this book is available from the British Library

ISBN 978 1 78914 706 3

CONTENTS

Preface: If Only They Knew

GRUNGE! Everyone's least-favourite word.

Writing now, in 2022, it has hardly any currency any more – in music, anyway. Think about it. To say that you are 'into' grunge today is a bit like saying you are 'into' the gavotte or something. The word immediately evokes ancient history, past rather than present, a sad attachment to hollow abstractions and empty hype. Few bands will straightforwardly self-describe as 'grunge', and few promoters will sell a show in this way, unless of course they are courting the attention of a very specific, probably middle-aged white male audience, all society's bad backs and bald patches, yesterday's news, not today's. Revivals are reluctant, and strangely literal: search 'Sun Puddle'. And academic thought still prefers punk to grunge as the true domain of its subcultural studies. Only, really, in the lexicon of fashion do grunge and its resurrections persist, in couture rather than cacophony.

Yet grunge was, once upon a time, as legitimate a genre as any other, in musical and social terms. That much is clear from the countless artists of the early 1990s who rejected it as a label that they wanted nothing to do with – a typical gesture, this, in response to the awareness that a genre had firmly and meaningfully taken root. Why, then, the rapid decline into embarrassment? A bubble burst. The massive media hype surrounding grunge, and the frenzy that descended on Seattle and the Northwest in those days, badly damaged its claim to authenticity. Critics wondered if it had ever actually existed in any genuine sense at all, a creation of someone other than real local artists themselves. In turn this generated a stark division between paranoid Seattle 'insiders' (who despise the term 'grunge') and exploitative, ignorant 'out-of-towners' (who use it freely).[1] I note in this regard that two of the most widely read books on grunge are 'oral histories'. That is, their (New York-based) authors minimize their personal presence by offering only very short introductions to their own books, otherwise relying on direct quotation from those who were there – or thereabouts – at the time. These author-editors have to use the word 'grunge', or else their intended international audiences won't be drawn to their front covers. But they also almost completely remove themselves from the picture, precisely for fear of becoming part of the hype problem their interviewees lament.[2]

It's not just a matter of media hype, however – or what we usually mean when we say 'the media'. Record labels, those who 'mediated' the music in the first place, are obviously also implicated in the rise and fall of grunge. Here there are multiple targets of different kinds. Yet it doesn't seem fair to blame the tiny northwestern independent labels with the elaborate punk names, many of which folded quickly, or, if they survive, remain unprofitable to this day. Likewise, if the problem is hype, it seems futile to arraign the massive multinational labels – Geffen and A&M and Reprise – for doing what they did best in releasing Nirvana's *Nevermind*, Soundgarden's *Superunknown* and Mudhoney's *Piece of Cake*.

A more promising culprit for the demise of grunge has proven a label somewhere in the middle. This is the most famous Seattle indie rock label of them all, Sub Pop Records, officially founded in 1988. On the one hand, Sub Pop and its creators, Bruce Pavitt and Jonathan Poneman, are now celebrated worldwide as having brought to our ears countless artists that defined that late 1980s moment through their loudness, their abrasiveness, their awkwardness and their poignancy – Bands that Could Be God, to use a punk phrase of the time.[3] Mudhoney were Sub Pop's house band, while Nirvana and Soundgarden were among their early roster; it is hardly surprising that Sub Pop very deliberately became as synonymous with the 'Seattle sound' as Motown with Detroit, or Factory with Manchester. Yet, as is sometimes forgotten, the label also released the first singles and early recordings of Hole, L7, Afghan Whigs, Smashing Pumpkins, Flaming Lips, Fugazi, Dinosaur Jr and endless others. As the presence of these non-Seattle bands testifies, Sub Pop was instrumental in launching the first wave of American 'alternative' rock in the early 1990s, refocusing the rock music industry so that it took note of its most out-of-the-way corners.

On the other hand, Sub Pop destroyed its key scene at the same moment as it showcased it. As the label's notoriously hyperactive publicity machine invited the world to listen to Seattle rock as principally commodified within its wares, it inevitably changed the scene for good and, in the eyes of most 'insiders', for the unalterably worse. To paraphrase the view of one of Sub Pop's earliest artists, Chris Eckman of the Walkabouts, the label excelled at overselling what was supposed to be undersold.[4] Blown up into a worldwide phenomenon, Seattle rock could no longer be the small, friendly, intense, ignored and therefore 'pure' or 'family' environment that it had once perhaps been, that it increasingly appeared to be in retrospect, and on which Sub Pop had fed so profitably. Instead it could only be a lumbering behemoth on the brink of collapse – and collapse it soon did, taking numerous high-profile lives with it. Grunge died when it was born; and back in the late 1980s it was Sub Pop, the most influential of all the genre's labels, that pulled the trigger.

To take one example only of this interpretation of the label, I have in front of me the book *The Strangest Tribe* by the American historian Stephen Tow, published in 2011. This is clearly invested in the huge importance of Sub Pop, the unique place from which it emerged, and the power of the music it sold. But still I sense Tow's righteous indignation in passages like the following:

> Sub Pop was not the first independent label in Seattle. It was, however, the first label that had serious aspirations beyond the region. Sub Pop would act as a major label, sans the funding. Unlike previous local and national indie labels, Sub Pop would brand and unabashedly hype itself and its bands. Sub Pop bands would emerge in the Mudhoney mold: Play loud and distorted music. Don't be too sincere. And preferably sport long hair, don shorts, and wear Doc Martens.[5]

For Tow, Sub Pop was an independent that crossed a line, in that it behaved as a major, dishonourably and insincerely commodifying what it found, turning itself into a cookie-cutter or sausage machine that then churned out all these long-haired, shorts-wearing clones – ultimately starting the process that made grunge and Seattle into the embarrassing things that, much like the fashion choices, we might now rather forget. But more even than that, it is implicitly Sub Pop's efforts that motivate Tow's overall quest for authenticity, to get back behind and underneath the commodification process to find some 'real' Seattle scene, some greater truth lying just out of sight. 'If only they knew!', he writes in introduction, of the way that the global public ('they') cling to stereotypes of the grunge artist as propagated by the likes of Sub Pop.

I want to preface the present book by admitting that, now some three decades after grunge's peak popularity, I do not share this confidence in the search for the 'real' Seattle. To be sure, the books I mention above are remarkable collections of research, their sheer level and intensity of detail perhaps unprecedented in music writing of this kind, and the pleasures they bring to fans of this scene uncontested. Is any ground as hallowed, or as well trodden, as that of Seattle grunge? Nonetheless, I see an irony in the project of trying to look away from Sub Pop as from a distorting lens, since *this* label, as much as any institution of its day, was responsible for making this Seattle music a special subject worthy of investigation in the first place. Without Sub Pop, I am sure, we would not attempt to speak of a coherent and meaningful Seattle 'scene' or 'sound' (as opposed to a hot mess of musical entrails like anywhere). Far less would we talk in the glowing terms of 'fusion' rock, or of Seattle as a 'melting pot' – the home of a 'rag-tag cabal of misfits from all quarters of the region who converged in tiny ugly spaces and made them beautiful and alive', as Jonathan Evison once poeticized it, writing of Sub Pop's inaugural band Green River.[6]

I am not so interested, then, in trying to distinguish between a real and a hyped Seattle scene, Seattle's true music from grunge, Sub Pop from 'genuine' independent labels, what actually happened from what we think happened, insightful insiders from interfering out-of-towners, art from capital. Instead I begin from what I suppose is a more realistic position, one that keeps Sub Pop in the centre of the picture as a creative force playing profitably across these divisions. Whatever its claims to independence from a corporate mainstream, whatever its presentation of total loser ineptitude ('Going out of Business since 1988' was an early slogan), and whatever the small scale of its initial operations, one thing is certain. Sub Pop worked fully within the commercial capitalist framework of popular culture. The challenge it met was that of living well within capitalism, not independently of it, and to do so it mobilized all kinds of well-worn rock attitudes of the 'alternative', the countercultural, the sick and angry, and the forgotten and primitive – furious, violent, broken loser men in search of the great god riff, or maybe just a good time. In this, actually, it closely resembled many of its 'indie' competitors;

what set Sub Pop apart was that it enjoyed enormous and sustained success. It continues to do so today, almost forty years on, its identity partly still based around the grunge freehold on which it gathers its rents. And that in turn prompts the question that I want to ask across the chapters of this book. Clearly, exponentially growing numbers of people wanted to buy. But what exactly was it that Sub Pop was trying to sell?

Introduction: Big Dumb Rock

> If every time you write a piece you realise you are stealing
> from someone, why do you keep playing?
> Guido Chiesa to Kurt Cobain, September 1989[1]

THERE ARE, OF COURSE, many responses to the question I posed at the end of the preface. What was it that Sub Pop was trying to sell? An 'alternative' is one obvious answer. An 'alternative' music, specifically an 'alternative rock', a genre that seems rooted in commercial independence and contrary punk attitude, and that countless listeners, and countless authors, have found to be straightforward, naive, serious, special, unique, personally resonant and expressive, and across all these various senses 'authentic'. That is, a pure thing that is true to itself and nothing else, a treasure worth finding and defending against those who would taint it, particularly by selling it like sweets to as many people as possible. Sub Pop's early advertising often made exactly these kinds of claims about the musical products they sold. They were 'pure' and 'honest' and 'fun' and 'real', created by innocent backwoodsmen with no experience of the 'industry', in a distant out-of-the-way town forgotten by bands and agents and ignored by their tour routes. Many critics have since followed suit.

At the same time, it is equally easy to argue that Sub Pop offered no alternative to anything whatsoever. What it sold was cast in standard formats (7", EP, LP, CD, cassette), divided up into standard-sized chunks (three-minute songs, or thereabouts), and almost exclusively performed by white men often indistinguishable from their rock forebears. It was, in other words, a commodity immediately familiar, recognizable and assimilable to many, despite – or, actually, because of – its abrasive exterior aspects, the screaming voices and whining feedback for which it became famous. Moreover, though Sub Pop's earliest releases may have reached only a few select audiences, theirs was a commodity soon placed far and wide by distributors in an effort to gather more and more listeners worldwide; the label aimed, in short, at a standard commercial narrative of growth. And anyway, before we even get to that, isn't 'alternative rock' a tautology in the first place? Hasn't rock always been a rowdy and rebellious and liberating alternative? If so, its opposite number is 'pop', which rock's advocates deem clichéd, anodyne, unchallenging, factory-produced, something you could bake a soufflé next to (to paraphrase a quip of Gina Arnold's).[2] From this perspective, Sub Pop's grunge was no alternative at all, but simply a latter-day 1980s descendant of the same ageing family line of rock patriarchs.

Actually, the people most aware of these contradictions – these alternatives that were no such thing – were Pavitt and Poneman, the founders of Sub Pop themselves. So powerfully aware, in fact, that they built them directly into their brand identity and their ways of engaging with their growing fanbase. Alongside all their claims of purity and integrity went constant self-effacing and self-undermining quips about how what the label was peddling was a 're-hash', a 'rip-off', a 'scam', 'reactionary' – that it was simply a case of making money from old rope by means of empty 'hype' (in fact, 'hype' became a key Sub Pop buzzword, second only to 'loser'). One of the label's earliest admirers and promoters, the British rock journalist Everett True, reflected on this in 2001 in the following way: 'John [Poneman] and Bruce [Pavitt]'s stroke of marketing genius was to push rock'n'roll as rebellion – an ancient credo – while allowing people to listen to big dumb rock and retain their hipster credibility.'[3] This is perfect.

It captures the core principles of the entire Sub Pop operation. Even better, what it indicates is the paradox at the heart of rock culture, namely that rock is simultaneously anti-mass ideology ('rebellion') and yet greedy for mass commercial success ('marketing genius').[4] Or to put it another way: rock sells individuality and exclusivity to anyone and everyone. This was Sub Pop's house paradox, and ultimately they made it quite literally part of their name. The 'subterranean pop' from which it is derived is really, if you think about it, a contradiction in terms.

The same paradox also provides the key to much of the label's image and much of their marketing. An Australian compilation of 1989, part of Sub Pop's early expansion worldwide, brings together the tracks from the label's first five singles, released over the prior two years. Its song titles recall all of rock's rebellious pet topics of pathology, crime, rage, libido, oppression and liberation: among its tracks are Mudhoney's 'Touch Me I'm Sick', Soundgarden's 'Hunted Down', Swallow's 'Trapped' and Blood Circus's 'Six Foot Under'.

In a brutal pun that draws attention to the mass commercial viability of this stuff, however, the compilation is named 'Fuck Me I'm Rich'. It is not clear how this phrase is supposed to be parsed. It might be a command of the swaggering rock-star masculine libido variety ('Fuck me, I'm rich'), or perhaps an exclamation of surprise that anyone could make money out of such a desperate rock rehash ('Fuck me! . . . I'm rich!'). And that very ambiguity seems to be part of the point, and part of the fun. In his sleeve note Poneman assures the reader – again, sarcastically or not, it is hard to tell – that while *you* might still be buying into 'romantic notions' of rock music's importance, *he* is using the proceeds of the record to buy 'houses, cars, villas on the Costa del Sol! *That's* rock 'n' roll! See you by the pool!'[5]

Originality and Conformity

Comedy, then, was clearly one important part of Sub Pop's appeal and hipster credibility. The hilarious and stylish verve with which Pavitt, Poneman and their colleagues wrote about their operations, their bands and their music, and the biting sarcasm with which they routinely attacked themselves and their fans, were aspects of identity and strategy that set them apart from other record labels, whether 'independent' or 'major', and remains so to this day.

Still, comedy is one obvious register only of the Sub Pop 'scam' of the late 1980s. I think we need to begin by exposing some of the other, rawer nerves surrounding it. If the label's principal joke was that it was making money from an exhausted genre, this also meant an implicit acknowledgement that rock was now at base a charade, something stale and empty, torn apart by its own contradictions and so at best in a perpetual state of crisis. On this point, it is worth noting an interview of September 1989, in which the Italian fanzine writer Guido Chiesa got hold of an unusually candid Kurt Cobain, in those days still a Sub Pop artist, on the phone. In these early interviews, Cobain typically evades scrutiny of himself and his band by saying something brilliantly weird or surreal or out of context – for example when, in a discussion of the relationship between Sub Pop and American youth, he told *Amok* fanzine in 1989 that he used to be 'chairman of the YMCA'.[6] Or when he said to Joe Preston that he got '4 × 8 feet of wood paneling and a turtle neck sweater' for Christmas, and that he had been most inspired musically by the record *Ford Motor Company Presents: Winnebago, the Climax of Life* (apparently 1971 – if it ever existed at all).[7]

The Chiesa interview, though, strikes an entirely different tone, a very much more honest and depressive one. Introducing his conversation with Cobain in print, Chiesa first writes of his impression that the phenomenon of rock has now reached its creative limits. '[W]hat can the future hold', he asks, 'for a music that, less than 25 years after its unofficial birth, is already forced to recycle itself?' One answer, he thinks, is that it will continue its slide into 'irreversible decadence', at best attracting media attention on account of its bare minimum of 'originality' (*originalità* in Chiesa's Italian). In other words, try as they might to write new songs, all the rock artists of the late 1980s can do is move around the same old building blocks, regurgitate the same old mush. They may make headlines, but they can no longer be truly original.

The thing is, Cobain largely agrees with this perspective. Viewing himself for once historically, he says that it is now almost impossible to make anything new as he would like. For every three hundred songs he writes, maybe only one won't have been unconsciously stolen from somebody else. 'We are nothing but the shadow of something that has already been,' he says, wistfully. The best he can do is accept the presence of these ghosts of the past, 'make do' with them; he agrees with Chiesa that the best outcome is that other people might find them as 'honest and agreeable' as he does, that, like him, they might feel the same old 'illusion' conjured up again. This provides just about enough incentive for Cobain as a songwriter; as he explains, writing songs is just what he does, he never wanted to be a 'doctor or a reporter'. But he also agrees with Chiesa that this bleak view of songwriting links to an 'existential nihilism' that sounds out plainly from his music, a sense of there being 'no tomorrow', of living as a 'minority on the verge of extinction'. This is an existence made worse by the 'ridiculous society' of contemporary America, made up almost entirely of 'idiots', of people that he won't try any longer to change or save because they 'don't deserve it'.[8] Cobain's dilemma is as much philosophical and political as it is music-creative; he comes across here as a disillusioned punk-messiah.

These themes would come up again and again over the next few years. In April 1990 a similarly reflective Cobain remarked to Bob Gulla:

> Every band since the mid-'80s has surfaced as a revival act. It's a sure sign that rock is slowly dying. There's nothing like wallowing in the past when everything in the future looks bleak. It happens in every art form. When they're afraid of what's in front of them they always look back.[9]

And again in the lovely, and now little-remembered, liner notes that Cobain wrote for the Nirvana compilation *Incesticide* (Sub Pop/Geffen, 1992), when he described how it was that his band came into existence in the first place:

> We just wanted to pay tribute to something that helped us to feel as though we had crawled out of the dung heap of conformity. To pay tribute like an Elvis or Jimi Hendrix impersonator in the tradition of a bar band. I'll be the first to admit that we're the 90s version of Cheap Trick or The Knack but the last to admit that it hasn't been rewarding.[10]

At least in this statement, I suppose you can say, the older, newly world-famous Cobain sees personal reward rather than just empty repetition and shrinking territory. And it was precisely this kind of double vision, it seems to me, that also holds the key to the situation for Sub Pop. Like Cobain, I think Pavitt and Poneman were well aware of the bleakness of their enterprise in founding a heavy rock label in the late 1980s, swimming against the tide of a post-punk popular music culture in which, as Everett True put it with some disdain, 'you couldn't pick up the *NME* . . . without someone like Toyah or Gary Numan telling you that guitars were old and dead and phallic symbols of repression.'[11]

They knew their early artists and releases were being called the 'ultimate rehash' and 'the last wave', rock's 'epitaph' or, more plainly, 'retro bullshit', and that their best acts were attracting media attention for what seemed their 'parody' and 'mockery' (Soundgarden liked to leave the stage with 'We're Black Sabbath, thank you and goodnight'), if not for their outright 'stealing' (Mudhoney).[12] They knew that their much-vaunted 'Seattle sound' was actually a close relation of the 'New York 1973 Sound' (in the words of one early listener).[13] As critics, they knew their marketing vocabulary was riffing on rock criticism commonplace since the 1970s: even the key term 'grunge', sometimes assumed to have been a Seattle coinage, had been around for well over a decade. And as ideologues, they knew they held no credible political stance to compare to some of the independent punk and hardcore outfits that had inspired them, beyond, perhaps, the fun they made of the capitalist system they embraced. Never did the early Sub Pop label take a strong political stand, and one marker of this is that – unlike, for example, SST Records – only rarely did it publish its artists' lyrics.

At the same time, though, Pavitt and Poneman surely realized that the whole package might itself serve as an attractive identity, a selling point in the market, particularly if grounded in a distinctive regionality and a tone of 'semi-jocular debasement' that emphasized that what was to be taken seriously about it was that none of it was to be taken too seriously.[14] Theirs was a record label, in short, as hipster in-joke about the death of rock, within which it was easy to stress a simple and pointless 'fun' – a crucial early Sub Pop term that evokes the alleged purity, childlike naivety and drug–booze frenzy of the Seattle rock scene, as well as the frivolous 'pop' of the label name. As Poneman claimed, 'It was just a bunch of people having a good time.'[15] Many of the label's bands seem to have soaked this point up. 'Nobody wants to hear a preacher,' says Cobain in a fanzine interview of 1990, taking direct aim at the political hardcore rants of earlier times. 'If you play guitar, you're supposed to have fun.'[16] Or Danny Bland, after the demise of his Sub Pop band Cat Butt in the same year: 'It was an exercise in self-destruction. We were born to destroy ourselves and we did. It was really fun. What I learned was uh – uh – nothing.'[17]

Even so, the label would inevitably have broader appeal than an in-joke might imply. Just because every monster riff was a huge rip-off of something – Soundgarden of Led Zeppelin and Black Sabbath, Nirvana of Motörhead, Mudhoney of the Stooges, as early critics constantly pointed out – Sub Pop's music would still carry that kernel of rebellion in it for a new generation who might not know the hard rock canon of decades past. It could confer, in Cobain's word, the *feeling* as though you were crawling out of conformity's dung heap, even as the label simultaneously drew your attention to the fact that it could offer no such escape, and that you were a loser for thinking this in the first place. Take the most famous grunge riff of them all, Nirvana's 'Smells Like Teen Spirit', a song written in the band's Sub Pop days, and very nearly released by the label. As Cobain told *Rolling Stone* a few months before his death, he was painfully embarrassed by it, not only because he had to play it so often, but because it was 'such a clichéd riff . . ., so close to a Boston riff or "Louie Louie". When I came up with the guitar part, [bassist] Krist looked at me and said "That is so ridiculous." I made the band play it for an hour and a half.'[18]

Still, isn't the fame of 'Teen Spirit' explained by the fact that it has also held the sonic signature of teen rebellion for many: an intensely personal revelation, even as it was experienced through its MTV video alongside millions of other listeners? And, as much as it might pour irony on rock's posturing, doesn't it also simply recreate it? Whatever else it is, isn't it, as Everett True might say, just the big dumb rock all over again, channelling the same aggression and primitivity and toxic white masculinity? This was why, in the continuation of the *Incesticide* notes cited above, Cobain felt the need to make the following demand, finally smuggling in a liberal political position as if by the back door. He had heard that two men had raped a woman while singing one of his songs: 'At this point I have a request for our fans. If any of you in any way hate homosexuals, people of different color, or women, please do this one favor for us – leave us the fuck alone! Don't come to our shows and don't buy our records.'[19]

Energy

This is one of the main things I want to say about grunge in this book. Whatever the hipster cred it once held, whatever its reputation nowadays as a more enlightened alternative to hard rock, and however outspoken certain artists, including Cobain and Cornell, became against various types of discrimination: grunge was still supposed to be *nasty*. The stuff of rock aggression and transgression was threaded through the DNA of its music and lyrics. Its bands loved to shock, to smash the taboos of 'mainstream' society in a way that connected them with their hardcore punk idols and sometimes with fringe social and political views ('no rules means no rules', as hardcore ideologue Steve Albini put it in 1983).[20] This was as true for Sub Pop as for any other 'grunge' label, whether they were releasing the music of artists now fallen into obscurity – Cat Butt's psychotic murder ballads and Swallow's dead-body songs – or those that have become more famous: Cobain's songs about child abuse and murder, Mudhoney's of giving fatal diseases to girls, or TAD's vivid imaginings of captivity and torture.

Of course, all this was easily seen as part of the alternative offered by the label: that its artists were simply honest, liberated by rock to explore the darker side of men's natures, authentically unconfined by the nice rules of what can and cannot be said. In the hands of a clever artist like Cobain, the effort could be poignant. His fractured songs sometimes seem to pity the perpetrator of horrible acts as much as their victim, drawing a tragic loop around the whole of experience. But it was by no means all so sensitively and ambiguously done. As is easily overlooked nowadays, one early Sub Pop Singles Club 7″ was provided by Albini's new band Rapeman (SP40, August 1989). And if this single was a one-off only, the same cannot be said for Dwarves. Dwarves were from Chicago, not Seattle, and in musical style they were more obviously hardcore punk than what most would call grunge; but still, a fact forgotten now, they were one of the label's most prolific artists in the period from 1990 to 1993, second only to Mudhoney, releasing five singles and three LPs. Many of the songs and images on these recordings seem to revolve around themes of misogyny and paedophilia. 'She's Dead' is one of Dwarves's early Sub Pop single titles (SP50, February 1990); *Thank Heaven for Little Girls* is the LP of a year later (SP126); the cover of *Sugarfix* (SP197, 1993) shows a young girl sucking a lollipop. And then there is the climactic line of the song 'Let's Fuck', in which, if the girl is old enough to 'bleed', 'breed' and 'pee', then she's old enough for the singer. This comes from the LP *Blood Guts and Pussy* (SP67, July 1990), the infamous sleeve photography of which manages to convey all its title nouns in one lurid colour image.

It is easy to argue that these kinds of lines and images were never supposed to be taken at face value. From this perspective, they were so exaggeratedly vile that they obviously didn't *mean* what they meant. They were ironic, in other words, a shtick like any other, Dwarves as base as other hardcore bands were fast or loud, poking fun at the excesses of 'horror' punk of an earlier decade while piggybacking on its shock value. But that view very much depended on the listener understanding the cues in a certain way. Many no doubt did, and still do: one response to the thirteen-song, fourteen-minute *Blood Guts and Pussy* might be to laugh or even marvel as a kind of land-speed record for invective is broken ('Blag is a legend!' runs the top YouTube comment on 'Let's Fuck', referring to Dwarves' lead singer). Yet it is equally clear that not everyone responded like this, even among the staunch Sub Pop insiders of the late 1980s. Cobain wasn't so sure, for one, and cited the label's commitment to Dwarves as one reason he wanted his Nirvana to leave it.[21] As he reflected to Everett True in 1992, there was a very real danger that Sub Pop had simply become what it sought to caricature.[22]

Something similar can be said about TAD's song 'Sex God Missy', the opening track for the label flagship compilation *Sub Pop 200* of late 1988. It has been argued that Sub Pop's rock, as part of grunge more broadly, held greater appeal for women, drawn in by its curious humour and promise of an alternative to rock's conventional machismo; perhaps, even, there were more women in Sub Pop's early show crowds (though this is now hard to gauge statistically).[23] Even so, in early 1989 Dawn Anderson reported that 'Sex God Missy' was a song that 'a couple people told me they had trouble listening to', while Veronika Kalmar specified that it 'seethes of misogyny'.[24] Had these women failed to get the inside joke? Or had Sub Pop and TAD simply got them exactly where they wanted them, in a place of confusion, wondering whether this was rock or 'rock': irony about the thing or the thing itself, something knowingly progressive and yet powerfully regressive, the realm of the violent male loser who was nonetheless cool? Indeed, Kalmar perhaps accepts this when she goes on to write that 'Sex God Missy' was the song 'every female I know hates, because it's done so well', as if acknowledging that there was a misogynistic front put on here, a kind of act that only the in-crowd would understand.[25]

But what and where, in that case, was the real thing? The difficulty of such questions was another reason why, I think, Sub Pop liked to disarm through 'fun' and, particularly, by placing emphasis on blazing live performance. This came in handy when trying to drown out awkward questions about what they really stood for, and about what they found acceptable to release into their ever-growing mass international market. '[W]hen we're in the throes of doing it, it doesn't matter,' said the TAD bassist Kurt Danielson when confronted by Anderson about the violent nature of their lyrics.[26] Or, as True put it in early 1989, with obviously defensive rhetorical flourish, in one of his British propaganda articles for the label:

> To me, there's nothing regressive about the emotional impact
> or sheer physicality and sexiness of seeing these bands up
> and in your face. This sort of texture and exhilaration is
> timeless. The regressive angle just depends on your outlook.
> If someone sees that as damning, well what can you do?[27]

This claim of exhilarating timelessness relied on, for its effectiveness, a peculiarity of the Seattle environment itself. Perhaps it was because Seattle was a relatively small rock scene, with restrictive licensing laws on younger audiences and only a few venues and practice spaces; or perhaps it was because of the wide transit of hard and soft drugs, typical in a port city; or perhaps it was because of the presence of lots of new bands, each trying to outdo one another, without a sure sense of boundaries that a stronger attachment to a market might have given them. Whatever the reason, many Seattle rock bands seem to have played like it was the last show of all time

– and it was this unbridled liveness, the 'alarming' impression that it could 'all fall apart any second', that Sub Pop encouraged and made their mission to capture on record as local identity.[28] As Pavitt told *Dazed and Confused*: 'for us, the live show was everything. In those days, that was our No. 1 criterion when it came to who we would sign. Just: did that band absolutely rock the house?'[29]

From their now completely forgotten bands – the Fluid, the Walkabouts, Blood Circus, Swallow – to those who became household names, every Sub Pop reputation was staked on the renown of the live show, in which all kinds of retro triggers would be pulled as influences slammed together onstage. The bizarre Cat Butt were perhaps the epitome of this, a band seemingly incapable of writing anything that wasn't a twelve-bar blues, riddled with quotations from earlier rock songs (not to mention disco hits and TV shows). Such bands could be ear-bleedingly loud, heavy, and weirdly psychedelic, punk-violent and gross. Or – through 'bad working class' personas to thrill and threaten their early audiences – backwoods folksy, or monstrously primitive, or just comically, intoxicatedly clumsy. 'We do seem to fall down a lot,' said Mudhoney's guitarist of their live show in 1989.[30]

Or they could be purely destructive. Again I think of Nirvana, who would smash up their equipment at the end of their live show, even very early on when they were not yet the 'big, rich rock band' that Cobain would joke about on *MTV Unplugged* (1993). Definitely guitar, amplifiers and drums would get this treatment, sometimes bass guitar as well. This, once again, was in one sense more 'retro bullshit' (the Who's antics of the 1960s spring to mind). It was also a powerfully live display of the nihilism that Guido Chiesa had put his finger on: the end of rock, every night, symbolized by the destruction of its instruments – an act performed regardless, whether Nirvana felt they had played a bad show or a good one.

Above all, however, the destruction was nothing other than a hyper-aggressive masculine rock spectacle, a finale that would keep the crowds streaming in to witness, as one early critic put it, the band 'purge themselves in search of the great exalted god riff'.[31] There exist literally hundreds of photos of this routine, both amateur and professional. It was great box office: fully in tune with that part of the Sub Pop project that wanted to sell you overwhelming liveness as a primary commodity, over and above anything discomfiting the songs and their violent destruction might seem to 'mean'. ('They crafted melodies of eye-watering mercy, and then beat the fuck out of them,' as Terri Sutton wrote of the band.[32]) Tellingly, bassist Krist Novoselic once remarked that 'Uncle Jon Poneman' was happy to put his hand in his pocket to pay for replacement instruments the morning afterwards.[33]

Losership

Perhaps, ultimately, everything I have described above was nothing more than a late wave of punk. That is, punk reborn a decade after the fact, with Pavitt and Poneman playing the Malcolm McLaren role. 'No future' could hardly, after all, be more of a punk slogan; Greil Marcus could have been talking about many Sub Pop bands when he wrote that the Sex Pistols 'used rock 'n' roll as a weapon against itself', and Virgin's *Great Rock 'n' Roll Swindle* (starring, incidentally, the Sex Pistols) pre-dated the Sub Pop 'scam' by almost a decade.[34] Still, as a late 1980s phenomenon, Sub Pop's grunge necessarily had more overview than its predecessors. It included punk in what it voraciously ate up and spat back out. This is one reason why, in my view, its bands often made far more

Kurt Cobain goes on a post-show rampage at the Pyramid Club, New York City, April 1990.

interesting and engaging music than many in earlier punk or hardcore.

In that case it might be better to say that grunge was an 'archaeological' rock of the kind that David Buckley envisages when he says that, by 1979, a 'great rock band now needed . . . a pop *historian*, someone with a sense of what had happened and what could be done with it that might interest us'.[35] Certainly there were avid record collectors among the Sub Pop bands – Cobain was one of them – and certainly terms like 'dweeb', 'geek' and 'nerd' also became common journalistic currency for capturing their skinny, plaid-wearing ordinariness and curious offstage obsessions. At the same time, the bookish idea of a 'historian' is far too prim. What it can't capture is the adrenalin-soaked liveness evoked above – the domain of the 'total fucking godhead' (a label nowadays attached to Soundgarden's Chris Cornell, if not Cobain himself), in all its destructive implications. Nor does it cover Sub Pop's pervasive sense of parody and comedy: the hilarious rock rip-off, the staggering, swaggering act of 'redneck' entertainers fresh from the fringes of northwestern forests.

'Fusion' rock is all too similarly clinical, and rarely does justice to the mass of influences that coagulates in a given song. This is music, after all, not physics; to call the likes of Cat Butt a 'fusion' act is to risk hearing them precisely the wrong way up ('confusion' or 'diffusion' fits better). And if Grant Alden once got at something when he called grunge a 'postmodern reconstruction of punk, metal and psychedelia (along with any other loud music of the past twenty years)', then his point can only be taken so far.[36] 'Postmodern' captures something of the sense of free play with existing sources, as well as grunge's sometimes ironic humour and even, I suppose, its lack of commitment to any particular point. But still grunge rarely allows for any closer theoretical engagement with postmodernism. Most of its sources are, after all, ultimately stolen from the same narrow rock canon, whether in homage, parody or somewhere in between.

Personally, to answer my own question earlier on, I would prefer to say that what Sub Pop was selling was a 'loser rock'. This is dismal; certainly it is another tautology. Wasn't rock, whether alternative or not, always the stamping ground of the 'loser', from the Stones to the Stooges to Motörhead and to countless others? It is also another cliché, as well as something of a label trademark. The word 'loser' appeared, and appears, everywhere in Sub Pop products, marketing and merchandise, from song lyrics and titles to T-shirts to the recent collectors' 'Loser Editions' of classic releases. As if in confirmation of this ownership, the song 'Born Loser' (1966), actually by the Texas garage band Murphy and the Mob, is falsely attributed to Pavitt and Poneman in the credits of Cat Butt's *Journey to the Center Of* (SP 41, 1989).

Because of this density of its appearances, the word 'loser' takes on a heavy significance for Sub Pop. The label played freely with it as commercial identity in much the same way as its bands played with it as musical identity. First and foremost, Sub Pop participated in, and contributed to, what has now crystallized as the standard definition of the 'loser': in Clark Humphrey's words, the 'lovable, well-meaning (if sometimes addled) dropout from corporate career-ism; more concerned with having a good time than with making a fortune'.[37] This kind of loser was central to the early *Sub Pop* fanzine from which the brand emerged. As such it provided a linchpin for, and levelled the territory between, the label's bands, their music and their personas on- and offstage, the personalities standing behind the label (including Pavitt and Poneman as the most visible), and the consumers who bought the products.

At the same time, this all-uniting drop-out anti-corporate stance – 'losership' is perhaps the best name for it – implied several other important things. For one, it guaranteed the quality of the Sub Pop product, according to the aesthetic principle, beloved of fringe artists for hundreds of years, that true art must be created independent of commercial links. For another, it underlined a kind of rock-star masculinity – isn't the 'loser' always implicitly a white male? – even as it teased at and questioned what this masculinity could mean, making use of marginal characters familiar from rock history and elsewhere in popular culture, and thereby tapping simultaneously into the negative connotations of the word 'loser': the sex pest, the idiot, the aggressive working man, the stumbling drunk, the hinterland primitive, the serial killer and so on. These is no shortage of these rock characters among Sub Pop's early bands. They played no small part in creating the desired impressions of liveness, energy, danger and offence – and, bearing in mind that all were susceptible to exaggeration for effect, slightly pathetic comedy.

Ultimately, there is another layer still to this losership. To call Sub Pop's product 'loser rock' is fitting because it gets at the 'scam' identity that the whole enterprise wore on its sleeve, and that characterized its specific moment in the late 1980s, at the apparent death throes of rock as a spent, unreflective, dated genre. Certainly the bands were naive losers for taking part in this scam, while the label, as its owners often said, were shameless losers for trying it on in the first place. But most of all, the fans were losers in the specific sense of commercial dupes, taken in and energized by hyped products, even as their sense of losership reassured them that those products must have something important to tell them. To say that this was a clever piece of business doesn't go far enough: it approaches genius. These were the fans who would follow the 'Sub Pop Sold Here!' signs and ask their local record store for the latest Sub Pop release; they joined the infamous 'Sub Pop Singles Club' and indulged the obsessive practice of record collecting, hoarding monthly coloured vinyl 7″ releases (some of them nowadays changing hands for three-figure sums), even as the label actively branded them as 'losers' for doing so.

This behaviour was in many ways 'really weird', as Nirvana's Krist Novoselic remarked in late 1989. It was unusual, even in that world of small post-punk DIY label start-ups, to encounter a level of brand loyalty normally reserved for artists themselves. It made the fans cohere in the eyes of some critics into a Sub Pop 'movement' (a term with vague political resonances), or a 'cult' (with religious ones), and to acquire collective nouns like 'Sub Popians' and 'Sub Popists' and 'Sub Poppers'.[38] It would be hard to imagine the same thing happening to a many-armed million-selling giant like RCA Records, as Novoselic points out.[39] The success was testament to Sub Pop's cleverness in crafting a line of 'independent' and 'local' products, in evangelizing the power of those products, and in enlisting a following to consume them. 'Loser', in the many creative forms that the label deployed it across the 1980s and '90s, was central to these operations.

No Recess

An iconic example may help to sharpen these focuses a little. 'School' is the fourth track from Nirvana's debut album *Bleach*, released by Sub Pop in June 1989. It is among the most famous of their early songs and long remained a staple of their live show, often as the opener. Is there any rock that is bigger and dumber, as Everett True might say? The song has only about fifteen words in it, and, as its title suggests, seems very much on the ancient theme of rock 'n' roll's teen rebellion against adult authority, centred on the loser outcast at its heart. Its music, moreover, could hardly be any simpler. Guitarist or not, you could go and play most of it right now. The main riff's jagging rhythm is built on the alternation of only two guitar notes, one of them played straight, one of them bent harshly upwards. These two notes form the 'devil's interval', the tritone (that is, roughly six guitar frets apart), and they are far from the song's only heavy metal cliché. Its rhythm is rung out ominously at the bell of the ride cymbal throughout, while the double bass pedal thuds away underneath. And the bass guitar plays in its very lowest register, miles below Cobain's lead, individual notes almost imperceptible through sludge.

Okay – so, described like this, 'School' hardly sounds very promising. But the thing about this song is that, actually, it is extraordinarily intense. Part of this is Cobain's skill as a songwriter, his ability to derive so much from scant materials, to force opposition into tiny insular spaces. Why such power for a juvenile complaint about school? Why summon all the dark forces of metal for something so meagre? ('[W]hat's the matter, don't the kids have a union?', as one early reviewer asked.[40]) Part of the intensity is surely down to the performances: Cobain's 'anti-solo' is one of his best on record. But part of the song's effect is in its recording by Jack Endino, famously the Sub Pop 'engineer' responsible for the rawness, liveness and power associated with the 'Seattle sound' of so many grunge bands. With 'School', Endino further honed the art he was in the business of creating. For one thing, I think he must have stuck the microphone right in Cobain's face. The recording is red hot: that is, you can hear every nuance of the singer's increasingly fevered breathing throughout, as well as the feathering of his fingers on the guitar strings as he anticipates the first riff and the return of the chorus at the song's end. It is also soaking wet: almost everything is heavily reverbed, an effect that stands out most in the scream that splits upwards before the last chorus, Chad Channing's cymbal bell, and the song's last word, which echoes into the void Endino prepares for it.

Everything about 'School', then, makes it a direct, powerful and easily recognizable rock statement about antagonized loneliness, liveness, anticipation, loser masculinity and furious primitivity. Reinforced by the label's indirect forms of marketing – Everett True claimed that if Nirvana weren't doing this, they'd be working 'in a lumber yard, or fixing cars' – and a string of raucous live performances, it became one of the best-known tracks on *Bleach* and contributed to its early commercial success.[41] Particularly once the really big Nirvana wave began in late 1991, Sub Pop capitalized on this success as far as they were able, re-pressing the record in at least ten different vinyl colours (some of them now worth thousands) for their growing army of collectors, and striking licensing agreements with other labels worldwide for the record to appear on a variety of formats. Even today, scarcely a year goes by without another vinyl colour of *Bleach* being released or authorized by Sub Pop somewhere in the world: 2021 saw moon grey (USA, a Walmart exclusive), violet (Benelux countries), opaque red (Germany) and silver (Japan). The record remains, unsurprisingly, the label's biggest ever seller. Their anniversary deluxe edition of 2009 was accompanied by a second LP with a 1990 live set from the Pine Street Theater in Portland, opening with – of course – 'School'.

But one more thing about it. As Gina Arnold has pointed out, the song's obsessive refrain line 'no recess' is cleverer than it sounds at first. It doesn't just mean 'no school breaktime': it also means 'no nook', no hideaway, 'nowhere to hide'.[42] This reminds us of two things. First, that Cobain's lyrics are typically far more subtle than he would acknowledge, and second, that 'School' is on some level *about* the experience of public scrutiny in becoming a Sub Pop celebrity.[43] The song's working title was apparently 'The Seattle Scene', and the line its bridge repeats over and over again is almost identical to something Cobain wrote in a letter of the time to Dale Crover of the Melvins. 'FUCK I'M IN HIGH SCHOOL AGAIN!', he screams (the capitals are his), expressing his alarm at his band being made into Sub Pop 'socialites' to secure their record deal: the attendance at a 'zoo-event' (with its 'scene luminaries' and 'flashes of cameras'), and the need to impress Poneman ('Mr Big – money inheritance, right hand man of Bruce Pavitt').[44] Yet at the same time Cobain loved Sub Pop. He had first encountered the brand in the mid-1980s when it was still only the name of a newspaper column devoted to American independent rock, and possibly he knew it in its fanzine incarnation even before that. So by the time he was in a position to revile the label's 'zoo-events', Sub Pop had already shaped his belief in the value of independence from a mainstream and his suspicion of the media circus, just as it had structured his opposing belief in success, in getting signed, in reaching an audience with his music. As Cobain told Guido Chiesa in 1989, 'we said to ourselves, "this is the best label we could possibly record for"'.

In other words, written into Nirvana's 'School' is something like the Sub Pop paradox, the scam, the crisis itself. Inscribed in it is the avid belief in the communicative power of rock, particularly independent rock, at the same time as the painful awareness that, by the late 1980s, to wield it must make you at best a money-hungry fake, at worst a regressive monster. This is the conflict that charges the song's obvious emotional intensity, the trace sense, as Poneman put it of Cobain in 2002, of someone who 'wanted to be true to his friends and his culture' but simultaneously 'wanted to be fucking rich and famous'.[45] It is hard to overestimate the label's importance in making that precarious existence possible, at least for a short time. Sub Pop may have declared, in good humour, the death of the big dumb rock. But it also made it speak again.

Another Rehash

This book is designed in part as a history of Sub Pop, during what I consider to be the first phase of its existence, roughly the fourteen years or so from 1980, when the name first emerged as the title of a fanzine, to late 1993. This is in itself, of course, nothing original, the ultimate rehash. Sub Pop is a world-famous indie rock label, and there are many histories that establish the outline facts of this period. All of the Seattle-focused books I mention in the Preface offer chapters, or at least sections, devoted to Sub Pop, as do the major biographies of bands and artists associated with the label. As I have suggested, they could hardly do otherwise. Similarly, survey-ing numerous 'underground' bands of the era, Michael Azerrad's classic *Our Band Could Be Your Life* (2001) devotes a chapter to Mudhoney, which in effect becomes centred on Sub Pop. And most recently Gillian G. Gaar's book *World Domination* (2018) is an impressive feat in that it attempts to survey the whole history of Sub Pop – almost up to its continued existence in the present day – in just 140 pages. This means that Gaar makes mention of the bands and artists that have perpetuated the label's notoriety in its later, post-grunge phases: the Spinanes, Sunny Day Real Estate, the Shins, the Postal Service, Sleater-Kinney, Flight of the Conchords and Shabazz Palaces. I name only a few of the most prominent.

My aim is more specifically critical, by which I mean that this book is an attempt to reconsider some of the details of Sub Pop's first phase and to question the foundations on which the body of literature above is built and that it tends to reinforce. For example, it is well known that, like Touch and Go, Bomp!, Flipside and countless other rock labels of the 1970s and '80s, Sub Pop started out as a small-circulation music fanzine, in its case mostly written by the student Bruce Pavitt and collaborators such as Calvin Johnson (the founder of another well-known northwestern independent label, K Records). Contrary, however, to what is often assumed, this did not mean that Sub Pop would champion *any* music, provided it could be identified as regionally 'independent' in the face of what the fanzine rejected as the centralized corporate 'mainstream'. Instead, as Chapter One suggests, Pavitt's idea of an independent 'subterranean pop' was by no means all-inclusive. On the contrary, it was carefully constructed to be exclusive. The 'losers' who made it and consumed it were drawn together from American regional post-punk scenes, particularly rock and early industrial ones, and actively ignored the other major post-punk markets, particularly Great Britain.

Chapter Two follows this shaping process through to the founding of the label and its early multi-artist compilations, *Sub Pop 100* (1986) and *Sub Pop 200* (1988). These it places within the trend for 'Seattle' compilations of the early decade, designed to showcase and sell the city's post-punk 'scene' and to make it the next in the line of regional success stories, following cities like Minneapolis and Boston in the earlier 1980s.[46] At the same time, these Sub Pop compilations were a response to that trend, a kind of market coup to take charge of it and steer it in a particular direction. In particular, the lavishly produced box set *Sub Pop 200* was clearly designed to oust all other pretenders to the 'Seattle' title. Taking up the cue of the c/z Records compilation *Deep Six* (1986), *Sub Pop 200* homed in on a 'heavy', specifically masculine 'fusion' rock as Seattle's characteristic product and as Sub Pop's main claim to brand identity – even as, typically, it masked this consolidation with a bunch of goofy fake-corporate humour.

There were influential critics who loved *Sub Pop 200*. The influential British DJ John Peel, for example, found it to be standard-setting in terms of its coherent 'Seattle' sound. Others, however, found that the compilation was simply reactionary, too clever and knowing for its own good, not an innovative benchmark at all. It was, in other words, both visionary and a pathetic case of massive overmarketing, and these impressions provide the two poles between which the label shuttled as it developed its 'loser' identities over the next few years after 1988. Chapters Three and Four examine early Sub Pop products – the releases of Soundgarden, Blood Circus, Green River, Swallow, Nirvana, Dwarves and so on – and consider the brand armoury these built up: the well-known live 'drag shutter' snapshots alongside less famous posed imagery, 'secret' messages on the run-out grooves of records, the label's strong emphasis on 'limited edition' collectable coloured vinyl releases, and the Singles Club (through which many of these collectables were available). Together these focus the breadth of losership that united bands, label and fans early in Sub Pop's operations.

There is little doubt that at the beginning of Sub Pop's history as a label, the three new bands Mudhoney, TAD and Nirvana stood at the heart of its work as representatives of the new genre of grunge. These were the three acts who performed at Sub Pop's legendary 'Lame Fest' show (Seattle, June 1989) and then travelled to Europe that winter for the label's first major tour outside the U.S. The next three chapters examine each of them in turn, combining comment on music, image and marketing to identify how they delivered this 'lame' in creative cooperation with their label. Mudhoney performed mental and physical sickness that could turn anything bad: look at what they did to Bette Midler's famous piano ballad 'The Rose'. TAD – as 'bad working class' personas including farmhands, lumberjacks and abattoir workers – easily slipped into standard horror stereotypes, as is obvious from many of their songs and the onstage antics of their frontman. With Nirvana, however, these Sub Pop losers became less obviously rigid and comic, turning instead into the more seductive figure of the victim. This was a transformation that went hand in hand with Kurt Cobain's express wish to write 'very, very heavy pop' songs, a desire that represented both an homage to Sub Pop's origins and an escape route from them.

The epilogue to the book jumps closer to the present to consider Sub Pop's 25th-anniversary celebrations in 2013. It is notable that, whatever the label had brought to prominence in the intervening decades, this anniversary would trigger a wave of grunge nostalgia aimed at those who had experienced it the first time around. But what else did it bring back? Amidst the raft of collectors' 'loser' editions of classic records and merchandise celebrating the genre's key artists, a particular point of interest was the release in that anniversary year of another multi-artist compilation, *Sub Pop 1000*. Like its late 1980s namesakes *Sub Pop 100* and *Sub Pop 200*, this represented another attempt to establish the label's authority as a kind of curator – except that, some thirty years after that first wave of 'alternative' rock, it was not nearly so clear what the object of curation was intended to be, a problem that could not be entirely smoothed over by more of the same old rehash humour.

What *Sub Pop 1000* really gives, I think, is an opportunity to see in recent action the same drives that brought Sub Pop into existence in the first place. Sub Pop, 49 per cent owned by Warner Bros since the mid-1990s, may still just about be 'independent'; but it has also now become the Seattle institution from which other small labels take their cue in flying the flag of a heavy rock that never dies, as the example of the Seattle-based 'power violence' band and record label Iron Lung demonstrates.

1
Subterranean Pop

Only by supporting *new ideas* by local artists, bands, and record labels can the U.S. expect any kind of dynamic social/cultural change in the 1980s. This is because the mass *homogenization* of our culture is due to the claustrophobic *centralization* of our culture. We need diverse, regionalized, *localized* approaches to all forms of art, music, and politics.[1]

RADICAL WORDS FROM the young Bruce Pavitt. In May 1980, at 21 years of age, this resident of Olympia, Washington State, had produced five hundred copies of the first issue of his new music fanzine, titled *Subterranean Pop*. The quotation above is a central paragraph of the fanzine's opening manifesto, and captures its key terms, each emphasized in Pavitt's original. According to this, American music and culture were becoming – had, perhaps, already become – choked out of existence by the centralizing of power, money and influence into a few elite strongholds: New York, Los Angeles, San Francisco. Driven by a fanzine like Pavitt's, localization into a network of small regional scenes promised freedom from this stranglehold, and in turn offered a glimpse of cultural and social transformation. I am already giving you the long version, however. A few issues of the fanzine later, Pavitt presented a 'supreme statement of purpose' that, point by point, forged the same ideas into a list:

1. Culture is controlled by large corporations. It is bland.
2. Sub/Pop combats this by supporting independent systems of

expression: cassettes, records, publications, video, public access
cable television, whatever.

3. We are very big interested in regional trends, movements,
ideas, slang, record labels, what have you . . .

4. A decentralized cultural network is obviously cool. Way cool.[2]

Even some forty years later, these remain stylishly compelling words
– all the more so because they quickly found an audience. In the
immediate term there was success in distribution. Apparently
with little introduction, Pavitt sent these five hundred copies to
Systematic, a San Francisco distributor closely allied to independent labels along the West Coast. They promptly sold out of their
copies.[3] There followed eight more issues of *Subterranean Pop* (soon
abbreviated simply to *Sub Pop*), printed copies alternating with
tape-fanzines that offered the chance to hear some of the regional
music featured, and, from April 1983, a monthly column in the
Seattle music newspaper *The Rocket*, increasing Pavitt's readership
from a few hundred to many thousands. Finally, a few years later
Pavitt transferred the name 'Sub Pop' over to what became his
famous Seattle-based independent record label.

It is that label and its bands, of course, that will form the focus
of the present book. Even so, I begin with the *Sub Pop* fanzine, since
I want to understand how it might have paved the way for this future
success and the collection of ideas that supported it: the original Sub
Pop ideology, in other words. At the same time I don't want to get
carried away with this train of thought. However persuasive or
seductive Pavitt's initial manifesto, there is no reason to assume that
the resulting Sub Pop ideology was particularly coherent, or easily
translated into the basic principles of a record label. Actually I think
it was anything but coherent, a mess of sometimes contradictory
influences that need unravelling.

The first question, then, is what made up this ideology and its motivations. Clearly Pavitt's belief in regionality and locality is a good place to start. Clark Humphrey has suggested that changes to American tax structures at the beginning of the first Reagan administration in the early 1980s resulted in large record labels absorbing many smaller ones.[4] In turn this intensified a process of polarization within the music business that was easily romanticized and politicized: the greedy majors pitted against the struggling, upstart independents. For the young Pavitt, already the product of several 'alternative' educational institutions in the Midwest and Northwest, and the host of a late Friday night independent-music programme on the Olympia community radio station KAOS-FM, an emphasis on regional and local acts was one way to continue to fight the power.[5] To focus on bands in the little-known Minneapolis and the Midwest, or the unknown Seattle and the Northwest, promised freedom from the controlling centres of New York and LA where the big corporations were based, or at least from where their influence emanated.

What this ultimately came down to, as Pavitt frames it, was the struggle for American culture. To buy a record, he makes clear in his first *Sub Pop* manifesto of 1980, is not just to indicate personal musical preference. It is to buy into the 'values and lifestyles that are implied by that artist'. Centralized, corporate culture (the creation of the 'fat, cigar-smoking dough-boys at Warner Bros.') supports only 'macho pig-fuck bands whose entire lifestyle revolves around cocaine, sexism, money and more money' – as do you ('yes, you') every time you buy one of its records.[6] Decentralization must mean stepping outside this closed loop. It would also mean finding new sounds – 'the most intense music, the most original ideas' – and through them, new 'cultural heroes' and new ways of living for the dawning 1980s. In Pavitt's manifesto, a focus on the regional means social and cultural change for the better.[7]

The purpose of his new fanzine would be to build a network, a 'possible series of links between points and points between lines' that would confront the 'CORPORATE MANIPULATION OF OUR CULTURE', the hated legacy of the 'fab 70s'. It would do this by reporting regularly on invisible scenes around the country and the independent music within them. 'EXPLOSIVE artistic hanky-panky is everywhere,' Pavitt writes in his inimitable way, if only his readers would realize it and give it their support by writing to the band addresses given in the fanzine and buying their music.[8] I especially like 'hanky-panky' here. As a somewhat old-fashioned euphemism for secret sex, it is both typical of the way Pavitt engages his audience and chimes with his emphasis on fun and mischief and risk and randomness: the local 'anarchy and invention' in which the likes of Warner Bros have no share.

But 'hanky-panky' is also good because it suggests a kind of natural, haphazard, organic activity that will go on whether you like it or not, an unstoppable creativity rooted in ordinary people and invisible to those 'machine-like organizations' and the 'wealthy biz-execs who sit in their air-conditioned penthouses.'[9] So in its very beginnings Pavitt's Subterranean Pop landscape is all natural, green shoots and grass roots. Fertility, fecundity and mischief lurk just under its surface.

Loser Wins

The resulting narrative is very easily written. Many have joined up its dots. The independent, regional-focus fanzine of the early 1980s becomes the independent Seattle-focus record label of the mid-'80s. The label finds Nirvana, Soundgarden, Mudhoney and countless others waiting in the invisible northwestern wings. Members of its bands – most famously Kurt Cobain and Chris Cornell – echo

Pavitt in speaking out against corporate rock and 'macho pig-fuck' culture while making their own alternative brand of rock. For most critics, this has proven the easiest place to leave the legacy of the original *Sub Pop* fanzine.[10]

There is a lot more that can be said about it, however, and many additional ways it fed into the record label to follow. For one thing, Pavitt's insistent repetition of 'new' – new sounds, new ideas, new heroes – in his manifestos is certainly part of what makes them invigorating and exciting. It is also part obscuring, though, since what is being presented here is actually a rehash of an artistic attitude as old as the hills, something that had enjoyed a resurgence in recent rock and punk. Call it disinterest: the drive to look beyond selfish gain alone (here of money, sex, drugs) to locate a greater good for art and the artist. Disinterest has often been associated with the artistic avant-garde, the technical experimenters and risk-takers; that Pavitt has something like this in mind is indicated by his own lofty use of the term 'avant-garde' to describe what was going on within his 'traditionally boring' locales, and by his references to the 'great music' being made there.[11] His occasional collaborator Calvin Johnson has recently put the same point in terms of the most classic 'disinterested' slogan of all. Pavitt's fundamental revelation in the *Sub Pop* fanzine, Johnson states, was about the value of 'art for art's sake'.[12]

Though he was actually talking about European literary elites of the nineteenth century, the French sociologist Pierre Bourdieu coined several phrases for describing this disinterested relationship between artists and their market. One is the 'economic world turned upside down'.[13] Another is the 'generalized game of "loser wins"', and this is especially useful here, not least since it is one way of linking the term 'loser' to the early Sub Pop brand.[14] According to Pavitt's fanzine, his losers *do* win: it is lack of profit, lack of fame, lack of notoriety, lack of training, lack of centralization that the fanzine values and that it finds as stamps of identity, quality and authenticity. As the playful words of the front page of *Sub Pop* #6 put it, what the fanzine is interested in is 'a decentralized network of regional and local bums who refuse to get an honest job'.[15]

More than that, if it is a national network that is envisaged, bands are only one of the nodes in it. Listeners are also there, both as consumers of recorded media and in the crowds of shows that the fanzine reviews. Regional writers are part of it too, chronicling their home scenes. And so, importantly, are readers, who might also be all of the above. As the fanzine scholar Alison Piepmeier once wrote, the very 'materiality' of a fanzine like *Sub Pop* suggests a distinctly human character that lends a personal presence (or 'interpersonality') to the reader's experience. Holding the original *Sub Pop* fanzine means noticing its small, xeroxed, non-standard paper format, the marks of production and distribution embedded in the paper itself – the results of the 'X-Acto knife and press type and a typewriter' about which Pavitt has recently reminisced.[16] This materiality offers human connection in a way that Piepmeier calls 'embodied' ('The reader can revisit it, and although the text will stay the same, the artefact itself will change in subtle ways, like a body itself'), while the general messiness of writing and image contributes to the same effect, endearing the fanzine to its audience by suggesting qualities like vulnerability, openness, and, again, the presence of friendly human contact.[17] Unconfined by the strict machine margins of professional typesetting, this kind of presentation also generates 'visual energy and fluidity', as Piepmeier calls it, that binds readers into the experience, carrying them from page to page.[18]

Perhaps the best example is the first page of *Sub Pop* #3 (Spring 1981), on which there is a pair of black-and-white photos of Bruce Pavitt. Poorly photocopied and mismatched in size, they represent him as vulnerability itself. His eyes are turned towards the floor

Hi there —

My name is Bruce and we have to decentralize our society and encourage Local art and things and music. SUB/POP can be an outlet for this kind of subversive entertainment perspective but only if you help me by writing local gossip and sending it in right away to me with money and photos of you and your friends playing rock star. Send it in and I will print it. O.K.

x Bruce

Bruce Pavitt's 'letter to the reader' on the first page
of *Sub Pop* #3, Spring 1981.

and he sports a plaid shirt and cardigan, the very outfit of local ordinariness, of the frigid and 'traditionally boring' environment. Underneath, a handwritten note – not so much a letter as something you might find stuck on the fridge – relates the following:[19]

Hi there – my name is Bruce and we have to decentralize our society and encourage <u>local</u> art and things and music. SUB/

POP can be an outlet for this kind of subversive entertainment perspective but only if you help me by writing <u>local</u> gossip and sending it in right away to me with money and photos of you and your friends playing rock star. Send it in and I will print it. O.K. Bruce x

In the small space of a 7 × 8.5-inch page, this note achieves a surprising amount. It introduces the ideological buzzwords 'decentralize', 'local' and 'subversive'. It also emphasizes the urgency and emergency of the project ('right away', 'only if') and levels all barriers between editor and contributor, submission and acceptance ('gossip', 'send it in and I will print it'). These features, combined with the self-portrait photographs, the messy handwriting, the curiously juvenile run-on grammar, the first-name terms and the kiss at the end, conspire to create Piepmeier's 'sense of openness and availability for human contact that creates pleasure for the reader'.[20] Pleasure, indeed, is key: opening *Sub Pop* #3 and happening upon this note, the reader becomes immediately positioned as a friend, receiving some personal, perhaps private, correspondence, or even as the honoured recipient of a gift given for little purpose other than pleasure. The impulse to turn the page is hard to withstand.

In short, reading Pavitt's fanzine doesn't so much feel like 'consumption' as a 'process of involvement' (to put it in the terms of *Sub Pop* #8's interview with a local northwestern band, Calvin Johnson's own Supreme Cool Beings).[21] Language, design and materiality conspire to create the fanzine's identity as a 'non-commercial' alternative, operating in a network of physical spaces away from the established music business centres. This network is humanely connected, not corporately disjointed: it is populated by fellow losers invested in the pursuit of art for art's sake – or at least a little bit of artistic hanky-panky.

Punk into Pop

It feels almost like sacrilege to point out, then, that the sense of involvement was actually little more than a feeling. There was no guarantee that Pavitt would publish anything his readers sent in. While *Sub Pop* had numerous occasional correspondents based in regional scenes, and while Calvin Johnson often contributed record reviews and other copy, the fanzine never had a true letters page, and was never full of photos of readers 'playing rock star'. Also, commerce and consumption do inevitably rear their ugly heads, albeit on a tiny scale. Very few of the five hundred or so readers who received the early fanzine would actually have known Pavitt, and even fewer would have got it for free, that is, literally as a gift. As the request for money in the note above emphasizes, *Sub Pop* typically cost 50 cents to $1, with cassette tape issues around $5. A subscription could be taken out for a few dollars. Of course, it needed this financial input from readers to keep going.

It seems like still more sacrilege to try to focus what 'independent music' really meant within the fanzine. Pavitt's manifestos use it as a catch-all, always implying that any music is acceptable fare for promotion, just so long as it is created and distributed in some way that is 'independent' of the despised majors. 'Narrow-minded bigots need not apply . . . we want to hook up with *open-minded* people who flip on all kindsa music,' he promises in the tape-fanzine *Sub Pop* #4, and this is an ethos that still recommends the fanzine to this day, now that it has been reprinted and anthologized in a glossy volume.[22] But, honestly, this was more the approach of *Sub Pop*'s sister magazine in Olympia, John Foster's *Op*, which really did survey independent releases across a range of genres, from art music to jazz to rock. (In May/June 1984, for example, its 'W' issue reviewed not only Portland's Wipers, but also music by Robert Wyatt, Mal Waldron, and the Viennese early twentieth-century modernist Anton Webern.) Pavitt's fanzine, conversely, always remained within 'post-punk' limits – that is, the range of styles and genres that had emerged out of punk in the 'New Wave' of the first years of the new decade, including hardcore and homespun, usually tape-based, experimental music (perhaps best called early 'industrial').[23] This fundamentally 'guitars/machines' approach, as the label would later call it, aligns *Sub Pop* with many other local and regional American fanzines of the time: San Francisco's *Maximum Rocknroll*, Cleveland's *Cle*, Chicago's *Matter*, Lansing's *Touch and Go* and so on.

This does not mean, however, that Pavitt clung to 'punk' as a genre label, or as a broader descriptive term. Actually the word appears relatively infrequently in *Sub Pop*'s pages, and sometimes then in a negative sense as a worn-out commercialized form typical of corporate centres. Los Angeles is early on dismissed as the '"punk rock" capitol of the world', which is certainly not intended as a compliment ('If you want to be ugly and hate people, go to L.A.').[24] This pushes the emphasis away from punk as a valid term of identification. Instead, as the name 'Sub Pop' already suggests, Pavitt's fanzine gets much more strongly behind an alternative to 'punk' – namely 'pop'. The Spring 1981 abbreviation of the title's original 'Subterranean' is important in this regard. Shortened to 'Sub', it stands ambiguously for 'subversive', 'submissive', 'substitute' and 'sub-par', all adjectives that invest in Pavitt's loser economy. But it also stops the multi-syllable 'subterranean' stealing the limelight from 'pop', and allows an easy stylization into various striking and balanced typographies. 'SUB/POP', as in Pavitt's note above, becomes one standard. Later, the two words were stacked on top of each other with go-faster carets in between the letters to make what became the official label logo.

Sub Pop certainly wasn't unusual in stressing pop over punk in this way. Pop would prove to be, after all, a useful term for many punk critics in the early 1980s. For one thing, it highlighted musical traits from the 1960s that were then flooding back into guitar-led songwriting: an emphasis, for example, on sung melody and vocal harmony, high bass lines, folk elements, and certain kinds of instrumentation, structure and arrangement ('jangly' and 'Beatles-esque' are two words that often crop up).[25] At the same time, 'pop' provided a deliberately oppositional stance for independent music, in that to identify as 'indie pop' was to invite comparison with the subject-matter and lyrical content of Top 40 pop while simultaneously implying that the indie alternative was different and superior.[26] Take, for example, Pavitt's description in November 1980 of the original 7″ version of the Dead Kennedys' song 'Holiday in Cambodia':

> Suspence . . . Drama . . . Intrigue . . . fluttering,
> accelerated snare drum, I-spy lead guitar . . . this is
> definitely a soundtrack: starving, naked villagers run
> slip-sliding through the muddy backroads . . . Sweaty,
> paranoid Jello Biafra tortures his quavering vocal chords
> . . . Exciting: gut-shredded pop; as distinctly original
> as their first 45 (and a heck of a lot more convincing,
> gosh dammit).[27]

Pavitt focuses here on much that is striking about this song, not least Biafra's urgent delivery of its memorable melodies, and East Bay Ray's haunting delay-and-reverb guitar effects, directly inspired by bands of the 1950s and '60s. At the same time 'gut-shredded pop' (the last word chiming weirdly with the song's closing climb-out on the chant 'Pol Pot') grasps something of its lyrical content, since the song gleefully imagines the torture of complacently affluent American college kids at the hands of the Khmer Rouge. It is clearly a different kind of 'pop' to the chart norm, then: something 'original' and 'exciting', meant for listeners (most likely college kids themselves, incidentally) who despise complacently affluent American college kids and the mass culture they inhabit. This is one way in which Pavitt's *Sub Pop* reviews call out to their core audience.

Pop and Rock

As the Dead Kennedys example shows, 'pop' is also one of the main triggers for Pavitt's remarkable linguistic invention. Calvin Johnson has said that one of the *Sub Pop* fanzine's special qualities was that it 'made readers want to hear the music they were seeing', and this seems exactly right, testament to Pavitt's emphasis on both local uniqueness and pop creativity.[28]

According to reviews in the fanzine, three- and four-piece guitar bands like the Nurses, Hüsker Dü and Soul Asylum represent scenes in Arlington, Virginia, Saint Paul and Minneapolis, respectively, but they are also proponents of 'econo-pop', 'raw pop' and 'intense post-thrash pop'.[29] The Delinquents (a four-piece, with prominent keyboard, from Austin) are described as 'fun, garbage pop', while Steve Fisk's tape-looping collective Anonymous (Seattle) play 'the best electro-pop to come out of the u.s. all year'.[30] Wazmo Nariz (Chicago) has delivered an 'underground pop classic' with his single 'Tele-Tele-Telephone' of 1978; Epicycle plays the 'most dynamic set of power pop' in the same city ('Buy it or I'll kill you,' says Pavitt of their new EP).[31] And so on. Local pop becomes an intensely adjectival experience in the fanzine. It is ultimately as if there is little music in Pavitt's independent network, past or present, that cannot be labelled with some verbal riff on the term. In that sense it holds the whole project together, and even contains new pop's claim to be a flourishing subculture, as in the editorial of July 1983:

There are thousands of unusual, local artists in this country, expanding the concept of 'pop' music. Ideas and trends come and go, evolve and splinter into more ideas, more change. How does one gain access to this elusive, 'underground' information? 'Fanzines', publications put together with enthusiasm by fans, manage to document the most provocative local artists . . . Through a network of independent distributors, noncommercial radio, and the aforementioned fanzines, avant-garde pop music is being heard, talked about, and debated in cities across the U.S. and around the globe. All this without the visibility of a major label record contract. For people truly interested in the future of popular culture, these local, independent artists and publications can't be ignored.[32]

This is not to overlook that, for all his inventive emphasis on pop, Pavitt could also be called a critic in the American *rock* tradition. In many ways, this is just what he is, as is made repeatedly clear by the way his fanzine's reviews value liveness, rawness, originality and sincerity of expression, as well as the way in which they downplay consumption and seek to cultivate 'involvement' between a select group of musicians and their no less select audiences.[33] All this is about as rock as it gets. The point, as the editorial above shows, is that he works hard to marry this messily to the commercial practices and vocabulary of 'pop' and merges the result into the legacy of punk. The consumers Pavitt envisages are 'teenage' (sometimes quaintly spelt 'teen-age'). They buy and swap 'pop 45s' by the 'most promising pop combos of the year', ranked according to the fanzine's regular charts of 'fave' hits, sometimes called 'pop raves'. They listen for hours a day on community-college radio stations like KAOS-FM, and they know just how 'danceable' their favourite bands are live. They know, in a word, how to have 'FUN' (the capitals are Pavitt's).[34]

There is obviously a kind of nostalgia for an imagined world of the 1950s in this, a reaching back to a naive American idyll in which popular culture centred on the vinyl record first emerged. This is reinforced by the fanzine's visual style, which throws together cut-and-paste pictures of couples dancing, promotional images of early 45 players (like the RCA Victor), and the 'noir' slicked-hair comic designs of Pavitt's fellow Evergreen student Charles Burns.[35] It is also embedded in Pavitt's self-consciously dated language ('gosh dammit', 'rock 'n' roll' in place of 'rock') and, consequently, in the fanzine's curiously ironic atmosphere, which sometimes makes it difficult to tell what he really values in any given record – aside, of course, from its independence.

Ultimately, however, the most important point about this 1950s nostalgia is that it allows a leapfrog clean over the 1970s: the era of the 'handful of large, multi-national corporations' eventually challenged by the first wave of punk.[36] It is a journey backwards to a healthier age that, as Pavitt puts it in his very first manifesto, is simultaneously a journey forwards into 'tomorrow's pop'. So an independent pop is the key *Sub Pop* badge of identity and a way of grounding it in American music history. But it is also a post-punk route beyond what seemed to him, in 1980, the stale deadlock of punk, chart pop and macho rock.

No Rules

The other thing about labelling a song 'pop' is, of course, that it forces it to resonate with innocence and purity, with leisure and pleasure. This may be fairly straightforward in some cases: when Pavitt calls an EP by Seattle's Visible Targets 'pure pop, pure product' in August 1982, he captures something of that band's catchiness, the fact that they will 'probably receive heavy college radio airplay'.[37] To say, on the other hand, that punks like the Dead Kennedys play 'pop' is to draw attention to the band's obvious melodies and guitar effects, and simultaneously to downplay its extreme anti-authoritarian and anti-plutocratic politics (see the shock value of the band name). Sometimes these kinds of pop descriptions seem like a deliberate turning away or inwards from direct political engagement, back behind the defences of the enclosing local scene.

It comes as a surprise, then, when the front page of *Sub Pop* #6 (February 1982) is suddenly not so friendly any more. The tone is angrily political, in fact. This is a different kind of issue altogether. The U.S.-letter size pages allow for long columns to run down both sides of the fanzine's front page. On the left is Calvin Johnson's denunciation of Reagan's 'corporate bullshit' America and a call to musicians to use their audience's attention to 'do something other than getting a hard on'. On the right-hand side is Pavitt's homage to hardcore punk, which, as if in direct continuation of Johnson, presents it as a solution to America's political problems ('Fuck Authority. I hate war and I hate big business and I'm glad that other people feel the same way . . . RISE ABOVE').[38]

As this issue makes especially clear, the momentum of hardcore was another important inheritance for the *Sub Pop* fanzine, and something else it merged into the legacy of punk-as-pop. Hardcore provided another incentive for its localism, as well as some of its heroes ('Rise Above' is a slogan from Black Flag, the band whose live show Pavitt elsewhere calls a 'religious experience').[39] It also gave the fanzine an enemy:

> 1981? Simple enough . . . Britain gave us New Romantic white/ electro/disco/funk and America gave us what? Hardcore . . . Surprise. Today's Hardcore teenage army is the most dominant, the most *obvious* scene in the American music underground.

Hardcore is intense, honest American music, burning red, white and blue images confronting specific American problems. Anthems like 'Justice For All', 'Six Pack' and 'Guns or Ballots', band names like the Dead Kennedys, The Minutemen, and yes, even Jody Foster's Army. Does this sound British? No![40]

To an extent, these are just national caricatures exaggerated for comic effect: 'Howdy neighbor. Put down that gun and pick up this magazine' is one of the salutations on the same front page. Still, looking across the entire run of *Sub Pop* fanzines and columns, numerous echoes of this attitude towards Britain (or often 'England', used synonymously in the American fashion) are easily found. Many of them, in fact, go beyond dismissal and imply the threat of British music to Pavitt's American indie project. See the introduction to the tape-fanzine *Sub Pop* #5: 'In the next two minutes, you can read about great *American* bands. Or you can toss this book and spend big bucks on the latest hype from England.' Or the anxiety in July 1983 that the indie labels of a 'tiny rock in the ocean called England' had recently outproduced their American counterparts. Or certain bracketed asides to the reader: a compilation of New York bands 'recorded live in (cough) England'.[41] The overall effect is to maintain music from Britain as a persistent enemy lurking in the background.

In one sense this antagonism is just conventional wisdom, an Americanness that has constructed itself against Britishness since at least the Revolution.[42] Fine: Americans are real, gritty, honest, direct, self-made, hardcore; Brits are ineffectual, histrionic, evasive, fake, slaves to fortune, soft. It had, however, flared up again and taken particular shape in the independent rock scenes of the early 1980s. Gina Arnold gives numerous examples of 'Amerindie' radio stations, listeners, bands and their celebrities (R.E.M.'s Peter Buck, for example) rejecting British music, refusing to buy it or listen to it or play it. That this embargo extended even to Pixies, an American band, because they were signed to a 'farty English label', demonstrates that this was really all about competition in a crowded market, rather than, say, ethnic hatred.[43] British independent music, seemingly everywhere on import or licence, threatened to drown out local independent American voices, and that meant that, for the American project to succeed, it had to be shunned. For his part, Pavitt has confessed that the (British) label Rough Trade was his 'favourite' in the very early 1980s, and that he was directly inspired and assisted by its distribution network in the U.S. But this adulation was precisely the problem: recalling the beginnings of the *Sub Pop* fanzine, he complains that 'everyone was reading the British papers and buying Rough Trade singles' and so he felt forced to take action.[44]

Clearly this complicates what the *Sub Pop* fanzine really stood for. Here was another example of independent music that didn't fit the bill. The picture becomes even more complex if you follow the American–British opposition back to some of Pavitt's immediate influences. Take Steve Albini, for example, whom Pavitt praises throughout *Sub Pop*, whose 'really brutal reviews' for Chicago's *Matter* fanzine he cites as a central inspiration, and whose presence as producer was later important for Sub Pop as a label.[45] Infamously outspoken, and a true believer in hardcore's 'no rules means no rules', Albini rarely held back in the early 1980s.[46] Here is a rant from *Matter*, inspired by Albini's own circumstances as a musician and aimed at the British artist Boy George:

This is one of those weeks where I get incredibly depressed. I'm completely broke. Not just ain't-got-no-pocket-money broke but wolves-at-the-door broke . . . It's things like that (and those wolves) that make me boil when I find out how

ridiculously well-paid some of the lamest of the lame ripoff
artists are. Boy George, former hairdressing student, former
buttboy for [British punk] Kirk Brandon, former artschool
dropout, former (torn) clothes saleswimp, has just cleared the
million mark. A million dollars. Shit, that little fart doesn't
deserve the twenty-bucks-a-blowjob he'd probably be making
on Carnaby Street if he weren't such a good friend of Malcolm
McLaren. Put that in perspective – that's 20-grand-a-year
for fifty years. He doesn't have to do anything but tease his
dreadlocks for the next fifty years, and he'll make more
lounging around than most good bands make in their
best years.

The major-label British band Duran Duran, then enjoying their
greatest success in America, come under attack in the same column:

> When I heard [a Duran Duran single] on the radio the
> other day . . . I almost peed myself laughing. It didn't just
> suck – it sucked like a Hoover. How could they have fooled
> even the least selective of us? Because they were English,
> of course. These bozos started this whole silly Buy English
> Disco Records Trend. Duran Duran Duran Duran have
> a new record out. The album *Seven and the Sycophants*,
> or some such thing, is selling like southern-fried ludes
> at a Memphis homo convention.[47]

Sub Pop never descends into outright homophobia; it never quite
caught what Arnold calls the 'macho virus' of hardcore.[48] But I cite
Albini's words at length because a trace of his Chicago noise-rock
machismo does sometimes operate in the background of *Sub Pop*
reviews, even when independent music is back in the spotlight, and

even in cases where British music is not specifically evoked. In the tape-fanzine *Sub Pop* #5, the Wichita band the Embarrassment are reviewed as 'a great rock and roll band: simple, honest, sophisticated ... [They] are real Americans; they do not wear sashes and make up.'[49] The directness makes it hard to tell, as usual, to what extent Pavitt is being ironic; still, read in the light of the British dismissals, the review underlines the fanzine's fundamental position: American rock 'n' roll honesty, not British New Romantic sash-wearing theatricality. And this in turn makes it difficult to believe the original manifesto position, the anti-macho anti-sexist rejection of corporate rock. It prompts a difficult question, in fact. How exactly is hardcore macho punk rock better than corporate macho rock? Does the alleged commercial 'independence' of the former really make it more acceptable than the latter? The fanzine seems caught in between hardcore devotion to free speech and the social contract of equality for all.

There was, admittedly, a partial backtracking from this awkward position and an acceptance that, as one critic of the fanzine put it, this pro-American attitude 'was just as narrow as the Anglophiles'.'[50] If *Sub Pop* #6 was expressly 'all-American', then the next issue begins with what sounds like an apology: 'Fellow comrades, I have read your letters and you are right – Nationalism is the father of Fascism. So while we will continue to embrace grass-roots American pop, we will also open our arms to any and all contributions, both national and international.'[51] Again, these readers' letters were never published. Nonetheless, I think a resolution is made here to move away from uncompromising hardcore and its dangerous overlap with extreme right-wing masculinity (Albini insists on his right to 'make jokes about gays, women and cripples' – and, it seems pretty clear, Brits and other foreigners). Instead, making good on the *Sub Pop* #7 apology, the tape-fanzine *Sub Pop* #9 (June 1983) boasts that its 'new format is international'. There is still no British music, but it does feature a track by the French band Magnétique Bleu, two anonymous songs 'brought in from behind the Iron Curtain' and shouted in Russian, and a tape mash-up of Pavitt's seemingly created from, and titled, 'Random Swedish Radio'.[52]

Undoubtedly this 'international' indie avenue was a productive idea, and it turned up at least one celebrated find. This was the Japanese all-woman band Shonen Knife, whose music Kurt Cobain loved and which both Pavitt and Johnson would later release in the u.s. Nonetheless, what this brief international experiment ultimately emphasizes are its own limitations. Looking closer, only one song on *Sub Pop #9* (Magnétique Bleu's 'Virgin Boy', sung in English) definitely originated outside the USA, and so the claim on the tape's spine ('4 countries, 14 cities') is at best questionable, at worst desperate. (The later advertisement for it that promised '21 groups from 14 countries' is even harder to justify, and perhaps relies on assessments of the artists' distant foreign heritages.)[53] What these 'international' claims really do is reinforce the Americanness of the 'subterranean pop' network as a concept in the first place. In fact, that concept is precisely what Pavitt would devote himself to over the next few years, as the fanzine transformed into the *Rocket* column under a new and decisive title: *Sub Pop USA*.

Independence?

Reading the *Sub Pop* fanzine this closely reveals tensions operating at every level – points of conflict that, only a few years later, would necessarily become those of the famous record label. Sub Pop USA and Sub Pop International. Anti-British and inspired by Rough Trade. Hardcore masculinity and anti-sexism. No rules and rules. Independent and commercial. Rock and pop, punk and pop. Offensive and inclusive. Underground and visible. Local and national.

That this mix often feels contradictory is unquestionable. Sometimes, in fact, it is left to the reader to untangle it. Reviewing Black Market Baby in 1983, Pavitt accepts that they are 'reactionary, sexist pigs' but cannot conclude which is better, 'stupid, powerful music like this, or lame "politically correct" rantings like the latest dud from ['positive punk' band] MDC': 'You decide', the review fizzles out.[54] Even so, the same tangle of contradictions was uncontestably influential. Likely it was part of what made *Sub Pop* attractive and unique for many readers. One person affected by it – only the most famous – was the young Kurt Cobain, who is known to have read *Sub Pop* as a northwestern teenager in the early 1980s.[55] Cobain was devoted to independent music but also knew its limitations. He was a rock star who spoke out against sexism; possibly it was sexism that contributed to his decision to leave Sub Pop. But still he sought out Steve Albini, already the producer of his beloved Pixies and Breeders, to record Nirvana's final LP. Also, perhaps, the fanzine's influence lingered in his writing. Cobain's *Journals* includes a page of record reviews, all done in something like Pavitt's one-liner style. In response to Wipers' LP *Is This Real?* (1980), an Americana favourite of the fanzine, he writes simply: 'Yeah it is.'[56]

The question was how *Sub Pop* would continue to grow its influence, and that again brought up the problem of what 'independence' really meant. In the inaugural 'New Pop Manifesto', page 1 issue 1 of *Subterranean Pop* in 1980, Pavitt had pointed out that big stars like the B-52's, Devo and Patti Smith had once been independent-label artists. As you might expect, this invites his scorn for their having since sold out: 'drop dead Patti', he writes. Yet when he adds that some of these artists had retained 'a sense of strength and adventurousness' since joining major labels, he makes what sounds like a big concession.[57] Sometimes, major labels *do* release great things, music worth paying attention to and spending money on.

Gerard Cosloy, another American fanzine writer (*Conflict*) who became an independent-label founder (Homestead), once said that 'in the old days people went to a lot of effort to convince themselves it wasn't a business. And denying it just made people rotten business people.'[58] A similar realization must have occurred, I think, for Pavitt. Better that he allow himself to be a good businessperson, turning his fanzine into a kind of regional new-music broker, an A&R board for bigger labels, themselves already becoming interested in forming their own 'independent'-style imprints and boutique labels – and, in so doing, turning 'indie rock' and 'indie pop' into their own genres, regardless of how the music was made and distributed. Included in the recent anthology of the *Sub Pop* fanzine is the reprint of a letter from Howard Thompson, Talent Acquisition at Columbia Records, enclosing his $5 and requesting the *Sub Pop* #5 tape. This serves to emphasize the 'suits taking notice' of the indie scene, as the page's title indicates ('really got a kick out of this one', Thompson scribbles at the bottom, apparently in a note-to-self).[59] But the attention clearly goes the other way, too, and demonstrates the range of *Sub Pop*'s potential reach. Pavitt has said he was 'flattered' by Thompson's attention; contrast this with his original pledge to 'sabotage the corporate record industry by ignoring their system completely'.[60]

Amidst all the attention, however, brand Sub Pop might itself continue to grow, all the while retaining the carefully honed 'edge' (as Charles Cross has termed it) of the local punk indie as identity and exploiting it as a selling point.[61] I note that Pavitt and the *Sub Pop* fanzine had been singled out by an article in *Rolling Stone* magazine in March 1984 as a reliable underground source for 'excellent music' by 'regional New Wave bands'.[62] It had, in other words, been seen to accrue a kind of subcultural capital: a distinctive position against the mainstream, as well as against other independent players, whether American or British ones. The opportunity now was to invest this capital into the formation of a label.

2
Sub Pop Rock City

so when did Sub Pop become a record label?

The question is more interesting than it sounds. Most commentators avoid giving a straight answer to it. This is probably because there isn't one. It all depends, of course, on how you define 'label'. In numerous senses Sub Pop had been a label since around July 1981, the month in which the 2,000 copies of Pavitt's first tape-fanzine (*Sub Pop* #5), featuring artists from Washington State to Maryland, had been distributed to consumers. Another answer would be 1984, in which Pavitt released his first 12″, the Seattle band U-Men's first EP – although admittedly that was under the label name 'Bomb Shelter', shared with the Seattle record store he briefly managed.

Or was the Sub Pop label born in July 1986, when Pavitt made a more decisive professional move, transitioning fully from tape to vinyl and releasing the multi-artist compilation *Sub Pop 100* – its title indicating a raising of the stakes on the last of the tape-fanzines (*Sub Pop* #9, June 1983), and its catalogue number (SP10) a direct continuation of it? Or July 1987, in which month, backed by money from Pavitt's dad and the band in question, the first single-artist Sub Pop vinyl release had appeared, Green River's EP *Dry as a Bone* (SP11)? Or, finally, April 1988, when Pavitt and his new business partner, the local DJ and talent agent Jonathan Poneman, moved into their new office at the Terminal Sales Building on First Avenue in Seattle and began to take on a few employees?

Any of these might be the best answer – depending on why you are asking the question in the first place. In this chapter, I want to work towards another option still. This is December 1988 and a vinyl release that appeared then: another multi-artist compilation, *Sub Pop 200* (catalogue SP25). True, it would be hard to argue that *Sub Pop 200* was the release through which Sub Pop became *a* label. That moment is contained somewhere in the timeline above. Instead I think December 1988 was when it became *the* label. That is, it marks the moment when Sub Pop became what it is, and what everyone has known it for ever since.

Seattle Syndrome

I must admit it seems like a heavy weight for a multi-artist compilation to bear. *Sub Pop 200* may now itself be celebrated, but still it is easy to look down on these kinds of compilations. Lots of artists on the same disc typically means lots of voices and lots of styles; compilations can easily collapse into a miscellany, lacking the cachet of something properly finished and coherent. They also carry the suspicion of having been slung together as a 'sampler' of various artists for the purposes of advertising a record label – as indeed many of them were from the 1960s onwards. As such they are the victims of the 'album culture' that emerged in the 1970s: they feel temporary rather than timeless, functional rather than aesthetic. This is only exacerbated by their precarious existence today. Whereas single-artist albums (or single-artist 'greatest hits'-type compilations) are remastered again and again, potentially gathering new audiences each time, multi-artist compilations are rarely revived and, particularly when they came originally from small independent labels, usually do not appear on contemporary music streaming services (even if their individual tracks, tied to their artists, might). Sometimes, thanks to generous uploaders and hazy copyright positions, they are found in their entirety on sharing platforms like YouTube.

But often there is little trace, perhaps indicating that the physical artefacts are lost, or remain in tiny numbers of hands only.

This dubious contemporary existence stands in contrast to the importance of multi-artist compilations for independent rock labels in the late 1970s and early '80s. Typically these labels had little capital and only a few artists on their books; in turn, those artists had only a few songs and little money for time in the studio. Multi-artist compilations provided one obvious creative product in this situation, and endless numbers of them appeared in rapid succession. More than that, whatever their miscellaneous impression today, these compilations were a powerful way to suggest momentum and gathering group identity. They encouraged listeners, guided by titles, images and other cues, to make connections between artists, ideas and sounds, with the label at the centre as organizing force.

Countless compilations brought together artists from a particular locality or region. If Touch and Go's *Process of Elimination* EP (1981) surveyed the hardcore and post-punk scene in the Midwest, primarily Michigan and Ohio, Gerard Cosloy's *Bands that Could Be God* (Conflict, 1984) did something similar for Boston and Massachusetts, as did Oblique Records' *N.O. Experience Necessary* (1980) for New Orleans. *The Sound of Hollywood Girls* (Mystic, 1983) showcased women punk groups from southern California; *Live at Target* (Subterranean, 1980) documented some of San Francisco's new 'industrial'-experimental bands as recorded at the Target Video Studios. As detailed in Chapter One, Bruce Pavitt's early *Sub Pop* tape-fanzines took this regional principle one step further, stringing artists together into an American network of rock scenes united by the notion of independence from the big corporations. SST's vinyl compilation *The Blasting Concept* (1983) was in some ways comparable: while obviously a label sampler intended to turn consumers on to SST's back catalogue and merchandise, its artists promised to deliver a 'turntable education away from media outlets' (in the words of Harvey Kubernik's elaborate sleeve note).[1]

Other compilations aimed more obviously at curating rock history into an inspiration for the present. Lenny Kaye's well-known *Nuggets: Original Artyfacts from the First Psychedelic Era* (Elektra, originally 1972) brought together mid-1960s American recordings and began to consolidate them into a genre that would become known as 'garage rock' (though Kaye called it 'punk-rock').[2] The bootleg series titled *Pebbles* (from 1978) homed in on more obscure 'original 60s punk classics', while the spin-off *Highs in the Mid Sixties* (AIP, 1983 onwards) added a regional focus to each of its volumes.[3] All of these attracted re-releases and additional volumes as the 'archeological dig into the bizarre splendor of the mid-sixties' (Kaye) continued into the 1980s.[4] Reviewing the seventh edition of *Highs in the Mid Sixties*, Pavitt's *Sub Pop* column of May 1984 held it up as 'manic sixties garage punk' that would be a 'must for fanatics of roots rock 'n' roll' – that is, an important contingent of his fanzine's intended readership.[5] As this suggests, buying a collection like this could confer a typically rock superiority on a listener: knowledge of secret classics and ancestors, nuggets like gold, that not everybody would know.

Clearly, then, multi-artist compilations held many advantages for producers and consumers. They could be inventive, inspiring and consolidating, as well as pragmatic. Indie rock labels in the Pacific Northwest were no slower than those elsewhere to catch on to this. In fact, to attempt to survey the compilations dedicated to that region in the first half of the 1980s is quickly to get out of your depth. There are numerous examples from big cities like Portland, Seattle and Vancouver, as well as from the much smaller Olympia. Even survey-ing Seattle on its own provides no small challenge. There were, for example, the Green Monkey tape compilation *Local Product* (1983) and its vinyl follow-up *Monkey Business* (1986), both of which promoted the label as a hub for Seattle's retro rock and synth bands, and centred on label founder Tom Dyer, who played on and produced many of their tracks.[6] *Pravda Volume One* (Pravda Productions, 1982) attempted a similar consolidation around the music of members of the Seattle band Student Nurse. More obviously experimental, *Life Elsewhere* (1980) and *Absolute Elsewhere* (Mr Brown, 1982) offered what the latter called 'unusual rock music from Olympia and Seattle', mainly played by the Evergreen State circle comprising John Foster, Steve Fisk, Calvin Johnson and Bruce Pavitt's own short-lived band, Tiny Holes.[7]

These were narrow in terms of personnel, however, the product of relatively small groups of enthusiasts. There were also multi-artist Seattle rock compilations that made more obvious attempts to promote a broader sense of a popular 'new wave' across the city and wider region. The two volumes of *Seattle Syndrome* (Engram, 1981 and 1982) and *The Sound of Young Seattle* (Dust Bunnie, 1984 and 1985) have become the best known. These traversed a range of bands and stereotypical post-punk styles, often with synths and drum machine, and sometimes with a gentle reggae influence, as well as sixties psychedelia, fifties rockabilly and 'industrial' sound collages at the fringes. At any given moment, you might hear allusions to American bands like Devo, Sonic Youth, the Ramones, Talking Heads, Patti Smith and Black Flag. Roughly contemporary British artists obviously loom in the background too: those with some claim to 'independence' (the Clash, the Fall, Joy Division and John Lydon's PiL) as well as mainstream chart-toppers like Duran Duran.

As Pavitt once wrote, the problem with these local compilations was that 'half of the bands are history' by the time of their release – or, actually, had never existed in the first place, coming together only once to play for the recording at the producer's demand.[8] They should not be heard, then, as an accurate snapshot of Seattle's live rock scene. Instead, what they demonstrate is a struggle against one another – as much as against any 'mainstream' – to confer a musical identity on the city, a 'Seattle sound', and through it a youth sub-culture identity that could keep step with anywhere else in the U.S. and wider world. Engram's direct marketing for *Seattle Syndrome*, for example, promoted it as a 'sampler of the *Seattle* sound' (the emphasis is original), by which it meant 'everything from head-banging rock to slick pop to floating electronic sounds'.[9] Conversely, in reaction to this diverse definition of musical identity, the tape compilation *What Syndrome?* (Deus Ex Machina, 1983) was an uncompromis-ing forty minutes of low-fidelity Seattle punk, most of it played at hardcore speeds. Seattle, it made clear, should not be located in such a broad set of styles as Engram claimed – and, perhaps especially, had nothing whatever to do with the handsome sounds of the British New Wave.

Undoubtedly these Seattle-defining projects were not confined to small independent rock labels alone. As Peter Blecha has pointed out, one of the biggest-selling independent artists of late 1980s Seattle was not Soundgarden, nor Nirvana, nor Mudhoney, but the DJ, rapper and producer Sir Mix-a-Lot, whose 'Posse on Broadway' (1988) actually refers to the street in Seattle, not the famous one in New York. The track seems designed, in other words, to place Seattle on the map against what might be its competitors; Mix-a-Lot him-self quickly became a player in public debates over what made Seattle's true 'street music', and his label Nastymix became a venue for Seattle's rap and hip-hop artists (as well as the occasional thrash band).[10]

It seems to have been in rock culture, nonetheless, that the now familiar image of Seattle came through most strongly. This was the out-of-the-way, forgotten, creative and primitive city, a model environment for rock's long-standing obsession with life at the fringes. On first hearing, some of the associated catchphrases sound negative. 'Seattle Syndrome' refers to the inevitable fact that all talent will eventually abandon the backwater for somewhere better, probably California, or, according to Clark Humphrey, that you could write and play brilliantly and no one would hear or care.[11] Even so, these catchphrases were clearly also a positive statement of identity that would later be built into label branding. It wasn't only that talent and brilliance *were* born in this remote, desolate place, allegedly away from commercial influence and interference. It was that they *had* to be born there, under these inhospitable conditions: that the most ignored was also the most 'independent' of independent places, the most rock of all rock's innovation sites. Arguably it was this, in fact – let's call it the Seattle mystique – that gave these compilations a support, a reason to exist and an added line of appeal. It stopped them collapsing into what they often were, that is, heavily derivative of the familiar post-punk styles of the early 1980s.

Fusion

What has become by far the most famous of Seattle's multi-artist rock compilations is *Deep Six*, released by the new label C/Z Records in early 1986. Already its title signals something tightly organized. On the one hand, 'deep six' refers to the six Washington State bands – Green River, the Melvins, Malfunkshun, Skin Yard, Soundgarden, U-Men – that populate the record, and implicitly pitting them and the label against the 'Big Six' major record companies, which, in Gina Arnold's estimate, controlled 95 per cent of record releases by the beginning of the decade.[12] On the other, to 'deep six' something is to dump it overboard into obscurity. In short, *Deep Six* is a perfect expression of the Seattle mystique, with an obvious trace of danger and violence mixed in. Reyza Sagheb's cover design shows a fracture running through an urban sidewalk, inside which fragmented images of Seattle's secret underground bands can be glimpsed.

The sound of *Deep Six* is similarly tight. All the record's bands use the standard rock ensemble of vocals, guitar, bass and drums in comparable ways, and this means that the arrival of the main sonic exception, Ben McMillan's saxophone solo in Skin Yard's 'The Birds', comes as a powerful surprise. It also means that, like *What Syndrome?* before it, *Deep Six* feels strongly reactionary when placed against indie predecessors like *Seattle Syndrome*. Again it seems to deny that the music of the Northwest was anything so broad, instead making an attempt to shift the musical agenda on to narrower rails, and underlining its point largely through newly formed bands (the U-Men were the only contributor with any prior recordings to their name). Daniel House, the Skin Yard bassist and subsequent owner of C/Z, later confirmed this reactionary intention and its successful reception:

> At the time there weren't really bands playing music like this. What was big was synth-based New Wave. Everything that the bands on *Deep Six* were doing was basically a 'fuck you' to the popular music of the time. But locally, it was a big deal. After that record came out, we had no problem getting shows at all. *Deep Six* got a lot of radio play on [Seattle college radio station] KCMU and acted as a beacon for more people to begin starting bands, ones that were a lot more guitar-heavy and maybe dark or angry.[13]

Of course, the 'popular music of the time' could (and probably did) refer to almost anything, indie releases as much as 'mainstream' ones.

Skin Yard in a later incarnation for Sub Pop; bottom right is Jack Endino,
the celebrated label engineer and architect of the 'Seattle sound'.

c/z was in a battle with its friends as much as its enemies, and Skin Yard were, for the time being, one of its flagship bands.

Famously, there is something more compelling and historic about *Deep Six*. No reviewer ever fails to find a strong metal influence on the record, and that, measured against other Seattle compilations of the time, feels like a novelty. Metal, after all, had long been treated as its own scene in Seattle and the Northwest, a genre not requiring representation on the rock compilations noted earlier. By 1986 it had its own independent label (Ground Zero) and its own compilation series (*Northwest Metalfest*), its own fans and clichés, its own suburban territory close to Seattle (Bellevue) and its own regional history, spearheaded by 1970s hard rock bands like Heart and brought forward into '80s metal by Queensrÿche and others.[14] Even if some contributors disdained metal's presence on *Deep Six* – the U-Men suspected the other bands of being 'too heavy metal' and hastily recorded only one track on the way out to Idaho[15] – most critics welcomed it and found in its presence on *Deep Six* another key aspect of the city's developing rock identity. Whatever the reactionary intent of its makers, this compilation confirmed Seattle as something seemingly more progressive: the home of *fusion*.

The idea of 'fusion' itself was certainly nothing new in rock. Steve Waksman is surely right that it had existed since the advent of hard rock in the early 1970s, part of a constant story of opposition and recombination as metal solidified and punk 'arose as a dream shared by a small coterie of critical voices concerning what rock should be and could become'.[16] Fusion formed a necessary part, in other words, of the negotiation, always ongoing, between the two genres, and many indie rock labels of the early 1980s inherited its language in capturing what their music was all about.[17] Even so, fusion has become especially strongly associated with the Seattle scene. This is in part because it appeals as a piece of music history: the rock fusion that critics heard on *Deep Six* would soon become named 'grunge', or the 'Seattle sound' – metal music fused with punk attitude, or something along those often-repeated lines. Fusion also works well in social terms, since it seems to reconcile what were clearly antagonistic subcultures in the northwest, in turn easily written back into the 1960s history of the region: the Wailers who 'wanted to be big stars' versus the Sonics who 'couldn't play their instruments'.[18]

Perhaps most of all, 'fusion' is useful because it hints at the special conditions of the Seattle of the early 1980s. These include the city's famously restrictive licensing laws and lack of performance venues, recording studios and practice spaces, which meant that close-quarters sharing was unavoidable. The Mudhoney frontman Mark Arm vividly recalled one Seattle venue of the early 1980s where 'you'd see these punk rock dirt bags mixing with kids in pink spandex and teased hair', since metal and punk shows were going on simultaneously in different rooms (it is interesting to speculate what this sounded like).[19] Nils Bernstein, later a key Sub Pop publicist, paints a rosier picture:

There were a lot of punk rockers and metal heads and hippies, and there were a lot of punk rock hippies and metal punk rockers. Everyone lived together, everyone jammed together, everyone hung out and went to the same shows and had the same record collections. And when one person bought the first Big Black record, everyone did.[20]

By 1986 critics were poised to take advantage of Seattle as rock fusion city and to exploit its possibilities as identity. Reviewing *Deep Six* in the Seattle *Rocket*, Dawn Anderson, for one, points out that three years previously she had published a few issues of a fanzine specifically dedicated to 'breaking down some barriers by featuring bands like Mötley Crüe alongside bands like D.O.A'. At the time this seemed like an 'utterly ludicrous thing to do', but now, with the release of *Deep Six*, she triumphantly says 'I told you so', and stresses the obvious influence of metal on the compilation's acts, both in their onstage look and in their music:

> The fact that none of these bands could open for Metallica or the Exploited without suffering abuse merely proves how thoroughly the underground's [*sic*] absorbed certain influences, resulting in music that isn't punk-metal but a third sound distinct from either.
>
> Some of these influences are apparent visually; blatant posing on the stage is acceptable again. I've seen all but one of these bands live at least once and a few of the musicians, along with many of their fans, could pass for members of Ratt. Some people find this distracting, as it seems to have little to do with the style of their music. I personally don't mind boys in makeup . . . Heavy metal influence is also apparent in the music itself; in the showy guitar playing, horrendous screaming and the length of the songs.[21]

In fact, Anderson continues, the bands on *Deep Six* had learned valuable lessons from their influences. Though their songs might be as 'multi-dimensional' and full of 'musical intricacies' as any of their metal models, still they knew that they had to trade on 'noise value alone' to win over the 'casual listener'. The new Seattle 'third sound', in other words, was everything to everyone. It had a depth that would reward repeated listenings, but still its creators had realized, unlike 'most heavy metal bands', that 'technical finesse should never be an end in itself.' Screaming the listener into submission was a far more effective strategy.

Bruce Pavitt, on the other hand, makes a typical attempt to capture the experience of these bands' music through a slogan. 'It's slow SLOW and heavy HEAVY' is his summary verdict in April 1986.[22] Not all of the record is slow in a literal sense: the second Melvins song, as one good example, is an explosive 39-second rant. 'Slow' and 'heavy' are better taken as the reactions of Pavitt as young punk (and self-proclaimed hater of metal) to the obvious inclusion of metal techniques on *Deep Six*, including the thickening out of the bottom end of the sound to make it 'heavier' (sometimes by down-tuning instruments), the use of certain melodic and harmonic turns of phrase, extravagant solos and specific guitar effects like the shimmering 'chorus' sound. All of these apply to Soundgarden, who have three tracks on *Deep Six*. One of them, 'Heretic', even introduces some Spinal Tap-esque cod supernatural content, another stereotypical feature of metal. ('"[M]etal" songs have little basis in reality,' Pavitt writes elsewhere, 'emphasizing satanism, fantasy and mythology. But it's all rock 'n' roll.'[23])

From this punk point of view, 'heavy' and 'slow' function as words that reveal the presence of 'fusion', and Pavitt consistently applies them when he later mentions *Deep Six* or its bands in his fanzine.[24] Significantly, he is also willing to name *Deep Six* as holding 'THE predominant sound of underground Seattle in '86', and tells his readers to 'BUY THIS RECORD OR MOVE' – as in, *this is it*, this record sums up Seattle's new local musical identity. Most tellingly of all, he also signals his own ambitions by suggesting how it might be perfected. Instead of the closing U-Men track, by far the most stereotypically pogo-punk three minutes on the record, he suggests that a less 'out of context' choice would have been a 'fat slab from skull thumpers My Eye'. This was another new Seattle band whose demo tape, then doing the rounds, more obviously ticks the 'metal' boxes listed above.[25]

Punk-metal fusion is undoubtedly useful for placing *Deep Six* in the history of Seattle rock, as well as for capturing what its early local critics found in it and chose to mobilize. Where it quickly wears thin is as a tool for approaching individual songs on the record. The Melvins' 'Scared', for example, can be heard on one level as connecting hardcore punk (Matt Lukin's lightning solo bass riff, returning several times) with hard rock or metal (the main guitar riff).[26] But to leave it at that is by no means to do justice to this remarkable song. Indeed it is to smooth out the basic strangeness of this music, in which a complicated twist of performed (con)fusions is self-consciously the point. Buzz Osborne's astonishing vocal sounds like Alice Cooper being slowly fed through a mangle; it just about holds together the exaggerated speed changes that drag the song reluctantly from one style to another, the stadium rock moments in which the whole band shouts ('Do it!/ Well alright now!') above the hammering drums alone and, most of all, the curiously tuneful frame that surrounds the central song and keeps interrupting it. This frame is filled with falsetto whooping, frantic cowbell hits, strokes of the hanging chimes, and finally an extended singalong for the band with its own outgoing riff – as if all the Melvins were joining in with their favourite TV theme tune, a punk Beach Boys on (more) acid. Overall, 'Scared' is bizarre. It seems to issue a smirking challenge to the listener to make head or tail of it ('Look at me!', Osborne wails in its very first line, 'and I'll look at you').

To be sure, not all the songs on *Deep Six* are so conspicuous or confrontational. But there are other cases where the attribution of a simple punk-metal 'fusion' is similarly restrictive. Take another of the record's outstanding tracks, Malfunkshun's 'With Yo' Heart (Not Yo' Hands)'. Already the band name signals something outside of punk or metal: 'Malfunkshun' is presumably a reference to Con Funk Shun, a Californian funk-R&B act with a string of chart hits throughout the 1970s and '80s (see also the 'yo's' of the song's title). And, while the tritone riff that swings like a pendulum throughout much of the song is easily labelled 'doom metal', Andrew Wood's vocal licks match Malfunkshun's stage act in their glam displays of outrageous spandex masculine power. The woman addressed by the song is a 'lost little woman', and the singer is obsessed with his own libido. 'One time for the man!' becomes a catchphrase. Kevin Wood's solo guitar, meanwhile, is something else again, a thick smog of atonal feedback, distortion and frantic lead-playing that both generates much of the song's glowering atmosphere and descends through it in a series of mechanized whines.[27]

Perhaps the best way to sum up 'With Yo' Heart (Not Yo' Hands)' is to say that it is claustrophobic – 'heavy' in yet another sense. The song never opens up, has no space to breathe at all; the recording is notoriously terrible, but this of course only intensifies the overall effect. The handclaps that suddenly mark the beat after the bridge might evoke the easy psychedelic styles of Marc Bolan or Mott the Hoople, all the honking swing of the 1970s bari sax. But somehow they don't. And Andrew Wood's Steven Tyler-style stuttering and scatting at the end of song sounds not so much glam-ecstatic as straitjacketed, fighting off the demons unleashed around him in a dense overlap of screams, not the chorused hordes of lost little women. In hindsight, and with the specific knowledge that in 1990 Wood was to be one of the earliest grunge artists to die of a heroin overdose, the song becomes quite uncomfortable to hear.

So I don't think that 'fusion', specifically 'punk-metal fusion', always fits the bill, as compelling as it is in some ways. Anderson is surely just as incisive when, again in her *Deep Six* review of 1986, she writes that 'bands today can get by with rifling rock history for any cheap thrill they can find,' and praises the compilation's 'lack of direction', its realization that musicians need to 'concentrate on music rather than fitting a style'. Indeed, they 'toy with [style] rather than live by it'.[28] This description certainly captures something of the Melvins' humour in 'Scared', and the endless rock allusions they hit as they pinball between the twin foundations of punk and metal. It also gets at something in Malfunkshun's 'With Yo' Heart' – except that to sum up this song as only a 'cheap thrill' would be to miss what is compelling about it (perhaps this is what Anderson acknowledges when she calls it a 'genuine lemon-squeezer'). *Deep Six* may have been a 'fuck you' to the 'popular music' of the time, as Daniel House put it, but the bigger point is that the retro cultures of rock were here repeatedly stirred up, revived and made monstrous. At the same moment they became ridiculous through parody and low production values. If you don't laugh, you'll cry. Perhaps that is the phrase to capture the appeal underlying what Anderson and Pavitt uncompromisingly heard as the new, heavy sound for the mid-1980s: the sound of Seattle, buy it or move.

Doubly Reactionary

Deep Six is in many ways a remarkable collection of songs. Still, another compilation, *Sub Pop 200* (December 1988), managed to up the ante on it, even as it closely imitated it. *Sub Pop 200* was itself quite a departure for Pavitt and Poneman's new Sub Pop label, since its previous compilation, *Sub Pop 100* (July 1986), had not been a 'Seattle' compilation at all. In fact, only a few of its artists are even from the greater Northwest region, and so it resembles the earlier tape-fanzine compilations, *Sub Pop #5, #7* and *#9* (1981–3), like these comprising material from new regional North American artists, an international indie band (Shonen Knife), and established 'alternative' acts like Sonic Youth and Wipers.

Sub Pop 200, on the other hand, is immediately notable as a narrow 'Seattle' compilation. Only one of its bands, Denver's the Fluid, comes from outside Washington State, and so the whole thing seems an obvious attempt by Pavitt and Poneman to enter the race to curate and represent Seattle rock. By late 1988 they could credibly stake their claim in this race. Their new label exclusively represented eight or so bands from the Pacific Northwest, and most of these were still together and active. All of them had tracks on *Sub Pop 200*, and so the compilation delivered on two intertwined objectives: it brought (in Steve Waksman's words) 'valuable attention to many of the label's own artists', and, through the non-label bands also featured, simultaneously established 'Sub Pop's broader role as the primary curator of Seattle rock, the conduit through which the local scene would become known to the world at large'.[29]

This makes *Sub Pop 200* a powerfully reactionary statement in two different directions. First, it was a clear response to C/Z's attempt, with *Deep Six*, to corner this musical identity and its market; there are quite a few anecdotes that suggest Pavitt and Poneman's efforts to oust C/Z as a competitor in what they were trying to shape as *their* scene.[30] Second, *Sub Pop 200* is an even louder 'fuck you' to the popular music of the time. Almost all of it is 'guitar heavy' and 'loud or angry' (to recall House's description of *Deep Six*), rock in unreconstructed form; notably, there are no longer any ambient or electronic tracks as there had been from the very first of the *Sub Pop* compilation tapes. Even the experimental Steve Fisk's contribution snaps largely to the standard rock ensemble (compare his track 'Go at Full Throttle' on *Sub Pop 100* and what the liner notes call its 'disorienting tape manipulation'). As such, it might be said that *Sub Pop 200*

shoves *Deep Six* entirely out of the picture by borrowing and mag-
nifying its basic characteristics. It was pressed in 5,000 copies rather
than 2,000, and it offers twenty tracks instead of fourteen, seventy
minutes instead of 45. This last fact means that it won't fit on a single
LP; it would fit on two, but it is actually split across three 12" discs,
functioning in effect like three EPs, three or four tracks per side.
These are necessarily presented in a box – textured black, with 'hype'
sticker – that includes within a sleek and shiny sixteen-page booklet
of accompanying photographs and credits. In short, *Sub Pop 200* is
self-consciously lavish.

Poneman has spoken of this presentation as a rejection of the
'*Bonfire of the Vanities*-type yuppie culture' of Seattle business, a
parody designed to attack 'corporate culture through grotesque
overstatement'.[31] This is consistent, of course, with the independent mission of the old fanzine, as well as with the tongue-in-cheek
delusions of grandeur that issued out of it. The spine of the *Sub Pop
100* vinyl sleeve reads as follows: 'SUB POP: the new thing: the big
thing: the God thing: a mighty multinational entertainment con-
glomerate based in the Pacific Northwest'. The *Sub Pop 200* booklet
combines corporate-style photos of Pavitt and Poneman in suits
('Supervisory Chairman of Executive Management' and 'Executive
Chairman of Supervisory Management' respectively), a massively
oversized representation of Washington State within the map of the
USA, a picture of a towering building named as 'Sub Pop World Headquarters', and the following introductory text (in which the label
name is actually the company logo):

DEAR CUSTOMERS,
Thank you for coming to [SUB POP] for your entertainment
needs. Our experienced and qualified staff is always ready to
serve you. We at [SUB POP] take great pride in offering you

the finest in Northwest ROCK. Remember, if it isn't [SUB POP],
it probably sucks.

Rocking you heavily, the staff at [SUB POP].[32]

Obviously all this is funny, a series of ridiculous exaggerations
designed to press home the point that exactly their opposites are
true: Sub Pop as small, non-corporate, informal, friendly, fantasist,
authentic and endearingly 'crazy' (the gradual breakdown of the corporate language in the text above suggests as much). At the same
time, the humour is disarming; it tries to conceal the commercial
ambitions of the label by placing them in plain sight. I assume that
the *Sub Pop 200* booklet's 'Direct-to-Retail Sales Hotline' phone
number is no parody, and nor is the consumer reassurance that
'American Express, Visa and Mastercard' were all acceptable as forms
of payment. These indicate the necessary financial apparatus of the
growing business. Likewise, the comic excess hides the torpedo-
like gesture of *Sub Pop 200*, its aim to blow competitors like C/Z out
of the water. I know of no estimate of how much it cost to produce
and distribute, but it must have been considerable. Committing to
5,000 boxed three-EP copies, with shiny booklet (in comparison to
the 2,000 copies or so more common for a Sub Pop single-artist
standard LP release) feels like a calculated business decision.

The same could be said of the compilation's content. Listening
across the twenty tracks, it is as if the label were staking claim to a
commanding position in the Seattle rock landscape, drawing on the
core of the *Deep Six* idea of the 'underground' and adding to it at
its fringes in numerous ways. At least one lineage runs through the
box set: Mark Arm and Steve Turner's old band, Green River, has a
song, as does their new band, Mudhoney, as does an older side project of theirs, the Thrown Ups; there is, too, a cover of a Green River
standard by the Fastbacks. Also present, far more so than on *Deep*

Six, is a folksy Americana, encompassing the folklore of Green River's 'Hangin' Tree', the freewheeling jangle of the Walkabouts, and the genre of the sixties protest song (with Terry Lee Hale). Girl Trouble's cover of 'Gonna Find a Cave', made famous on '60s kids' TV by the Banana Splits, adds a lo-fi juvenile, 'garage' quality into the mix. And while Steven Jesse Bernstein's entirely spoken-word track 'Come Out Tonight' momentarily silences the roaring guitars (in favour of something like poetic substance), even this, like almost all the others, was recorded and produced by Jack Endino – which suggests an obvious drive for identity of 'Seattle sound', another self-conscious improvement over *Deep Six*.

Bearing in mind this relationship to the earlier compilation, it is also no surprise to find all kinds of musical fusions and collisions running across *Sub Pop 200*. Some of these are plain to hear: the Walk-abouts' 'Got No Chains' bluntly integrates lonely harmonica and strummed strings into driving punk rock, something reminiscent of the R.E.M. of the earlier 1980s. Some are more fluent. On the one hand, Swallow's 'Zoo' contains what seems almost an embarrass-ment of riffs for a simple verse–chorus song, all of them coloured by ominous metal harmony and played by downtuned guitars. At half-speed it might sound like generic metal, then; but at its actual lightning pace it has a frightening energy, made visceral by the verse's brutal stab chords, the relentless drums, the lack of any bridge or solo section, and the tortured lead that screams over the introduc-tion to each of the later verses. Above it all, Rod Moody's vocal can be summed up as neither sneering punk nor metal growl, but instead a perfect attempt to capture the lyrics' image of the ravening beast locked tight inside the cage.

More obvious elsewhere are the 'cheap thrills' of rifling and rummaging through rock history, just as Dawn Anderson identified them on *Deep Six*. Another new regional band, Nirvana, contributed their song 'Spank Thru' to the compilation. The opening of this might be called a kind of doe-eyed country rock, all jangly guitar chords and honeyed words about pairs of lovers, flowers and mountains. As such it is also clearly a parody, perhaps of certain 1960s styles, as signalled by its overcooked features: the low doubling of Cobain's half-spoken vocals, as if trying to lend the banal lyrics more 'depth', and Chad Channing's chipper drum track. A short transition, however, turns the corner into quite another style. The doubling to Cobain's voice is suddenly cut and he moves into his higher, more familiar register, a scream ushering in an obsessively repetitive sludge-metal riff, apt for the lyrics' sudden turn from the cliché of happy lovers to the subject of masturbation.

The two parts of the song are in comic contradiction in every way, and it must be said that a lot of this is pure Melvins (Dawn Anderson, in fact, liked to refer to the early Nirvana as the 'Melvins' fan club').[33] Still, Cobain's ambition to join up disparate rock styles – equally obvious from 'Mexican Seafood', a song Nirvana contributed to a c/z compilation of this time – has an intensity and seamlessness about it that the Melvins were rarely interested in.[34] The fearsome scream that connects the two parts of 'Spank Thru' erupts furiously out of the mountain song and touches down in new subterranean musical surroundings. White-hot, it is calculated to fuse the song together with an energy later revisited in its raucous guitar anti-solo, an act of virtuoso masturbation if ever there was one, Cobain's strings bent almost to breaking point.

Perhaps the most striking 'fusion' of all on *Sub Pop 200*, however, is one that goes far beyond musical style. In an allusion to the Kiss song 'Detroit Rock City' (1976), Soundgarden's contribution is named 'Sub Pop Rock City', and fittingly it mimics 1970s hard rock with a panache that only talented players like this band could achieve. The mixing into the bridge of two (apparently genuine) answering machine messages, one from Poneman and one from Pavitt, achieves several additional things. It intensifies the sense of parody, gives the band – who had left Sub Pop early for SST – a joke at their debut label's expense, and most of all fuses music to commercial statement, transforming the style into a memorable advertising vehicle. The Sub Pop founders appear as power-hungry control freaks lording it over the Seattle rock scene – an exaggeration, again, that both conceals and reveals the intention of the box set through humour. In this regard, it is also worth noting that Chris Cornell's lyrics are largely on-message, describing, in the first person, a journey to the distant 'Sub Pop Rock City' of the chorus, and laced with Pavitt's buzzword 'heavy' and all kinds of drugs and sex and 'in-crowd' references. The song performs, in other words, a pilgrimage to Pavitt and Poneman's new rock Mecca in all its loser glory. Within a few months, the European press would be parroting exactly this image.

Sub Pop's Nirvana: Cobain, Novoselic, Channing.

Sub Pop's chief British advocate, Everett True, titled his March 1989 article for *Melody Maker* 'Sub Pop. Seattle: Rock City'. A German interview with Nirvana shortly afterwards describes them as the 'new child prodigies from Sub Pop Rock City, Seattle, WA.'[35]

Boring

In his *Sub Pop USA* column of January 1987 Pavitt wrote that the 'Seattle scene' was 'gearing up for a major explosion'. Again, in March of that year, he wrote that it was on the verge of 'world domination'. And yet again, in June, that the 'next few years will see the ultra-heavy rock of Seattle rival the *Motor City* scene of the early '70s.'[36]

Possibly he already had the *Sub Pop 200* project in mind by then, and was carrying out some early groundwork for its reception. Even if he didn't, recent critics have obliged by turning the compilation into a stick of dynamite. Justin Henderson finds it to be a document of a '"Seattle Sound," a.k.a. grunge', that was 'about to conquer the world'. Stephen Tow sees it as indicating 'the moment when Seattle music had reached fruition and maturity'. Gillian Gaar calls her recent book on the Sub Pop label *World Domination*; she cites the label's chief photographer, Charles Peterson, in calling *Sub Pop 200* a 'turning point', evidence of a 'pretty serious foundation of talent'.[37]

The label must also have been pleased that many contemporary critics found the compilation both authoritative and innovative. The British DJ and influencer John Peel, writing for *The Observer* in what was apparently *Sub Pop 200*'s first international review, dismissed the earlier compilation *Seattle Syndrome* (Engram, 1981) as unrepresentative of the region's music, aligned the name 'Sub Pop' with that of 'Seattle' in the mouths of true fans, and spoke in glowing tones of the label's 'house sound' (a 'thick, angry, pressure-cooker guitar/bass/drums/vocals turbulence'). It was almost as if he had been fed these lines as propaganda, and possibly he was; his histrionic ending ('The God thing is coming') is suspenseful in the extreme and repeats part of the spine slogan of *Sub Pop 100*.[38] Similarly, Dawn Anderson's magazine *Backlash* found *Sub Pop 200* to be one of the albums of the year, and calls it a 'time piece' – as in, something to show off with on your arm, as well as something to structure your life around.[39] And, writing for the San Francisco *Advocate*, Adam Block stressed *Sub Pop 200*'s preferred status as the 'premier indie-anthology box *ever*'.[40]

It was not all a story of immediate world domination, however, and this is as important to note as it is easily forgotten. There were negative critiques of *Sub Pop 200* too, perhaps the most extensive of which was that of the British critic Simon Reynolds in his review for *Melody Maker*. For Reynolds, the compilation saw the Sub Pop label self-appointing as 'a guardian of the true delinquent tradition of rock 'n' roll. The '56/'66/'76 axis, the lineage that runs through rockabilly, Sixties garage, punk, and between those pivots, Iggy, No Wave, hardcore, and the more dumb-ass metal of the early Seventies.'[41] The problem with this was that, in 1988, to keep walking this axis was to offer little more than a tedious continuation in the same direction. In a rock history littered with delinquents, to remain a delinquent was, ironically, to stay safely on the 'straight and narrow'.

As such, for Reynolds the bands on *Sub Pop 200* could show little exciting and nothing new. He writes off the Fluid, Blood Circus, Chemistry Set and Swallow as 'firmly in the mould of the Saints and late Iggy', their music comprising 'emphatic, telling guitar blows and anti-heroic bluster, riffs as trusty and blinkered as old warhorses, and raw-cuss vocals'. Beat Happening are similarly dismissed as a dire fifties rewind who like to pretend that they can 'recover the moment before the notion of "tradition" was even *conceivable*' (this might also apply to the comparably lo-fi Girl Trouble, Cat Butt and the Thrown Ups). And while Nirvana and Green River show 'cleverness and dexterity', even these have been outmoded by 'simplistic monotony' – the realization that 'last year the coolest thing to be was *asleep*', not furious.

Sub Pop 200 was, on this view, not at all revolutionary or explosive or game-changing, but the one thing that rock must never be, and that, as salespeople, Pavitt and Poneman would want to avoid at all costs. It was seventy minutes of *boring* (to use the word that Reynolds applies to, of all the bands featured, Nirvana). He arrives at the following conclusion about the compilation: 'Those old and foolish enough to hanker for the next "revolution" are wasting their time if they're looking here. For the real convulsions are being conducted by the cosmonauts of inner/outer space, not those who hark back to an obsolete model of teenage rampage "wild in the streets".'

As the first half of this chapter shows, I can't quite agree with all that this implies. There are all kinds of exhilarating moments on *Sub Pop 200* (and, to be fair, Reynolds does acknowledge some of these). Still, I think he is pointing to something extremely important about the costs involved in *Sub Pop 200*'s double reaction, its angry rock response to the 'drift of the post-Joy Division generation of bands towards cuteness' (as Peel puts it). For all the innovation critics have wanted to hear on the compilation, Reynolds is right: it can just as easily be heard as profoundly reactionary, *conservative*, a kind of setting-in-stone or keeping of American rock's flame of the thirty years that preceded it. For seasoned rock listeners looking for some new direction, *Sub Pop 200* was more of the same old.

Primal Rock Stuff

It is intriguing, then, to see where Reynolds locates the real 'revolution'. Sonic Youth's *Daydream Nation* (also released in late 1988) marks the actual way forward for rock in his view, a move beyond *Sub Pop 200*'s dated 'joint-trashing rumpus' and a taking up of 'more spacious and galactic forays' in the direction of 'rapture'. At first glance, it seems unfair to pit *Sub Pop 200* – a multi-artist compilation, in part a label sampler – against *Daydream Nation*, generally acknowledged as one of the great single-artist albums of the decade. On the other hand, it is worth risking the comparison. Throughout *Daydream Nation*, Sonic Youth play with rock's parameters in ways that *Sub Pop 200*'s bands simply do not: in terms of its sounds, its tunings, its song lengths and forms. To take only one example, the second track, 'Silver Rocket', is a verse–chorus rock song so formulaic that its bridge seems to rebel, breaking down into pulseless noise alone. There may be 'anti-solos' all over *Sub Pop 200*, in Steve Waksman's sense of an 'alternative virtuosity' that draws deliberately on sounds and techniques way outside the frame established by the song.[42] But the bridge of 'Silver Rocket' contains the true 'anti-solo' if ever there was one: a prime space for a solo in which the screaming guitars can force nothing coherent whatsoever, and rapture must stem from rock's disintegration rather than its affirmation.

What stops *Daydream Nation* ever being boring, however, is the same feature that is most unmissable and iconic about it. This is Kim Gordon's commanding vocal presence, from her mysterious incantations of the record's first seconds to the fizzing sex aggression with which she brutally intervenes on what would otherwise be its gentle fade-out ending. Again, there is nothing of the kind on *Sub Pop 200*. Across a cast of some sixty to seventy musicians on the compilation I can count only four women, and only two of these sing (and are in that sense 'visible'). One of these, the Walkabouts' Carla Torgerson, sings back-up. The other, Kim Warnick on the Fastbacks' cover of 'Swallow My Pride', is an obvious choice, since the song's lyrics are based around a boy–girl conversation; Warnick's vocals bring forward the women's backing voices that were anyway present in the original Green River song.

What I am trying to get at here is that the 'conservatism' of *Sub Pop 200* might be thought of as something more than a straightforward rock-*musical* conservatism. It extends to gender as well. Obviously this needs closer comment. Mark Arm has recalled, 'It wasn't an anomaly to have women in Seattle bands . . . There just didn't happen to be women in the bands that got huge in the '90s.'[43] This seems right. Pavitt's early *Sub Pop* fanzine overflows with northwestern bands that featured women musicians prominently (and sometimes exclusively): Chinas Comidas, the Enemy, the Beakers, the Girls, the Neo Boys, the Visible Targets and the Dishrags, to name only a few. So do many of the early 1980s Seattle compilations mentioned above. So too did the *Sub Pop* tape-fanzine compilations and *Sub Pop 100*.

The problem, then, is that Arm's statement makes it sound like a natural occurrence that none of these women made their way into the subsequent grunge spotlight ('there just didn't happen to be'), rather than asking whether it might have been a conscious decision of certain Seattle compilation makers of the mid-1980s to cut out women's bands in creating the 'Seattle sound'. When, in 2011, Everett True denied that 'grunge was overwhelmingly male' and claimed that 'women were totally represented', he wasn't remembering it quite right – or, at least, he was thinking of a later time, perhaps post-1990.[44] Likewise, Catherine Strong cites a Sub Pop grunge compilation of 1991 to support her view that the label offered a more 'healthy showing' of women musicians than earlier rock.[45] Maybe so, but still: on the early label flagship compilations like *Sub Pop 200* that defined the genre, grunge really *was* overwhelmingly male, and that appears to have been part of the design and ingrained in its background of influences. *Deep Six*, I note, has no women artists on it at all.

An obvious objection to this would be that, at least in 1988, there simply weren't any women's bands making what was now coalescing as the 'ultra-heavy Seattle sound'. Then again, what is *the* 'sound' on *Sub Pop 200*? Even if we could agree on that (perhaps using John Peel's 'thick, angry, pressure-cooker' line), it still makes sound and gender into things that can be separated. My point is that this sound and masculinity were here sold together, as one and the same: metal 'fusion' assumed masculinity, which assumed men's voices and men's bands, which assumed delivery to a core of implicitly male listeners and collectors in a thick no-nonsense black box like aftershave, completely free of ornament in the most stereotypically hardcore masculine way. The exaggeration is certainly funny: 'How much more black could this be?', asks Spinal Tap's Nigel Tufnel of the sleeve for their record *Smell the Glove*. But it also makes a point. In all the rock-critic universalizing grunge talk of the Seattle 'cabal of misfits' (Jonathan Evison), the roaring guitars as 'human reaction to the drum machines' (Everett True), and the exciting advent of 'primal rock stuff' (Pavitt), it should be remembered that the baseline of primal misfit humanity is always assumed to be male – that is, nowhere near the whole of humanity at all.[46]

This, in turn, threatens to affiliate *Sub Pop 200* and *Deep Six* with the world that Gina Arnold has described in the most striking terms: the late 1980s American indie scene that was *more* misogynistic than the mindless rock 'groupiedom' that it opposed, precisely because its misogyny was 'more a power trip than a sex one'. The impression of growing numbers of women in bands across the 1980s, Arnold continues, is deceptive, since indie rock was actually 'less welcoming to women than the punk scene before'. She draws attention, for example, to the almost complete dearth of women lead guitarists in that era.[47] (Others have argued that the woman bass player, well known in alternative rock, led to the instrument's role in the band being devalued by male critics).[48] And although Bon von Wheelie, the Girl Trouble drummer, says that she personally experienced no 'gender discrimination', her words suggest that sexist attitudes and language were so internalized they became unnoticeable:

> I think I've been in a unique position because I was always older than everybody else. That put me in a different category than probably some of the other female musicians playing at the same time. In other words, nobody thought of me (or at least not at that point) as 'datable'. Cute girls in a band can sometimes bring extra tensions. I didn't have that problem. In the band it was me and my 'three brothers' (one of them being my real brother). I'd been going to all those shows, and those other musicians already had seen me around and treated me as an equal. I never felt any type of gender discrimination. In fact probably some of those guys were scared of me because they couldn't figure out what an old broad was doing playing drums in a band.[49]

Actually, the same point about social conservatism can be pushed even further than this. When Simon Reynolds remarks in his review that *Sub Pop 200* preaches the 'Gospel according to Lester Bangs, in fact, although he eventually dissed all that in an essay called "The White Noise Supremacists"', it seems to me that he means to suggest something quite specific. In the essay in question (1979), Bangs, the celebrated punk critic, finally called out the New York hardcore scene for what could, at best, be called its conservatism, and at worst its engrained racism and fascination with fascist symbolism (he refers to 'swastikas, Iron Crosses, and jackboots onstage').[50]

To align *Sub Pop 200* with a pre-enlightened Bangs, as Reynolds does, is to insinuate something far more provocative than it first appears, and more than sexism alone. It locates the compilation within what Bangs identifies as the 'evolution of sound, rhythm, and stance running from the Velvets through the Stooges to the Ramones and their children', a trend that he sees as having gradually erased the profound black contribution to American popular music in favour of the 'purely white' New Wave.[51] In turn it places *Sub Pop 200* in the lineage described by one reviewer of *Seattle Syndrome Two* (Engram, 1982):

> The general impression is one of affluent white suburban kids desperately trying to avoid working for daddy by forming bands to imitate music that was already pretty narrowly defined a couple of years ago . . . I have to wonder if there are any blacks, hispanics or Italians in Seattle, because it sounds like the closest any of these bands ever got to listening to funk or soul was the Thompson Twins. Shoot an alligator for me.[52]

Or as Gina Arnold more vividly and provocatively summarizes a similar point:

> Because my world, the independent world of the eighties, for all its supposed liberality, was essentially apolitical: it was white, it was sexist, and it was cruel. Yes, it rebelled against conformity and greed, but it also reflected the whole era's selfishness in its ultimate dismissal of responsibility and kindness.[53]

Sex God Missy

Of course, there are all kinds of things that must be said in response to this. Pavitt's *Sub Pop* fanzine was never outrightly misogynistic or racist. It was certainly never *Conflict* or *Forced Exposure*, contemporary fanzines that Arnold cites for their sexist style, or (as Bangs writes) Florida's *New Order* with its posed shots in front of the headquarters of the 'United White People's Party'.[54] At worst the *Sub Pop* fanzine occasionally toyed with fascist imagery – Elvis with a Hitler moustache and combover to imply a point about the evils of music commerce – or gave positive coverage to artists who traded on a fascist mystique (see the Residents' *Third Reich 'n Roll*).[55] In general, however, misogyny, racism and fascist symbolism were not central to its interests and advertising strategy. In some ways, indeed, Sub Pop is notable because ultimately it did *not* set and police the boundaries of white masculinity in the manner of its hardcore and heavy rock influences. Its logo was a straightforward rendering of the label name (compare, for example, the 'Imperial Eagle'-like symbol sometimes used by fellow Washington State indie Amphetamine Reptile; or the infamous 'SS' in the Kiss band logo).[56] And on the discovery of the early Soundgarden, Bruce Pavitt has said that he was drawn to the band because the 'bass player was Japanese, the guitar player was Indian'. They were 'interesting' to him precisely because the metal scene their music referenced was so 'very white, very homogenous'.[57]

From this perspective the compilation *Sub Pop 200* might be seen as another joke, an exaggeratedly narrow base of white masculine rock from which to work away – Sub Pop leading the charge towards what Arnold identifies as the better days of the early 1990s, in which the generation after hers 'changed some of its focus'.[58] After all, alongside *Sub Pop 200* in December 1988 the label released a single split between Mudhoney and Sonic Youth – with Kim Gordon, no less, singing one of the lead vocals. EPs and LPs of this time appeared from Girl Trouble (September 1988, featuring Bon von Wheelie) and the Walkabouts (March 1989, with Carla Torgerson's vocals). A little later there was a sudden flurry of releases from all-woman bands, or thereabouts: L7, Dickless, Babes in Toyland, Hole. And this, of course, is only to consider musicians on record. As the extended *Sub Pop 200* credits also reveal, Nicole Messa, Lisa Orth and Alice Wheeler formed a key part of the Sub Pop creative team behind the scenes. (This was also, by the way, the case for *Deep Six*, for which Tina Casale, co-founder of the C/Z label, is named as co-producer).

Still, to argue this line about *Sub Pop 200* also seems too apologetic. It reminds me a little bit of the classic episode of *The Simpsons* where Principal Skinner tries to explain away his presence in a bordello: 'I was only in there to get directions on how to get away from there.' I don't think Sub Pop only wanted to *escape* rock's toxic masculinity. I think they wanted to maximize their appeal to as many fans as possible by indulging it at the same time as teasing at it: again, as Everett True put it, conferring the feelings of 'big dumb rock' and 'hipster cred' side by side, gathering up those with allegiances to both. Indeed, going beyond *Sub Pop 200* and surveying the approximately five hundred artists whose music Sub Pop released in its first hundred catalogue numbers (July 1986–May 1991), one statistic in particular stands out. Fewer than fifty of them are women; eight of those are anyway on *Sub Pop 100*, long before the grunge watershed of *Sub Pop 200*. Only a handful of these musicians would identify, moreover, as non-white, and so Rupa Huq's label for grunge as 'white noise', formed from a complex amalgam of white rock influences, is apt.[59]

To spell out what is obvious from a quick listen to almost any of these hundred releases, the label's early interest in 'primal rock stuff' is also an exploration of white masculinity. Specifically, this is a 'loser' masculinity that took its cue from the larger Seattle identity already established in the earlier 1980s – stuck out on the edge of nowhere, rude, raw, primitive, working, suffering and desperate, original; 'sarcastic first-person exposés of guy pathology', as Terri Sutton said of Nirvana.[60] As such, I think these hundred records also demonstrate a business decision. As the *Sub Pop* fanzine entered the riskier financial territory of a fledgling record label in 1986–7, it was no longer an optimistic matter of finding fun and pop and frivolous local hanky-panky only. It now needed to force a focus, to turn into a 'serious' and 'credible' business – a shift that, as Catherine Strong points out, has often been accompanied in popular-music history by the exclusion of women from the forefront.[61] A regional lesson Seattle-style, from the Gospel according to Lester Bangs, was likely the safest option. And if, in 1990–91, the flurry of releases by what have become iconic women's grunge bands (L7, Hole, Babes in Toyland, as well as Shonen Knife) seems a moment of impressively progressive novelty, that effect is in part because the early label had itself worked against the normalization of women's bands in rock over the preceding decade.

Nowhere is the nature of Sub Pop's 'primal rock stuff' more obvious than the flagship collection *Sub Pop 200*, which lines up one loser masculinity after the other like some freakshow identity parade. We hear Cobain's 'Spank Thru', a song in which the woman is literally discarded in favour of masturbation. There is the Fluid's on-the-road zipper blues, Chemistry Set's stuck-in-your-room getting high anthem; there is the surfer bum of Blood Circus, the jilted lover of the Thrown-Ups, the drunken antics of Cat Butt, the suicide allure of Green River. As the last verse of Swallow's 'Zoo' reveals, even the furious beast in the cage is as much a poser clamouring for attention as a primal (male) animal. Only occasionally is there what might pass for politics, but even this is as distorted as in a hall of mirrors. Steven Jesse Bernstein's cantankerous ode to Jackie Kennedy demolishes any sense of nostalgia for the American sixties. Terry Lee Hale's acoustic protest song implodes into howling feedback.

Of course, all these are frequently as funny and pathetic as they are threatening, and that is part of the charm of the collection. But it is hard to see and hear them as anything other than deeply invested in the masculine loser. The first seconds of the first *Sub Pop 200* record – the label's opening gambit on its most important release to date, remember – make this as clear as anything. They are given to another new Seattle band, TAD, whose first full release for Sub Pop (March 1989) would bear the 'heaviest' (also most male) title the band could think of, *God's Balls*, and would in early copies come with a promotional 'Manzine' ('MOTHERS: Hide Your Daughters' runs the line on its front cover). It is no surprise, then, that TAD's song for the compilation is heaviness so fully optimized that it verges on caricature. Beginning with deep 'tribal' drums alone, it builds anticipation for the metal guitars to tear in a few seconds later, at the very bottom of their ranges with a riff that can barely be described as a riff at all; really more a muscular power-chord chug with a sudden rhythmic turnaround in its tail, curiously reminiscent of car horns hammered in heavy traffic. The snarling main voice, meanwhile, describes lurid sex acts in crude metaphor, and the distorted CB-radio-mike repetitions of the 'trucker' backing vocal are largely unintelligible except for one word: 'pussy'. Several guitar anti-solos come and go, and the last one cannot be called a display of technical prowess so much as an act of musical strangulation. Single notes are throttled out of the guitar one by one, the pitches changing as if by the tightening of the grip. This song is titled 'Sex God Missy', a curious collision of nouns that means nothing so much as the self-destructive vice – sex, drugs, prostitution, suicide – that is made to seep out of the song's every pore.

As such, 'Sex God Missy' is both a powerful and deeply un-comfortable opening statement, something that became a badge of identity for band and label, and was soon revisited by Jack Endino for a so-called 'Lumberjack Mix' on the first TAD album release a few months later. Some, like Simon Reynolds, praise it as a highlight of *Sub Pop 200*, a 'brutish groin-grind' that was one of the compila-tion's only novelties. Dawn Anderson, on the other hand, used it as an example when confronting the band about the apparent misog-yny of their lyrics. This drew a response from the frontman that made it clear that, whatever it meant, it was far more than a joke: 'I don't think any of it is a spoof. It's all genuine. We basically sing about sickness and people can take it with a grain of salt if they like, if that makes them feel better, or they can take it totally seriously.'[62]

Exactly this ambiguity, I think, permeates the whole collection. It also surrounds *Sub Pop 200*'s most famous image, drawn by Charles Burns for the front of the compilation's insert booklet. Here, for the first and last time to my knowledge, Burns presents a musician for Sub Pop, grotesque in stark black and white, and with a prominent Brylcreemed quiff that points to the fifties reminiscences of his typ-ical style for the old *Sub Pop* fanzine. A cartoon, it surely invites the viewer to take it with a grain of salt. Even so, it is no simple carica-ture of Elvis the King. With one foot kicked out in front of him in punk rock spasm, Burns's musician is bent almost double, and since he wears nothing but underwear and shoes, we can see almost every sinew of his body, as well as the sweat pouring off his face and the rictus tongue clenched tightly between his teeth. What he is expend-ing so much energy over appears to be the (ironically cute, diminutive, Spanish-style acoustic) guitar he holds, and the strain of making his skeletal fingers produce the shaky notes sounding from it. Actually it is not only, though, the effort of rocking out that is bending him double, but also the weight of the monkey bound to his back. (To have a 'monkey on your back', as the old Aerosmith song goes, is slang for a drug addiction. It is the monkey, by the way, that holds the microphone and appears to be doing the singing.)

What you are about to hear, Burns's image seems to say, will really suck. Look how much effort his Elvis man is pouring out for his quavering musical notes, and look at the cartoon-like 'fume lines' that surround the central figure and form his background, as if, quite literally, he and his music stink. You might even have sympathy for him. In black and white, and curled up double, he is seen as if through the scanner's monochrome screen, a tiny blighted foetus hanging on to the guitar as to life.

Then again, there is something important about the ground on which he walks. It is made of broken records, stereo equipment, perhaps parts of instruments too, and he is crushing them under his feet. The stink lines come off these as much as him, as they might from a rubbish dump. So at the same time as he sucks he seems like a warrior, massive in his surroundings, the tiny head hanging from his guitar's fretboard a token of primitive victory. It is what would become a typical Sub Pop brand statement in the next few years: the God thing as much as the Loser thing. Compelling and comic, its caricature of violent masculinity destroys music as much as it stands victorious on it, contorting itself in its compulsion to play.

3
Lamestains

There are a bunch of you who have scored your Soundgarden, Mudhoney and Nirvana records thinking you have the grunge cred covered. No chance. 'Primal Rock Therapy' is the acid test. The thing that made Blood Circus so great is that they were everclear to every other band's whiskey. No statements; no irony; no arty pretense . . . it's just industrial strength rock. And since when is that not good enough?[1]

WHAT JONATHAN PONEMAN is talking about is a Sub Pop CD reissue that appeared in November 1992. By then the three named bands had largely stolen what had been Sub Pop's grunge limelight, defining the genre on an international stage and piling high its cultural and economic capital. All three had already moved on to major label deals; Nirvana's *Nevermind* had gone platinum already, and Soundgarden's *Badmotorfinger* wasn't far behind it. In this light, Poneman's allusions to primitivity – the CD re-release in question is titled *Primal Rock Therapy* – seem designed to remind his audience that his Sub Pop was, in its own estimation, the original Seattle grunge label, the real thing, the authentic roots of the whole phenomenon. Likewise his references to illicit booze and the 'scoring' of records. These place this reissue as a pure substance untainted by the 'grunge cred' to which so many were now pledging their allegiance, and that his label had been so centrally involved in generating.

In fact, these notes were not only a matter of reclaiming territory now lost to other, bigger, richer labels. Poneman's back-to-basics was also a continuation of a Sub Pop sales identity that had been built up over at least the past five years. Compare his last lines above, for example, with Everett True's propaganda for Sub Pop's Nirvana in *Melody Maker* in March 1989:

> Basically, this is the real thing. No rock star contrivance, no intellectual perspective, no master plan for world domination. You're talking about four guys in their early twenties from rural Washington who wanna rock, who, if they weren't doing this, would be working in a supermarket or lumber yard, or fixing cars.[2]

Just in case this didn't make the point strongly enough, the same article also dismisses Simon Reynolds's verdict that early Nirvana in their 'cleverness' were 'too complex for their own good'.[3] 'Fuck that guy,' responds Kurt Cobain in true lumberyard style, 'what does he know? He was probably in a bad mood or something.'

There are countless similarly 'primitive' Sub Pop band descriptions, notably peaking around the release of *Sub Pop 200* in late 1988. These often link 'industrial strength' with 'primal strength', a return to rock's eternal foundations of pure noise and aggression via its obsession with the working classes, mixing in turn with the compelling idea of a 'distinctive' Seattle sound made possible by the city's remoteness from the 'harsh demands of fashion' (in True's words).[4] All this may have started, in fact, with Blood Circus, who in 1988 said of their music: 'If the cavemen were playing rock n' roll, this is what it would sound like.'[5] But through journalists like True, the same idea quickly caught on everywhere. In June 1989 he described Soundgarden's *Screaming Life* EP (SP12) as a 'thrusting, primal scream of articulated rage'.[6] In October John Robb introduced TAD as a 'shit-stained rock beast', and quoted the band's singer as saying that

Seattle was an 'isolated microcosm not affected by any New York or LA trends'.[7]

As these make equally clear, however, this primitive superiority to all other rock was only one component of the Sub Pop band image. After all, 'back to basics' also meant back to *basics*, regression towards something less evolved. As much as they were the 'total fucking godhead' of their 'unforgettable' live shows (as True says of Soundgarden), the label's bands were also presented as an unholy mess, a degenerate fusion that demonstrated nothing so much as the inability of these backwoods northwestern sons to live up to what their rock fathers had achieved (that it was *sons* and *fathers* who were in question, incidentally, is always implicit).[8] 'If you thought Ted Nugent and Black Oak Arkansas were retarded,' ran one label advertising line for Cat Butt in mid-1989, 'you'll find the Butt Gang totally subhuman. Primitive genius knows no boundaries.'[9] In the case of Blood Circus, Poneman's sleeve notes for the CD re-release begin by reminding the reader that their original record got 'panned by the critics' and was 'one of the worst selling products in the history of our company'. Significantly, he isn't saying this is unfair; he isn't blaming it on the ignorant critics. He leaves it open. Maybe the divine Blood Circus were, well, terrible; probably the label made a mistake ('I think the word is "stupid"', he says of his own release policy). And definitely you are a dupe for buying the CD that made such a lame attempt (*Primal Rock Therapy*?!) to revive this minor Seattle band.

It is a useful reminder that, as much as they were ever an elite, Sub Pop's bands were always losers too, in several different senses, and that this was an identity that the label used to loop its audience in, to create an in-joke of 'losership' shared between label, bands and fans. This, in fact, was where they focused most of their promotional energies. Where SST, for example, would devote album sleeves to confrontational political rants and inners to meticulously reproduced song lyrics, Sub Pop preferred to focus its growth strategy on building the bonds of losership. As this chapter and the next one show, this was a total project that spanned the label's language, images, design, music, media and merchandise – and often all of these in the same release.

It is also worth saying again that the same strategy went far beyond the late 1980s. Speaking as of 2022, the label's current website slogan is classically self-effacing: 'We're not the best, but we're pretty good.' 'Going out of Business since 1988' is another long-standing one. These kinds of expressions have been a constant over the past 35 years. And, thinking about it, they are exactly what stand out in the most celebrated Sub Pop anecdote of all. As everyone knows, in late 1992 a *New York Times* journalist phoned up Seattle rock insider and Sub Pop receptionist Megan Jasper and pressed her to give details of grunge speak; apparently he was given her number by none other than Jonathan Poneman. Jasper responded by making up, seemingly on the spot, a bunch of 'Seattle' phrases and definitions, which were duly printed in the national broadsheet as authentic expressions of the local rock subculture.[10]

This anecdote is normally presented as the little guys getting one over on the big ones, an example of the mainstream media's gullibility when it comes to empty hype – in short, a comic instance of what might now be called 'fake news'. She made it all up and they printed it in the *New York Times*! But wasn't it also just more of the same, a creative trend that extended way back to Pavitt's *Sub Pop* fanzine and had then tapered down into the label's sales tactics? Jasper's phrases, after all, were largely a riff on fragments of subcultural 'slacker' language already in existence. They are equally as familiar as they are inventive. No one, not least fans of the *Bill and Ted* films and *Wayne's World* (1989–92), will be surprised to hear

Jasper's 'kickers' for heavy boots, 'score' for 'great', 'harsh realm' for 'bummer', and 'rock on' for 'a happy goodbye' ('swingin' on the flippity flop' for 'hanging out' may be more unique). And what I note above all is that Jasper's invented grunge glossary homed in on numerous different ways of being a loser: 'cob nobbler', 'tom-tom club', 'big bag of bloatation', 'lamestain' – and, with a curious trace of misogyny, 'bound and hagged', to describe someone (always implicitly a man) who is forced to stay home on a Friday and Saturday night.

In fact, building the 'loser lexicon' wouldn't be a bad way of describing what Jasper was doing in her phone call to the *New York Times*, a spontaneous version of something that Sub Pop had practised since its earliest days and has never stopped practising. It seems no coincidence that nowadays she is CEO of the company.

Totally Rocks

To understand this Sub Pop loser lexicon in more detail, a good place to start exploring is the direct-marketing inserts found inside the sleeves of the label's earliest vinyl releases. These inserts were standard among the indie rock labels of the 1980s and early '90s, and a vital commercial opportunity. You've bought one thing, they say, and so here is a catalogue of what all else we have to offer, whether different records, different versions of the same records, compilations, T-shirts, stickers or other promotional stuff. Combining descriptive text, sleeve images, price listings and mail-order forms, they often mimicked the style of a punk fanzine and so were one important way of grounding the new products for sale in what were often these labels' grass roots. To that extent their obvious commercial intent was disguised, as was the goal of establishing brand unity across a range of different products, in part achieved by the 'visual 'rhyme' effect of lining up sleeve images and introductory texts alongside one another in rows.[11]

Likewise, the written product descriptions fulfil several different functions at once. On the one hand, they usually hark back to a snappy, often brutal, fanzine summary style. On the other, they attempt to place their bands' music for potential consumers and make claims over what was familiar and what was innovative (and therefore worth buying) about them, often using the language of rock fusion. In late 1987, for example, the standard SST insert catalogue told listeners that 'we're here to blast your concept', a reference to the run of label compilations initiated a few years before. Its numerous product descriptions included that of Gone's LP *Gone II – But Never Too Gone!*: 'Greg, Sim and Andrew jump on their Harleys and ride roughshod through the sleepy towns of jazz, rock and blues. Like the fabled biker riots of the 1960s, Gone's sonic assault leaves the towns they ride through with the knowledge that things will never be the same.'

Das Damen's self-titled first EP is even more elaborately described, with obvious emphasis on the band's relationship to sixties psychedelia: 'Like four men running on empty, Das Damen (Philleopold, Lyle, Alex and Jim) breathe fumes and spark combustion like a four-wheel sex machine. Fill up your mind, and check your strawberry love oil levels with Das Damen. Six songs for six cylinders of molten love rock.'[12]

Sub Pop's insert descriptions undoubtedly fit right into these same indie practices. Even so, they were also distinct from those of their competitors. To be honest, many inserts of the time end up falling on the bluntly commercial side. Notwithstanding the descriptions above, many of the SST ones were actually dully factual, little more than long lists of tracks and influences, and reminders to buyers to state their T-shirt size when ordering. Sub Pop's, on the other hand, were more obviously a continuation of the original *Sub Pop* fanzine: roughly xeroxed in appearance, they were full of goofy one- or two-liners, either because they were written that way, or because they were selectively excerpted from reviews in other rock fanzines. The newly written ones were likely prepared by Bruce Pavitt, as certainly they display his curious genius for making the reader 'want to hear the music they [are] seeing' (as Calvin Johnson put it).[13] Alongside the insert's sleeve photos, they introduce release after release in an oddly fragmentary way, reflecting ambiguously back on to the quality of the artists and label, and the common sense of the buyer in choosing them. This is amusing and endearing, but it also creates a semblance of brand unity, the catalogue of the new Seattle rock label and its new Seattle rock bands, even though some of them were, in fact, no such thing.

Take, once again, Blood Circus, the flop band cited above whose one and only EP, *Primal Rock Therapy* (SP22, January 1989), was destined to be re-released on CD in 1992. Their name appears to have been taken from a corny pulp-fiction biker-gang novel of the 1970s ('They have a grudge against the whole square world . . . And an unholy taste for terror' runs the book's strapline in one edition).[14] In the Sub Pop catalogue insert of mid-1988, their initial single (SP13, May 1988) is described in twenty words like this: 'So what if they smoke pot? This sounds like Creedence and Motorhead in a head on train wreck. TOTALLY ROCKS.'

You might take away from this that Blood Circus are dangerous, transgressive, primitive, explosive; but also that they sound like an accidental and catastrophic mangling of old rock body parts. And as much as it is enticing, the description is undercut by its last words, the exaggerated capitals of which inevitably make it sound just a little sarcastic, as if the opposite is also implied. As Pavitt told the *Seattle Times* in 1989:

I think the whole psychology to our marketing is if you've got a weak point, you take it and spit it right back. I like to take something and oil it down to the obscenely simple. It's situated smack in the middle of stupidity, but there's something ironic there that elevates it.[15]

See also Swallow in this regard, whose debut single *Trapped/Guts* (SP14, June 1988) was the third to be released by Sub Pop. Pavitt's *Sub Pop USA* column of September 1987 had already identified Swallow as a 'local band, of the God variety', and had promoted their demo tape titled *Shooting Dope Gives Me a Boner* (this unfortunately appears not to have survived).[16] Their catalogue description runs as follows, a cute take on rock fusion as *con*fusion of a pathological kind, again loaded with what might be sarcastic capitals: 'These guys can't figure out if they're the Buzzcocks or Black Sabbath!! Melodic and psychotic MOTORCYCLE POP.' Or Soundgarden, for the time being a Sub Pop band through two singles and the EP *Screaming Life* (SP12, October 1987). They are presented as an 'Ultra HEAVY Zep rip-off', a statement expanded on by a longer quotation from the *College Music Journal*:

> Soundgarden has spent more of their fair share of time listening to Led Zeppelin and Black Sabbath, but sometime during their schooling, SOUNDGARDEN was also turned on to acid-drenched underground rockers like the Butthole Surfers. It might be hard to imagine what would happen if Gibby [of the Butthole Surfers] met Ozzy [of Black Sabbath] but it happens on SCREAMING LIFE.

Or Denver's the Fluid, their second LP *Clear Black Paper* (SP16, May 1988) given a comparable 'fusion' description, even though they were actually the odd one out – by no means new and not from Seattle: 'A GODHEAD record in classic Stooges/Stones form.' Or, finally, Green River, another older band whose recent LPs, *Dry as a Bone* (SP11, June 1987) and *Rehab Doll* (SP15, May 1988), had appeared first on Sub Pop: 'Gritty vocals, roaring Marshall amps. Ultra-loose GRUNGE that destroyed the morals of a generation.'

This last one has become iconic, of course. 'Grunge' was certainly nothing new in rock discourse, as a few moments with any American or British or Australian rock periodical of the 1970s will reveal (in 1975, for example, Greg Shaw had described Iron Butterfly as the one-hit-wonders of the 'heavy grunge psychedelic-punk era').[17] It was also part of more general vocabulary. To the homemaker it might have meant the gunk that collects round the edge of your sink. To the perplexed Blood Circus, 'grunge' meant 'something you scraped out of your bong when you were out of weed' (as their guitarist once put it).[18] But this is the point. It is both familiar and comically confusing, mundane and transgressive – and productively so. Here in capitals, like MOTORCYCLE POP, like GODHEAD, like HEAVY, it is the sales hook, situated smack in the middle of stupidity, that draws you in and sets the musical imagination in motion.

Life as It Happened

Words could not sell this music on their own, however. Alongside them was developing a distinctive visual style, another well-known part of the Sub Pop armoury. Charles Burns had created the macabre cartoons of the original *Sub Pop* fanzine and the *Sub Pop 200* compilation, but it was another northwestern Charles, the photographer Charles Peterson, who quickly became associated with the new label and, beyond that, was widely credited with creating 'grunge's hair-sweat-and-guitars look' (in the words of the *New York*

Times article above). Peterson's Seattle band photographs and sleeve designs had appeared from Green River's EP *Come on Down* (Homestead, 1985) and *Deep Six* (C/Z, 1986) onwards, and he has become particularly well known for his live-show in-performance shots. Among these are many in 'drag-shutter' style, a range of techniques that involved slowing the shutter speed, setting the flash off, and moving the camera during exposure, blurring things in motion while keeping other objects sharply outlined.

This 'drag-shutter' style is now celebrated for the way it communicates countless qualities dear to rock 'n' roll: liveness, spontaneity, abandon, action and the authentic grittiness of a home-grown music scene. Most such images are in black and white, a classic documentary effect. Steve Waksman writes of their striking 'intimacy' and 'intensity', and points out that, in the context of small clubs and tiny stages, photographers like Peterson had quite literally to get right up among the performers onstage in order to achieve their effects, often taking close-ups at strange angles.[19] Michael Azerrad adds sardonically that the 'blurs and streaks of light' all over these images signal another aspect of the real live experience of these bands, namely the 'disorientation effect of beer and MDA'.[20] To me they have other qualities still, near-magical ones. In the image on the back cover of the Fluid's single *Tin Top Toy* (SP57, March 1990), the guitarist James Clower's arm is thrown up in the air, having apparently just played a chord windmill-style. By chance, the angle formed by the outstretched arm and his bandana resembles the flashes of light that have been dragged all over the top of the photograph, adding a kind of connective visual motif to the chaos unfolding beneath as the shoeless singer John Robinson ducks and dives through the thicket of sweaty bodies onstage. The effect is sensational. It is as if you can see Clower's chord, live, as it echoes off the low ceiling and bounces round the room. The image fixes the audible in the visual, and becomes another means of whetting the appetite for this music.

Clearly Sub Pop was aware of the reinforcement this distinctive and documentary photographic style would give to its project. For one thing, flying blonde hair – virtually a label trademark – looks particularly great in it. But more importantly, in Pavitt's words, it represented the 'very essence of the indie live show – which is very different from arena rock photography'.[21] It also placed their output in the elite context of a kind of art form, specifically, as many have pointed out, the so-called 'snapshot aesthetic' of renowned twentieth-century photographers like Walker Evans, Garry Winogrand, Robert Frank, Diane Arbus and Nan Goldin (it is no coincidence that Peterson's images are sometimes credited on Sub Pop record sleeves as 'snapshots'). In the glossy presentation booklet for *Sub Pop 200*, it followed that Peterson's live drag-shutter images of the label's bands dominated, and the style would appear regularly thereafter on Sub Pop's products and everywhere else. The live band images for Skin Yard's single *Start at the Top* (SP47, October 1989) and Godflesh's *Slateman* (SP114, 1991) are good examples, as are the sleeve and insert shots of Soundgarden's LP *Ultramega OK* (SST, 1988), taken by various photographers. Ed Sirrs's live shots of TAD and Nirvana in London for *Sounds* in late 1989 (see pp. 180 and 185) share the same lineage again.

As this indicates, this visual style has come to signal 'grunge' or 'alternative rock' far beyond any individual label, and now serves as a trigger for nostalgia, real or imagined. This is in part because, since the mid-1990s, many of the most famous of these images have also been available in compilation format, within plush coffee-table-type volumes where they might be more easily appreciated as 'wonderful works of art' (in the words of Michael Azerrad). This may feel a little ironic, bearing in mind the liveness and spontaneity for which they are also valued, qualities seemingly incompatible with the comforts of the living room. Yet the following 2015 review from someone who bought Peterson's anthology *Touch Me I'm Sick* (2003) suggests that the different form of presentation has little bearing on what these images ultimately mean to people. If anything, in fact, the coffee-table format reinforces the connection to exhilarating, 'genuine' and alternative live performance that is now a thing of the past:

> Most (if not all) pics were black and white, raunchy, electric, and captured life as it happened – so in effect the perfect visual companion to a lot of this exciting music coming from Alice In Chains, Mudhoney, Nirvana, TAD, Screaming Trees, Soundgarden, Melvins, Pearl Jam etc.
>
> There were NO posey stupid shots of wannabe rock stars with pre-ripped jeans standing all static and primadonna like, as I see a lot of today (there are too many crap bands out there today that just try to look cool and talk the talk but don't 'rock the rock'!).[22]

With the documentary phrase 'life as it happened', this reviewer also hints at another famous aspect of Sub Pop imagery. This is the label's love of picturing the crowd itself, often in sharp relief against the dragged blur of the performers onstage, and at a level of detail that makes these small Seattle clubs bustle with random goings-on (even though, as many survivors have pointed out, there were sometimes only a handful of people there at early shows). Characteristically, Peterson has defined this crowd focus simply as a way of making his job more 'fun', of relieving the boredom of taking endless shots of 'guys singing into a microphone'.[23] But it also revived a basic dogma of the *Sub Pop* fanzine and extended it to the professional record label: that it could be anyone, that anyone could do it, that one aim of the Sub Pop network was to level the terrain between artists, label and fans. '[O]ur photos always, from the very start, showed the fans as well as the bands', explains Pavitt, 'so people could see the real intimacy between the two, so that they could feel "Yes! I could be a part of it!"'[24]

This point is very often made literal. On the reverse of the Fluid's *Glue* (SP64, April 1990), John Robinson is *in* the audience, apparently having dived into it backwards, bringing a range of stage equipment down with him, but still somehow the focal point is a young man in a leather jacket climbing on to the stage. On the back of Mudhoney's LP *Mudhoney*, the singer Mark Arm sits dolefully in the crowd, facing the stage and wearing a Sonic Youth T-shirt, a fan among fans. And in that Fluid *Tin Top Toy* sleeve mentioned earlier, someone at the bottom centre is also climbing up, following John Robinson to become part of the stage's performance and its chaos. The audience, as Peterson once put it, is made to look 'just as exciting as the band on stage'.[25]

In fact, one of the unusual features of Sub Pop's photographic style is that sometimes the crowd can be *more* exciting – in control, dominating and ridiculing the band and making their usual star status into a two-way street. The cover of Dwarves' single *She's Dead* (SP50, February 1990) shows the singer Blag Dahlia bent double, prone, with his trousers round his ankles and the microphone clenched between his teeth like a ball-gag. The crowd screams at him with arms in the air as if hurling things at him and the band. There is something medieval about it, of the stocks and the baying mob that mocks the dancing naked fool. Carnival humiliation, not humane connection, seems to be the intended effect. This is the fulcrum on which Sub Pop imagery very often sits.

Mindfucking

As vibrant as they obviously are, still there are a few dangers inherent in these famous live images. First, that the magic of their technique might blind us to their obvious symbolism, which is sometimes the same old 'technophallic' stuff of rock past, men with hands clasped tightly round electric guitar fretboards while women stare on enraptured (see Peterson's snapshot for Reverend Horton Heat's single *Psychobilly Freakout*, SP96, December 1990, for an extreme example of this).[26] The second danger is that these shots are nowadays left to represent the iconography of grunge and Sub Pop entirely, when really they only accounted for a small percentage of the many hundreds of images distributed with the releases of the time. Again, this has the knock-on effect of uprooting the label from the rock tradition in which it clearly stood, making it seem more exceptional than it actually was. For the first hundred Sub Pop records or so, it is worth remembering that there were other prominent photographers besides Peterson, such as Alice Wheeler, Michael Lavine and Arthur S. Aubry. And so, though Steve Waksman is right when he says that Peterson's drag-shutter style was one of the things that gave Sub Pop its consistent look, still there was a large amount of object and concept photography, and plenty of static 'ripped-jeans' shoots after all.[27] Undeniably, 'posey stupid shots' that 'talk the talk' rather than 'rock the rock' were also a key part of Sub Pop's grunge.

Some of these latter may have felt like 'going through the motions' (Peterson) but what they also indicate, then, is just how important those motions were: the label's need to keep within traditions of rock iconography at the same time as playing with them to suggest an 'alternative' take, to pose while denying the pose.[28] A persistent early aesthetic to this end was a set of 'funhouse' type effects, as if viewing the band through a hall of mirrors to distort the artificiality of the artist line-up. Green River's *Dry as a Bone* and the Fluid's *Roadmouth* (SP36, June 1989) fall into this category. Cat Butt's *Journey to the Center of . . .* (SP41, August 1989) raises the funhouse to a more general principle, the fancily dressed band being attacked by a green papier-maché head while coloured 'psychedelic' shapes whirl in the foreground. Similarly, Wheeler's band images for Nirvana's first single *Love Buzz* (SP23, November 1988) are obscured almost out of recognition by in-camera techniques, in this case the use of infrared film, and Michael Lavine's shot of Skin Yard (used on the back of SP47; see p. 70) matches the band members' bodily contortions with a heavy blur; his Nirvana, meanwhile, steeps the band, both intense and comic, in shadow (see p. 83). For the solo album *The Winding Sheet* (SP61, May 1990), Peterson places a moody looking Mark Lanegan on a backwards-facing chair. This approximates standard images of Jim Morrison, whom Lanegan closely resembles, except that the chair is at a rum angle and the whole image is flushed bright red.

Lavine's line-up for the original vinyl release of Blood Circus's *Primal Rock Therapy* offers another typical Sub Pop cover aesthetic, one closely intertwined with its claim to rock authenticity. It shows the band in chains and leather, like the hard rock biker outfits of the 1970s from which they were descended; they appear bored and moody, except that the singer, Michael Anderson, stands forwards out of the frame in forced perspective, confronting the viewer with his larger-than-life physicality.

The effect is reminiscent of Peterson's most famous live image of all: the cover of Mudhoney's EP *Superfuzz Bigmuff* (SP21, October 1988) is a live shot taken from above, with the guitarists' hair exploding upwards towards the lens, bodies and guitars and cables wrapped round each other. But the same confrontation effect could also be

Blood Circus, from the shoot used for the wraparound sleeve
of *Primal Rock Therapy* (SP22, January 1989).

used for more specifically provocative purposes. Pavitt has explained
that he chose the shot for the front sleeve of Soundgarden's *Screaming
Life* (SP12) precisely because Chris Cornell's muscular nakedness,
erupting forwards towards the viewer, would unsettle Sub Pop's core
audience, whom he clearly expected to identify as male and straight.
'I was basically saying, "This is homoerotic and I am going to push
that a little bit." And ooh boy, a lot of guys got really uncomfortable
with that.'[29] How exactly that discomfort was expressed has never
become clear, but Gina Arnold sees this homoeroticism – not just
images of Cornell, but the Afghan Whigs' Greg Dulli and the Fluid's
John Robinson – as one of the most distinctive aspects of the early
Sub Pop project, one 'compelling' thing that popularized its 'sound
and character' beyond that of other regional independents.[30]

Lavine's photography for the cover of Dwarves' *Blood Guts and
Pussy* (SP67, July 1990), on the other hand, moves beyond insinuation

to deliberate outrage, using the same confrontation effect for its three naked figures, set off at a weird angle against a blank white background. For Kurt Cobain this was a step too far: it was one reason, according to Clark Humphrey, why Cobain came to want to leave Sub Pop, as he didn't think that a stark cover image of 'two naked women and a bare-chested short man all drenched in animal blood' was compatible with his own anti-sexist views or those he had formerly attributed to the label.[31] On the other hand, the image probably titillated as many as it shocked, since it brings together at least two traditions of rock imagery: the ubiquitous naked women of hard rock past and the gore-streaked horror-punk and hardcore sleeves from earlier in the 1980s. (Big Black's *Headache*, released by Touch and Go in 1987, springs to mind as an extreme example of the latter; don't look it up.) True to form, Sub Pop used Lavine's shoot for all it was worth, making a special-edition vinyl 'picture disc' out of another shot in the same sequence, and placing still another on the sleeve of Dwarves' single *Drug Store* (SP81, October 1990).

As much as anything, what the above examples imply is that design was just as important to Sub Pop as its renowned photography. That is, as impressive as the famous live shots and less-famous posed shots are, they work within a larger graphic context that is itself in dialogue with rock sleeves of the past, as recalled by a wealth of specialist Sub Pop designers, including Lisa Orth, Jane Higgins, Art Chantry, Linda Owens and Pavitt himself. More than that, the overall concept is more cunning than it first appears. Chantry has spoken recently about his mercenary ideology of design:

> [Graphic design] is a language everyone can read
> and understand – and yet nobody recognizes that
> fact. As a graphic designer, it has been my job to
> use this language to change the minds of the viewer

– 'Buy this product! Go to this event! Vote for this
candidate!'

In that process, I use all the skills and knowledge
at my command to manipulate the viewer into thinking
the way that another interest – the client – wants to see.
I'm a virtual cultural propagandist of the lowest order
– a mindfucker. And I do this for hire.[32]

One common propaganda strategy was to pair a colour posed shot
of the artist with a live one on the back, as if poking fun at the fakeness of the posing tradition and, again, using it to stress the
authenticity of the Sub Pop musical experience. With the Reverend
Horton Heat's *Smoke 'Em if You Got 'Em* (SP96, November 1990),
the label entered into the revival of 'psychobilly', another 1970s
fusion genre that collided punk with country (or, more precisely,
rockabilly). For the front, Chantry uses a clean-cut portrait of the
Reverend by Michael Lavine, hands clasped, in sharp blazer and
string tie and 1950s colour scheme: he could be Jim Reeves or Gene
Autry or something, with grunge's grubby chequered flannels
transformed into smart plaid and matching shoulder patches. On
the reverse, though, is the 'real' Reverend and band in a raucous live
shot taken from below, with Gretsch guitar, double bass and
cowboy boots flying at weird angles. Overlaid is Carson Langtry's
parody essay, which merges Southern Baptist revivalism into the
live experience of this Sub Pop psychobilly revival: 'Reverend
Horton Heat looked straight at me and it was like all the devilment
was draining right outta my bones. And that's when I knew I'd done
been Saved'.[33]

Is it art, then? Insofar as it is design, Chantry thinks not: 'It's
anthropology and politics and economics – almost ANYTHING
except art. It is not a muse-driven masterpiece created by a single

Reverend Horton Heat, as seen on the front of *Smoke 'Em if You Got 'Em* (SP96, November 1990).

person in an edition of one. It is mass-produced manipulation and coercion created to maintain the current economic system of exploitation.'[34] Perhaps this is excessive; but still it serves as a useful corrective to all the waxing lyrical about the 'beauty and honesty' of the Peterson photographs, and the standard line on grunge images as 'flipping the finger to the dictators of culture'.[35] After all, the images and design are as dictatorial as they could be, much like Sub Pop's catalogue descriptions: they impel you to tip out the disc and prime you to experience the musical content in a certain way. The two sides of the Reverend Horton Heat LP, for example, visually set up the collision of psychobilly before the disc is even spun.

The graphic design may also complicate the music, and vice versa. The TAD–Pussy Galore split single *Damaged 1/Damaged 11* (SP37, June 1989) is a pair of covers of songs from Black Flag's LP *Damaged* (1981), which on the face of it might seem a direct homage to the famous hardcore band, one of the idols of Pavitt's *Sub Pop* fanzine. But the sleeve shows Peterson photos of these bands getting it all wrong: the microphone stand hitting one of the singers on the head, the microphone shoved fully in the mouth of the other, for once in decidedly un-erotic fashion. In the context of these images, the single is equally likely to come across as a clumsy cover by rock-addled dunces. In fact, listening closely, TAD's version of 'Damaged 1' restarts suddenly with the riff from the other side, 'Damaged 11', only for the singer to come in with the lyrics of AC/DC's 'Let There Be Rock' (1977), a song based on almost the same riff. It points, tongue-in-cheek, to hardcore's debt to the heavy rock of the 1970s, and grunge's debt to both, while also emphasizing these bands' inherited roles as half-witted descendants of both genres: rock fusion and confusion once again ill-combined.

Secret Messages

Chantry's point about design manipulation and coercion can be taken, too, inside the sleeve. It extends to the main item inside it – besides the catalogue flyers, promotional photographs and other forms of advertising that were common for Sub Pop. I refer, of course, to the vinyl record itself. Vinyl was the format that Sub Pop primarily invested in until 1990 or so, almost to the exclusion of other ways of selling its music. This flew in the face of the very small market share that vinyl enjoyed by that time. According to David Hepworth's figures, this was only 9 per cent of U.S. music sales, against 65 per cent for cassette tapes and 26 per cent for CDs.[36]

There were numerous reasons for this Sub Pop focus on vinyl. For 7″ singles, at least, one of them was cost of manufacture. Michael Azerrad says that, around this time, you could press 'a thousand 45s for $410 or a thousand CDs for $3,000', and this in turn was surely a key factor in Sub Pop's investment in limited-edition singles for collectors.[37] But whether 12″, 10″ or 7″, 45 or 33⅓ rpm, the physical nature of the medium was surely just as decisive. Vinyl is incredibly delicate, susceptible to everything – scratches and wear from being played, from being handled, from bad storage, from the paper inners that are supposed to protect it inside its sleeve, from the treatment of any past owners it may have had. As the music writer Joe Bonomo has aptly put it, it bears 'proof of people living' in a way that digital technologies cannot match, an impression of 'depth' and 'sponginess' that, on listening, somehow transmutes into the humane warmth that vinyl's advocates often claim they miss with digital media.[38] In this sense the vinyl record continues the home-made fanzine's impression of 'embodied community' (in Alison Piepmeier's words). Like Pavitt's original *Sub Pop* paper fanzine, it is an object that can be revisited time and time again, and that will 'change in subtle ways, like a body itself'.[39]

Underlining this potential for subtle and personal communication, there is a long tradition of scratching short messages onto the vinyl surface, far exceeding anything comparable found on cassette tapes or CDs. I mean the short messages inscribed in the so-called 'run-out' (or 'run-off') grooves of records, the wide expanses of dead wax found closest to the central label. Some of these inscriptions are a necessary part of, and have always referred to, aspects of the production process: catalogue numbers, 'matrix' numbers for reference of the pressing plant, the name or handle of whoever cut the lacquer master from which the disc will eventually be pressed, and other hieroglyphs that will mean little to anyone who works outside this industry. Since the 1960s, however, and particularly in rock genres, these production marks have often been joined by other phrases. It would be logical to assume that these messages are left there by the lacquer-cutter who prepared the master, as a calling card or as a comment on the artist or music or label. Sometimes it turns out that this is so. But usually there is little indication where they come from – or who is saying them, or to whom, or in what context. They are mysteriously disembodied, and so, further 'proof of people living', they urge connection back to someone as their origin. They are also likely to seem 'secret' or 'private', since they are almost invisible until you tilt the disc towards the light to read them, and they very often have the 'personal' touch of being hand-etched (in 'handwriting') rather than machine-stamped. Perhaps, indeed, not everyone who owns the same mass-produced and identical disc will have noticed these messages' existence, opening up another possibility to become an informed 'insider'.

As such, the important point about these run-out messages isn't so much *what* they say as that they are *there*, they say *something*.

They open a channel that seems to connect you, the finder, more closely and personally to the network of people who created the record – a channel that seems all the more significant because it stands apart from the standard visual and aural aspects of the record, and inevitably sets your interpretive wheels turning, eager to gain the insight that might come from deciphering what the secret words mean. This explains, I think, their widespread use among independent labels like Sub Pop, and speaks to these labels' typical stance against impersonal, 'corporate', ignorant musical consumption.

It also explains the fact that there are many hundreds of examples of these messages and that it is difficult to predict much about what it is they will say. The utterance can be almost anything. Some are apparently publicity: 'Buy Skin Yard' says the B-side of C/Z Records' compilation *Another Pyrrhic Victory* (1989), with reference to one of the label's best bands. Some confront the seeker directly: 'Why are you reading this', asks side A of the reissue of Circle Jerks' *Wild in the Streets* (Frontier, 1988). Some make a joke at the reader's expense. 'Ha Ha, Made You Look!' reads the B-side of Chemistry Set's single *Fabulous Stinking* (Fatbald, 1989), while side A of Das Damen's self-titled EP, reissued by SST in 1986, says, 'I thought I told you to shut up' (admittedly this may have been a phrase directed at the band).

Many are more elaborate, exploiting the two-sidedness of a vinyl disc to provide a set-up on one side and a punchline on the other. 'Looking for something??' asks side A of Poison Idea's EP *Record Collectors are Pretentious Assholes* (Fatal Erection, 1985), and then, perhaps predictably, 'you stupid asshole!!' Happy Flowers' *Oof* (Homestead, 1989) has the innocuous message 'Tiny little bunnies, playing in the grass' on one side, but on the flip side, 'Tiny little bunnies kick your fuckin ass'. And then there is GG Allin's *You Give Love a Bad Name* (Homestead, 1987). 'Q: ever fucked a Priest with a flaming broom-handle?' enquires one side. 'A: hasen't [*sic*] everybody?' asks the other, rhetorically.[40]

Some run-out messages build bridges to other artists, in some cases across labels, with the consumer as the implicit mediator. 'We love you Dinasour' says the B-side of Sonic Youth's *Sonic Youth* (reissue; SST, 1987), presumably referencing and advertising Dinosaur Jr with an 'authentic' spelling mistake. 'Chuck is bald Robo was' reads side B of Adolescents' *Adolescents* (Frontier, 1981), apparently a comment on the changing, and much-discussed, hairstyles of the members of Black Flag. Some appear to open a critical angle on the operations of the label, giving the impression that they stem from the free-thinking artist themselves. 'In the lap of the Gods ... / ... and in the hands of S.S.T.' reads Meat Puppets' *II* across its two sides (SST, 1984), sounding mildly critical. 'SST's gotta lotta nerve' reads the A-side of the Sonic Youth reissue above, perhaps much more disaffected.

A few run-outs are poetic, over and above anything in the lyrics of the actual songs. 'Silent aerials, this quieting/Worshipping volcanoes on virgin knees' reads Saint Vitus's *Saint Vitus* (SST, 1984), quite enigmatically. A few are easy to interpret politically, particularly in terms of anti-establishment positions: 'Ray Gun or Manson, its the same thing' reads Sonic Youth's EP *Death Valley '69* (Homestead, 1985), just after Reagan's re-election. Some, finally, appear to issue comment on the music itself, influencing it before or after you hear it. 'It was screaming but I couldn't tell where the mouth was' says the A-side of Dinosaur Jr's *You're Living All Over Me* (SST, 1987). This is a line that could be from a 1980s sci-fi movie, and perhaps it is. But it seems significant that it is etched on a record that begins with a furious scream that doesn't come from J Mascis, the notoriously lethargic lead singer.

The countless run-out messages on Sub Pop's vinyl releases are in many ways directly comparable, offering up yet more 'proof of people living' and drawing audiences ever closer through 'secret' statement. Again, some use this privileged space for publicity, made lamely ironic by the hidden status of the words. The final disc of the flagship compilation *Sub Pop 200* reads 'Buy Sub Pop' on both sides, while Soundgarden's *Screaming Life* (SP12, October 1987) seems all about advertisement for other Seattle bands ('Buy Green River/Buy Malfunkshun'), albeit ones now on their last legs. Many other Sub Pop run-outs are simply factual, if goofy: 'Recorded somewhere in France' is probably accurate for the French band Les Thugs' *Chess and Crimes* (SP29, February 1989). Some name-check other independent rock artists: 'Freeway to Gibby!!' appears on the Fluid's *Clear Black Paper* (SP16), presumably a nod to the Butthole Surfers' *Hairway to Steven* (Touch and Go, also 1988) and its frontman. And some appear to be messages from the label to the artist, again with the consumer in the middle to interpret. Nirvana had already left Sub Pop by the time their live split single with the Fluid, *Candy/Molly's Lips* (SP97, January 1991), appeared, and only allowed its release as part of the buy-out package. This, according to Kurt Cobain, was why the word 'Later' is inscribed on both sides of the single, a decision that had nothing to do with the band and everything to do with Jonathan Poneman's (probably sarcastic) farewell.[41]

Certainly the most famous of the label's run-outs is inscribed on the A-side of Nirvana's first single for Sub Pop, *Love Buzz* (SP23, November 1988): 'Why don't you trade those guitars for shovels?' This apparently comes from something that the father of Krist Novoselic, the bass player, once said to the band, and seems to shore up their punk rock credentials – their rebellious refusal to do something more 'useful' than playing abrasive music. Beyond that, however, it became a kind of slogan repeated over and over by the band in interviews. In March 1989 Novoselic used it to exaggerate Nirvana's comic primitivity to Everett True: 'We just want to ROCK!

Ninety-nine percent of music out there is bullshit . . . So quit! Give it up! Turn your guitars in for shovels! You guys suck!'[42] And in 1990 he evoked the same phrase, and Nirvana's alleged working-class roots, when he told Mimmo Caccamo that, were it not for the rock band, he would be 'Runnin' the United States of America . . . I'd plant potatoes'.[43]

What this indicates is that even these little messages were mobilized to reinforce the image that Sub Pop and their early bands were making for themselves. Hand-etched and hidden, they were a different form of communication to the more upfront efforts of the catalogue inserts and images, and may on those grounds have seemed somehow more insightful. It is interesting to note, then, that they were almost never political. In fact, I can find only two examples of messages that might have contemporary political implications. One is the Afghan Whigs' single *Sister Brother* (SP84, October 1990), and that is cryptic: 'Simon Leis sleeps in Mapplethorpe's grave'. The other is a violent take on the standard indie fanzine creed, found across the two sides of Cat Butt's *Journey to the Center of . . .* (SP41, August 1989): 'When the man from Geffen comes . . . / Shoot him with a gun' (and this eighteen months before Nirvana signed to Geffen).

Otherwise the Sub Pop run-outs all tend to turn inwards, focusing on some weird expression of band identity, or just plain old fun. The B-side of Blood Circus's single reads 'Killer Green Bud', presumably a reference to the 'So what if they smoke pot?' of their catalogue description. One side of Swallow's single reads 'Throbbing Bike', again recalling the catalogue and its 'MOTORCYCLE POP'. Numerous other run-outs were more obviously self-effacing; perhaps, ultimately, this was the most common category, aligned with the label's commitment to striking a string of loser poses in its early releases. Love Battery's *Between the Eyes* (SP45, October 1989) reads

'Dial M for Muzak', easily interpreted as a dig at the music you are about to hear (relative, perhaps, to Pussy Galore's celebrated *Dial 'M' for Motherfucker* of April 1989), as well as a reference to the Muzak distribution service in Seattle where many early Sub Pop artists had found employment. 'Pretend you like us' runs one side of Girl Trouble's *Hit It or Quit It* (SP20, September 1988), while the other says coyly 'Thank you'. And the first Sub Pop single-artist LP of all, Green River's *Dry as a Bone*, sets what became the overall tone, each side giving part of a joke phrase in quotation marks as if expressing a motto for band and label at its very beginnings:

SIDE A: 'I tried to love life ...'
SIDE B: 'But it wanted to be "just friends" ...'

4
A Collector's Label

THE SLEEVE IMAGES, run-out groove messages and marketing inserts surveyed in the last chapter all made, in more or less subtle ways, a series of key contributions to the Sub Pop project of the late 1980s and early '90s. All were component parts of brand identity and image, and as such they join a long list of other more obvious features. One, famously, was the idea of a 'Seattle sound' curated by Jack Endino at Reciprocal Recording. Another was the black-and-white Sub Pop logo, first hinted at in Pavitt's *Rocket* column in 1983 and later emblazoned across all of its products and events to such saturation that it became a frequent target for parody, not least by the label itself ('Pus Bop' and 'Sob Pup' were favourite anagrams).[1] The label also became known by the two-tone yellow disc label that gave its singles a consistent appearance from early 1989 onwards, and by the elaborate range of so-called 'hype' stickers on its products, sometimes featuring a map of the USA with 'SEATTLE' marked in capital letters or a hilariously exaggerated outline of Washington State.

While Sub Pop has often been praised for the power of all this branding, it didn't exist in a vacuum. A strong suit in this regard was nothing unusual among small independent record labels that, to put it bluntly, depended on attracting and maintaining a consumer base for their survival. To cite only a few of the most obvious rock examples, SST, Homestead, Touch and Go, and Dischord all exhibited comparable branding features, and in many ways served as models for the early Sub Pop. In Gillian Gaar's view, the 1980s

UK independents Factory and 4AD should be added to this list of influences, as should, according to Gina Arnold, the Californian punk label Dangerhouse.[2] Extending the same line of argument in terms of decade and genre, Michael Azerrad appends a number of much earlier labels to this list of influences – Sun, Stax and Motown – and places Pavitt and Poneman as diligent students of the way these 1950s outfits, some of them with a strong regional emphasis, applied a 'look' to their products as a means of encouraging customer recognition.[3] Pavitt himself has cited as inspirational the mid-century jazz label Blue Note and the small Scottish label of the '80s Postcard Records, itself clearly indebted to Motown.[4]

Actually, I would go even further than this. What all these independent labels were practising, I think, is what Naomi Klein once identified, ironically enough, as an innovation of corporate rock: the artist as 'brand extension'. They were keeping the label name, logo, look and sound centre stage and using their artists, big and small, to advertise it for them.[5] Sub Pop excelled at this above all, and it was a strategy that could cut several ways, as their most perceptive bands were well aware. In 1989 Kurt Cobain told Lena Jordebo of the widespread perception that empty hype had granted Sub Pop its rapid rise to popularity, and that this had led to the belief that the brand lacked 'any substantial bands to back it up'.[6] A year later he expressed his fear that fans only followed Nirvana because they were on Sub Pop, and spoke of his irritation at intended compliments, such as 'You're my favorite SubPop band,' that reduced the band to the label.[7] 'Just to be categorised in this world of five or six bands is kind of frustrating,' he said to *Lime Lizard* magazine in 1991, 'cos you wonder what they think of you compared to bands on other labels.'[8]

Still more interesting on this point is the following excerpt from an interview conducted by the Italian radio station Radio Onde Furlane with Nirvana in late 1989:

M[immo Caccamo (interviewer)]: I think this new Seattle sound – which Sub Pop includes – is one of the best things to come out. What do you think of this movement that comes around Seattle?

K[rist] N[ovoselic]: Well, it's weird that people focus on it as a movement. It's just bands, you know? People focus on the movement more than they do the bands, it seems like a lot of times. I don't – Somebody will give us a review and then they'll talk about Sub Pop a lot. It's like, well, when people review Madonna, do they talk about RCA Records a lot? I mean, it's really weird! I mean, if we were on a different label, would that mean that we were a different band, even though we sound exactly the same?!⁹

I know Novoselic intends the closing question rhetorically, but nonetheless it is one worth thinking about. Would Nirvana have been a different band had they not been on Sub Pop, with its logo, its imagery, its colour schemes, its weird run-out messages, its hold on regional identity, its quips about lumber yards, and all the rest? And, for that matter, *would* they have sounded 'exactly the same', bearing in mind that they would likely have moved in different circles, recorded with different people, and written and performed differently? These are tricky questions, and any hesitation over their answers implies Sub Pop's success in its branding and the resounding association it made between its name and a new regional rock. This was seemingly more successful, even, than noted rock independents like SST, and inevitably more successful than the efforts of sprawling monsters like RCA, far too massive to benefit from association with a singular 'movement', and yet simultaneously dwarfed by the fame of its biggest stars.

Clearly, then, Sub Pop's notoriously aggressive promotion and marketing were making good ground in the late 1980s. This took structure and process: the label hired dedicated staff and mounted, in the word of one indie competitor, a 'genius' direct-to-retail campaign in which record stores were bombarded with merchandise and test copies to play for customers.[10] But it also depended on turning the commercial screw hard on consumers, transforming them from what might have been casual fans into something more diehard, namely collectors of Sub Pop products, particularly vinyl records. Indeed, Sub Pop actively sought to become a label for collectors, and was well established as such by the time of its launch into Europe. In May 1989 the *NME* critic Edwin Pouncey put it to Mudhoney that Sub Pop was 'considered a collector's label', and inferred from this that its bands must also be keen collectors ('To a degree,' is the response, followed by an excited account of finding a rare Klark Kent single in the UK).[11] A few months later, John Robb wrote of Jonathan Poneman's 'Sub Pop collector's label'.[12] And only a short time after that, Novoselic recalled autographing the entire Sub Pop collection of an avid fan – not in the U.S., but in France.[13]

Record collecting is a curious practice. It has, of course, a long tradition in rock history, not least in the punk and metal fanbases to which Sub Pop was attempting to speak. It is therefore hardly surprising to find that it has always been dominated by men, and seemingly still is, whatever the occasional counterexamples of women collectors.[14] More than that, since it relies to some extent on qualities like 'mastery' of information, a cultivated and discerning 'hipness', control of resources, hunter-like competition and so on, it tends to reinforce sexist social structures that label these as 'masculine' attributes (and, by the same binary logic, the absence of these to be 'feminine').[15]

Even so, in Will Straw's words, record collecting has also always stood in an 'uncertain relationship to masculinity'.[16] Remember the protagonists of Nick Hornby's novel *High Fidelity* (1995)? They were men with names like 'Barry', whom Hornby describes not only as 'single as in no girlfriend', but also as 'single as in no friends' – except, perhaps, each other.[17] In situations where others might show emotion or seek productive confrontation, they obsessively make top-five lists and reorganize their record collections alphabetically. They are, to put a single word on it, nerds: they may have mastered their area of knowledge, but the useless information they amass comes at the cost of social adjustment, of fulfilling connection with others, and of personal curation and presentation (see also the inter-viewees in Alan Zweig's documentary *Vinyl*).[18] At the same time they stray into other un-masculine territory. Collecting records, like other forms of collecting, is typically about bringing objects into the home environment, 'domesticating' and preserving them, and is apt to suffer the accusation that it locates personal identity in material things outside the 'true' self. Understood within the same sexist framework I mentioned above, and from a 'masculine' perspective, it has a suspiciously 'feminine' conservation and consumerism about it.[19]

In short, I think the rock record collector made an easy and obvious target for Sub Pop to aim at. Turning fans into collectors, drawn in by the logo-heavy 'Sub Pop Sold Here!' signs and keen to get their hands on the latest releases, was a good way of staying afloat commercially. It also drove a lively resale market, full of audacious price gouging, that kept the label's cultural stock high. But most of all, the ambiguous practice of collecting was an important means of meshing fans, bands and the label into the Sub Pop loser economy. An advance notice of the release of Mudhoney's self-titled LP (SP44, November 1989) addresses itself to 'record collecting scum', and this underlines the point. Sub Pop incited the masculine practice of collecting as much as it mocked its weaknesses, placing the nerd on a pedestal as a loser in several different senses at once. Simply put, the label could have some fun with collectors, and all of it would be in the name of their brand.

Gimcrack Extras

There were many different ways in which the early Sub Pop enhanced the collectability of its products. Some of these were entirely standard across the industry for labels big and small: there were countless band posters and stickers and photos included in first and subsequent vinyl pressings. Others made use of more extravagant presentational forms. Fugazi's only single for the label (SP52, December 1989) has a kind of handprinted 'vellum' outer sleeve through which the contents can be seen; the layered effect of depth is quite impressive. Less subtly, the first 2,500 copies of Dwarves' single *Drug Store* (SP81, October 1990) included a pin-badge that said 'Fuck You Up And Get High' on it (very few now survive).

Collectability was also driven by the relatively small runs of discs, as well as by simple and time-honoured techniques designed to draw attention to these small runs and to intensify the impression of scarceness and desirability. This is not to say that genuine scarceness was never a problem: 'I think they take the limited edition thing too far . . . They could sell a hell of a lot more records if they pressed more,' observed the TAD frontman in late 1989; 'The tough part about Sub Pop,' reflected the radio DJ Bill Reid in early 1990, 'is that sometimes you can't get ahold of their stuff 'cause they make so many collectors singles and things.'[20] But the crucial thing was giving the *impression* that there might not be enough to go round, that demand far exceeded supply, whatever the reality. Marking the sleeves 'limited edition', for example, and indicating the number of copies made, was standard, and in one famous case – Nirvana's first single – a (handwritten) number was given to each disc in the pressing. Imagine being one of the owners of these! In its own way the effect was an analogue to the 'Charles Peterson effect' of the live photography – the vision of tiny Seattle clubs teeming with fans, as exclusive as they were inviting ('Yes! I could be a part of it!' was the intended feeling).[21]

Above all, Sub Pop raised the collectability stakes of their products through another technique, one that cast a critical view over the existing industry in numerous ways. This was the issuing of variant versions of a record on coloured (or clear) vinyl, as opposed to the more familiar and standard black, and it needs some introduction. Broadly surveying the history of rock from the perspective of a keen listener and collector, David Hepworth sees the resurgence of coloured vinyl in the 1980s as little more than a desperate gimmick of record labels, a last-gasp way of reviving sales for what was then thought to be a dying medium.[22] On this view, falling for the gimmickry of coloured vinyl made you a commercial stooge – you were letting the market manhandle you, the money-men exploit your 'weakness for shopping' and sell you unnecessarily fancy things you didn't 'actually want' or need.[23] It has also become part of the typical critique hurled by older generations at so-called 'hipsters' (or, more recently, 'millennials'), those allegedly desensitized to fads and gimmicks who know not what it means to be a *genuine* enthusiast. The title alone of music writer (and small-label owner) Mike McGonigal's 2015 article gets his point across: 'Colored Vinyl Is For Big, Spoiled Record Babies'. According to McGonigal, coloured vinyl 'always sounds worse' and is 'not pressed with the same well-formulated vinyl that your plant is used to working with'. He nonetheless makes an initial colour pressing of almost everything, so that he can hawk it direct to the 'big record babies' who have driven the vinyl resurgence of recent decades.[24]

Clearly both critics find coloured vinyl inferior, and both express this in ways that feminize (and/or infantilize) it and those who buy it, simultaneously normalizing and 'masculinizing' black vinyl. In so doing they echo a long-standing prejudice. From a rock perspective, coloured vinyl was always associated with 'other' purposes and 'other' repertories: historically, colour records were often promotional or test presses, and some large labels tried to use them to 'colour-code' certain genres (in the 1950s some RCA novelty children's singles were on yellow vinyl, country-folk were green, classical were red, and so on; consumers knew as much what to avoid as what to buy). As McGonigal also says, certain suspicions have always swirled around coloured vinyl: that it lacks some kind of mysterious strengthening additive found in black vinyl, and as a result is more fragile, more susceptible to warping, damage and surface noise.[25] The music in its grooves can therefore never sound 'as proper, as final, as definitive' as that of a black record.[26]

Perhaps all this is so, and perhaps, in that case, coloured vinyl should take its place in ignominy alongside the much-derided 'picture disc' of the same era. Yet the same verdict also overlooks just how important coloured vinyl was to small independents like Sub Pop, for whom, I think, it wasn't only a rearguard action, a 'gimcrack extra' or 'unsought enhancement' to increase sales, or a goad to hipster credibility. It was also an important badge of identity and commerce.[27] These labels often drew directly, I think, on coloured vinyl's impression of 'otherness'. In 1981, for example, when the DC independent Dischord Records issued 1,000 first-press copies of Minor Threat's 7" *In My Eyes*, they did so on bright red vinyl with yellow labels. This was an impressive commercial choice: red was a colour that set this single off visually from other records in a collection, as well as linking it with some colour punk and hardcore 7" singles of the late 1970s. It also symbolized something of the incandescent rage of the band's hardcore punk aesthetic through colour, as if power violence itself were spinning on your turntable.

It made even more commercial sense, however, for Dischord to press another 3,000 copies of the same single in black vinyl over the course of the next year. This gave the growing fanbase of the band and label a chance to own it, and maximized profits from a relatively small line of products. (Dischord only had about five records to their name at the time *In My Eyes* was released.) Simultaneously, it implied that the single was a 'classic' that warranted re-pressing and instantly turned the early red version into a 'rare' collector's item that you might want to seek out, if only you could still find it. Seen like this, issuing coloured vinyl was not just a gimmick but a potentially rewarding strategy, a relatively inexpensive way to shore up these labels' authority (they instantly became the issuers of 'classics'), to flatter the hipster's sense of superiority, and to indulge the rock collector's nose for the prestige that comes from the obscure, the rare and the abnormal. By 1982, after all, many fans would own the black version; only a select few would have the red one in their collection. Nowadays the latter changes hands for around $1,100.

Pretty Colours

What made Sub Pop different was not so much its devotion to coloured vinyl as the sheer scale of its commitment. Labels like Dischord and SST issued the occasional coloured disc as a first press, usually for their biggest artists or records (or those they hoped would become so). Conversely, most Sub Pop releases were on coloured vinyl. The first five singles issued by the label were pressed almost exclusively on coloured vinyl and, in general, for both singles and EPs/LPs, anything from 10–60 per cent of the run – usually at least the first 1,500 copies in total – would be on a colour, the remainder on black. Many subsequent releases appeared in at least two colour variants, and in some cases, like the Fluid's single *Tin Top Toy* (SP57, March 1990), at least eight distinct colours were pressed early on. Later, about 1992, some of what had proven the bigger-selling singles and LPs – by Mudhoney, Nirvana, Soundgarden and Hole – were re-pressed in countless new coloured collectors' variants (often referred to as the so-called 'Erika' pressings after the pressing plant involved).

Across these hundreds of records, Sub Pop necessarily expanded the palette for coloured vinyl. As in the Dischord example, many colour discs issued by other labels had been a striking transparent red or yellow, a music-appropriate reflection of the aggressive hard-core masculinity – Hazard Warning! Extreme Politics! – of their bands. Sub Pop certainly inherited this attitude, but moved out-wards in all kinds of colourful directions, as if deliberately stirring the feelings of 'nerdiness' and 'femininity' that might simultaneously lie beneath the pursuit of coloured vinyl, and simultaneously raising the stakes of the vinyl record as an aesthetic object in its own right. In addition to reds and yellows, they regularly made provocative pinks, purples, gorgeous greens and oranges, both solid and transparent. They also created many elaborate marble, 'splatter' and split effects that mixed two or more colours together.

These colour choices were sometimes tied in with the artist or title. There was red for the Blood Circus single and LP; green for Green River; a kind of black-and-white 'cowhide' for the 'cowpunk' Reverend Horton Heat; white for Nirvana's *Bleach*. Or, again with the importance of design in mind, they reflected some aspect of the sleeve: the red wash of the front of Mark Lanegan's *The Winding*

Sheet is matched by the red disc inside; Afghan Whigs' neon orange *Up in It* (SP60, April 1990) echoes the colour of the text on the front of the sleeve. To focus on these content links alone, however, misses the point that the colour vinyls themselves are *beautiful* and in many cases unique. Due to the fluid process by which their plastics are mixed, no two marbled discs can be exactly alike – and as a result, they are likely to seem more 'aesthetic' and less 'manufactured' than a cassette tape or a shiny metallic CD, something to admire quite apart from the mass process by which they are actually made. They may also be special in the sense that they protect something 'sacred' and share in its vulnerability, as Kurt Cobain told Bob Gulla in early 1990:

> I really don't go for the CD revolution either. There's
> something I like about records. I really can't explain it.
> I know it sounds stupid, but music to me is kind of sacred.
> You're supposed to take care of it. If you scratch it up, then
> heck, you'll have to go out and buy another record. You've
> ruined something, and if you really like the band, you'll
> have to go buy it again.[28]

Or they may even be 'sacred' in the sociologists' sense, in that, once acquired, these records may be taken out of practical use completely, hung on a wall in a special frame or placed on a special shelf or stand (many such bespoke things exist) – and certainly never grooved by something so hard as the stylus of a record player.

The 'sacred' status may also reflect, of course, that these limited-edition Sub Pop records have proven valuable, sometimes extremely so. 'People like pretty colors,' as one prominent Sub Pop collector has put it, and the label's coloured variants have almost always fetched higher resale prices than their black counterparts, even in cases where the latter are known to be in shorter supply.[29] This was a trend that emerged early on and rapidly drove prices of rarer variants skywards, a trajectory which in some key cases has never really come to an end, and has only reinforced the Sub Pop status as one of the quintessential indie collectors' labels. When interviewer Mark Shafer remarked to Nirvana in October 1989 that he owned a white vinyl first pressing of their LP *Bleach*, the band told him gleefully that it was now worth '50 whole bucks'.[30] This response was more than a little sarcastic in tone ('I'm getting one right now!' says Chad Channing; 'You can retire!', adds Kurt Cobain), and I guess the band's point was that $50 was not much in an industry where many artists were worth millions. Still, bear in mind the appreciation here and the lightning timeframe in which it had occurred. *Bleach* had been released only a few months earlier and Sub Pop had originally listed it at $8. (You would now have trouble securing one of these first-run white copies for less than $1,200.)

Perhaps the most Sub Pop touch of all is that this rapid appreciation effect has been exaggerated by confusion and ineptitude, some of it no doubt deliberately sown. All the pressing statistics I cite above are necessarily rough. Since the label's notes were always sketchy, and have sometimes been comprehensively proven to be inaccurate, it has never really been clear how many of each variant were pressed, and thus how many should be out there for collectors to chase. It remains likewise uncertain whether some variants actually exist at all. Rumours have always abounded in collectors' circles over, for example, a clear vinyl version of Skin Yard's *Start at the Top* (SP47, October 1989), a transparent green one of Hole's *Dicknail* (SP93, March 1991), an orange Walkabouts' *Rag and Bone* (SP56, February 1990) and a purple Dwarves *She's Dead* (SP50, February 1990). No evidence, so far as I know, has ever emerged of any of these. But the mystery is motivating.

These rumours probably arise from confusion with other records of the time, and perhaps from mis- or disinformation stemming from the label and the kind of 'telephone game' that goes on between collectors. They are also a consequence of the nature of the colour vinyl pressing process itself, which admits slight variation, particularly when other coloured plastics are introduced, or are left behind from another run. I might have what I call a 'teal' first pressing of Nirvana's *Sliver* (SP73, September 1990), and you might have what you call a similar 'light blue' one. Aren't they the same thing (like, 'blue')? Or are they true and deliberate variants, different runs of the pressing machinery, one rarer and therefore more valuable than the other? And how, exactly, should that difference be monetized? This is a situation that plays on numerous subjective factors, not least colour perception and naming. There exists no Sub Pop index or official information to fall back on, and this absence has tended to encourage sometimes wild fluctuations in desirability and price (I might claim I have the only 'aqua' copy of *Sliver* in existence and price it at $1,000; you might be tempted to buy it as a genuine rarity).

Clearly, all this is a rabbit hole. It is something intensely nerdy that can hardly seem important to outside observers, and that, in its obsession with pretty colours and consumables, may seem intensely feminine or infantile to those 'masculine' rock fans who fancy themselves as all about the music. Whether marbled or transparent, blue or teal or aqua, the music inscribed in the record's grooves will be identical, after all. And yet part of the Sub Pop effect is to make sure that it *does* matter, and quite apart from the music; indeed, as Nirvana knew, these records were collectable because they were Sub Pop, not because they gave access to any particular artist or song. And, if part of this appeal is one of aesthetic beauty, then the crucial thing is that this aesthetic aspect is ultimately linked to the kind of obscure knowledge that again reinforces a sense of 'masculine' mastery, financial know-how and control. To be able to tell the transparent pink first-press *Sliver* from the transparent pink second-press one, after all, is not only to do with discerning a slightly darker pink from a lighter one. In the current collectors' market, volatile as ever, it means a difference of more than $100.

A Singles Club

This brings me to the 'Sub Pop Singles Club', a justly celebrated part of the label's early operations, and in many ways its signal venture. Begun in late 1988, the Singles Club offered consumers the opportunity to pay upfront to receive a succession of the label's latest vinyl singles, one per month, with little advance idea of what they were going to get. It was a business success in that it created a win-win situation. Customers were guaranteed, at low cost, to receive 'limited edition' records largely unavailable elsewhere, and the label was paid money upfront to cover its production and running costs and ease cashflow and distribution problems that erupted as its reputation grew. According to Clark Humphrey, membership of the Club peaked in 1991 at 7,000 members.[31] Based on similar figures, Grant Alden estimates that, through the Singles Club, 'Sub Pop raised a cool $175,000 in up-front, interest-free capital.'[32] Understandably, the Club has sometimes been credited with keeping the label solvent in this early phase of its existence.

Despite its success, I don't think we should get too excited by the originality of the Singles Club as a business idea. At base, it is simply a form of subscription service, after all, which must be as old as humanity itself. Also it was clearly inspired both by the majors' record-of-the-month clubs (common since the 1950s) and by the attempts of other small labels to attract a following through collectable series of their wares: K Records' International Pop Underground, begun in 1987, springs to mind, but other examples can be found. What *was* clever – though, again, not original – was Sub Pop's strong emphasis on the vinyl single. As Michael Azerrad sees it, there was little actual profit margin on selling this inexpensive format in the late 1980s, but nonetheless it came with a 'valuable byproduct', namely, 'street buzz'.[33] Vinyl singles had long held a prominent place in the infrastructure of independent rock music, where labels had clung to them in defiance of the major labels' attempt to render vinyl obsolete. In so doing, they had made singles into badges of identity for the entrenched who still owned the disappearing technology, and who had a fondness for the cheap 'pop'-single culture, revived by punk, to which Sub Pop had always referred through its name.

Moreover, bands could record vinyl singles quickly and cheaply compared to CDs, and labels and their industry partners could fall back on the old argument that rock just sounds better when mastered to a 45 rpm single, allegedly because this higher-speed format loses less of the original sound information from the master tape, and allows space for more precise grooves to be cut; the result is perhaps louder, clearer, perceptibly 'heavier' music compared with an LP spinning at 33⅓ rpm.[34] Maybe this is part of what Pete Paphides is getting at when he says that a vinyl single seems an inherently honest thing. There is little room for anything other than one three-minute song on each side of a single, and this means that you are likely getting the very best this band could do – perhaps the only thing it could or would ever do – mastered at the highest vinyl quality it could be. As constraining and conservative as the single format may be, then, it would seem to hold no scope for deception. 'If I showed you a CD now,' says Saint Etienne's Bob Stanley in Paphides's article, 'you wouldn't know if it was a single, an album, a video game or the new

Tom Hanks movie. It's just a thing on which you store information.'[35] A vinyl single might also therefore feel more personally fulfilling, conferring a kind of hipness on its owner. 'Holding a killer package with a cool colored-vinyl single with two great songs on it,' says Tom Hazelmyer, founder of the early Sub Pop competitor Amphetamine Reptile, 'there's something that's deep-down cool about it that's not there with a CD.'[36]

On the other hand, the collector's coolness could be highly contingent. When Thurston Moore of Sonic Youth adds that these Sub Pop Club singles, with their consistent design, could become 'almost like trading cards' among fans, he aligns the Singles Club impishly with the baseball cards and football stickers of the 1970s and '80s, a concern of children and adolescents, not grown-ups.[37] His words also point towards those sad 'instant collectable' magazine regimes where you build up a collection of something mass-produced over time, like coins or model parts or figurines, and can sometimes buy a display stand for them at the end (I note that the fifth volume of the Singles Club, launched in 2019, includes a 'nice box to keep them all in').[38] This is a reminder that, as Moore also puts it, Sub Pop was looking to 'tur[n] the tables a little bit: We're geeks, we're record collectors, we're losers, we're pathetic.'[39] Its club was a *Singles* Club, after all: its heavy rock singles simultaneously played on nerdiness, on all those (always implicitly) men with a 'questionable relationship to masculinity', who, like Nick Hornby's characters, are single in the sense of 'no friends'. See the classic text that accompanied the insert promoting the club, found in most Sub Pop releases of the time, and apparently written by Bruce Pavitt himself:

> Hey loser. Wanna find some action? Tired of being left out? Here at SUB POP we've just started a special club for lonely record collectors like yourself: THE SUB POP SINGLES CLUB.

> Every month we'll send you a limited edition 45. All you have to do is SEND US YOUR MONEY. $35.00 for a full year, $20.00 for 6 months. Your subscription begins the month we receive your $$$.[40]

As if this wasn't bad enough, above the space where you had to fill in your name and address was the following line of consumerist auto-humiliation: 'YES. I am lonely and I want to join your SINGLES CLUB. Here is my money.' Even so, next to *that* was a list of bands projected for the next six months of the Club, by no means always accurate, but still gently enticing its members to trust the label's taste in turning them into connoisseurs of brand-new rock music. It is perhaps the clearest example of Sub Pop turning the badge of 'loser' upside down into something superior. Club members, after all, would have an exclusive first hearing on these singles, in what in many cases became valuable coloured-45 format, and sometimes featuring material not found on the band's LP and never made available elsewhere, whether store retail or mail order. Nirvana's *Love Buzz* (SP23, November 1988) was only the first and most famous of these Club singles, and it is now worth many thousands of dollars in its original version (even the many counterfeits sell for hundreds). Others in the first edition of the Club, which ran until December 1993 and spanned some seventy singles, were recorded by Sonic Youth, Flaming Lips, Rollins Band, Jon Spencer, Lou Barlow and Fugazi, to name only a few of what are now the most celebrated artists.

It is one of the more obscure ones, though, the ninth release in the Club, that sums up the ethos and effect of the whole venture most perfectly for me, what was both powerful and pathetic about it. Michael Lavine's front-cover photo for Das Damen's *Sad Mile* (SP39, July 1989) is a strange thing indeed. Dark eyes peer furtively from behind long hair. An arm is raised above a head. An elaborately

The pensive Das Damen, for the sleeve of their
Sub Pop single *Sad Mile* in 1989.

ruffed shirt – sort of pirate bourgeois – sticks out of an open waist-
coat. The singer stares thoughtfully at the floor and the drummer
is cut in half by the framing, which might be a 'documentary' or
'snapshot' technique, or might just be an accident; he doesn't look
entirely happy about it. The colour scheme is gloomy, and that is
perhaps one reason why this was one of the Singles Club releases to
appear on black vinyl only. Meanwhile, the back of the picture sleeve
is devoted to a clipping from a Seattle lonely hearts column:

FREEMAN ... Longhaired, Harley-ridin', music-playin', strong
and gentle INDIVIDUAL seeks women (mid-20s?) with class,
integrity, heart. Whimsy is fine, BS games aren't. Sun, Moon,
Wind, Thunder, Passion, Honesty. Do you know what you
want? All letters answered, photos returned. Write openly to:
Box 9495, Seattle 98109.

Maybe this is genuine; definitely it is tragic in its apostrophes and
its wind and thunder, and slightly seedy in its promise of 'photos
returned'. In combination with Lavine's line-up photograph, it
hints at a particular characteristic of Das Damen's music, namely
that, alongside their impeccable punk and hardcore credentials,
their songs always have an atmosphere of paisley melancholy to
them, far more obviously than anything in Sub Pop's existing 'heavy'
roster. The A-side track on this 1989 single might be in driving hard
rock style, but its lyrics are about a search to understand the enigma
of the Mona Lisa's smile; this is the only rock song I can think of
with the word 'nevertheless' in it. And then, just as you are pro-
voked to ponder what all this might mean existentially, you notice
the run-out groove, a common one at the time. 'Sub Pop Singles
Club Scam', it says, as if again you were being laughed at, ridiculed
not only for spending your money (the final 'S' was sometimes a
dollar sign) but also for sending it in advance to receive the washed-
out, self-conscious songs of these curious men. The band name
translates from (bad) German as 'The Ladies'.

Then again, do you trust Sub Pop? Perhaps you would be laugh-
ing with them: you might sign away your money, but you might also
make it back and then some. More than that, you might be the
owner of an exclusive by the next big thing in alternative rock.
Granted, this wasn't the case here. Das Damen never really became
a name to conjure with; you could buy up most of their vinyl back

catalogue now for a few pennies or cents. Yet that is a retrospective verdict only. Received in the mail in July 1989, the single must have sent signals of steely promise alongside its pathetic paisley ones. As the sleeve states, the single had been recorded by Wharton Tiers, a producer already associated with Dinosaur Jr, SST and most of all with Sonic Youth (the lead guitar on Sonic Youth's own Singles Club single, SP26, is credited to 'Alex Damen', stressing this inter-artist connection). And in early 1989 Everett True had made a big pre-emptive splash in the British music press for the band, naming them with confusing flourish as 'post-post-post-hardcore', a 'part of the new wave of bands mixing sixties pop with seventies power chords and eighties insight'.[41]

In reality, and as exciting as this makes them sound, Das Damen had been around for a while. Formed in New York in 1984, they were among the oldest of the bands that recorded for the Singles Club: Mudhoney had opened for *them* in their (Mudhoney's) first public performance at the Vogue in Seattle in April 1988. But via the Singles Club, Das Damen were now assimilated into the Sub Pop project, rather than the other way round. It is not unusual to see them nowadays categorized as 'grunge' (or, with their early 1980s origins in view, as 'proto-grunge'), even though they started out 3,000 miles (4,800 km) from Seattle. The Singles Club seems responsible for that.

THERE IS NO DOUBTING the importance of the vinyl single, for Sub Pop and for American alternative rock of the late 1980s more broadly. The Singles Club itself has been revived numerous times over the past thirty years, and, writing late in 2022, is just about to embark on its eighth volume. There have been other big rock dis-coveries in the intervening period: an early White Stripes single (red/white split vinyl, SP527, December 2000) would count as one of them. It has also inspired similar schemes at other small indie labels on both sides of the Atlantic, helping to prolong and even rejuvenate the life of vinyl. See, for example, the Estrus Crust Club and Clawfist Singles Club (both from mid-1990), the Rough Trade Singles Club (from late 1991), Kill Rock Stars' Mailorder Freak Club (from 1998) and the Too Pure Singles Club (from 2007). No doubt the Sub Pop example also stands behind the notorious case of Communion, the tiny Atlanta label, which in the middle of 1991 released a split Melvins/Nirvana single in so many colour variants that collectors, close to madness, are forced to speak in hair-splitting terms that sound like a paintshop colour chart. 'Emerald green', 'green marble', 'lime green', 'seafoam green' and 'green-grey' are only a few examples of names used to distinguish very similar colours. Inside every sleeve is the line that confirms the influence of Sub Pop and their house brand of humour: 'Limited edition of ____ (how many we can sell)'.[42]

Alongside the Singles Club, and drawing on its success, Sub Pop also used the format to release stand-alone singles, some of them from bands that became the household names of alternative rock in the early 1990s: Hole (SP93, March 1991), Dinosaur Jr (SP68, June 1990), Screaming Trees (SP48, December 1989) and Smashing Pumpkins (SP90, December 1990), as a few examples. All in numerous coloured vinyl variants, these are now collectors' items, in some cases with versions of songs that have never been released anywhere else. Clearly, as Billy Corgan put it in 1992, the 'Sub Pop affiliation really helped . . . it created a general interest and definitely helped us to get national.'[43] Equally it went the other way too. These bands helped the label fulfil one of the goals that had surrounded the name 'Sub Pop' since the early days of Bruce Pavitt's fanzine: to profit from a reputation as the curator of a national network of new rock, easily labelled with the buzzword 'grunge'. '[T]hey signed the one good band in every town,' says Blag Dahlia of Dwarves:

> There was no Chicago scene, but you could get one thing out of Urge Overkill. There was no San Francisco scene, but you get one thing out of the Dwarves. L.A. had L7 and Ohio had the Afghan Whigs. Basically, 'Grab the one band that's touring and hanging out, and make it into something.'[44]

This is clearly too reductive, and it is easy to take issue with the claim that there was no Chicago or San Francisco scene. It does, though, suggest something of the way in which Sub Pop expanded via its singles strategy, as well as demonstrating that it led as much by provocation as by influence. This explains why there were count-less bootlegs and unofficial parody imitations, some of them bitter towards Sub Pop's success with singles. A certain Ramones 7" from about 1991, for example, has all the Sub Pop singles branding, a satirical catalogue number (SP666), and at least two coloured vari-ants. It has nothing to do with Sub Pop, but its insert does have a noir comic strip in which a woman who hates the label and just wants to listen to her simple old punk records is violently bullied into submission and a 'LOSER' T-shirt. 'We now rule the world,' laugh a cartoon Pavitt and Poneman at the end, in an unmasking of one of their own ironic slogans.[45]

Perhaps the most important thing about singles and the Singles Club, however, was that they served to advertise the Sub Pop brand while rapidly expanding it, far beyond the cities that Blag Dahlia surveys. The 'maniacal release schedule' that saw the label releasing one Club single a month, plus a few stand-alone ones, plus EPs and LPs, meant branching out not only across the United States but North America more widely.[46] It led to focuses becoming established elsewhere, often under the mission statement to find the isolated rock scene that would be the 'next Seattle', the 'next grunge'. An A&R expansion to the East Coast took place in the early 1990s under Joyce Linehan, beginning with bands like Velocity Girl and Green Magnet School, and leading eventually to Eastern Canada and what has become known as the 'invasion of Halifax'. This included Eric's Trip (SP205, April 1993), Jale (SP235, November 1993), Hardship Post (SP262, November 1994), and the compilation *Never Mind the Molluscs* (SP198, March 1993).[47]

The same expansion also meant going international, turning to Japan with Shonen Knife (SP108, April 1991; actually a throwback to *Sub Pop 100*), to Australia with Lubricated Goat (SP65, April 1990), and even to Britain (Thee Headcoats, SP71, June 1990; These Immortal Souls, SP121, June 1991), which since the early 1980s had been marginalized by the label. Singles also gave the opportunity to assimilate a rapid succession of women's grunge bands – Hole, Babes in Toyland, L7, Dickless – across 1990 and 1991, countering the over-whelmingly male artist base of the label, and eventually to introduce some new instruments. As if heeding Grant Alden's 1990 warning that 'You can't make a label on one kind of music', the slap-style bass of Big Chief's single *Chrome Helmet* (SP53, March 1990) begins to hint at something more like funk rock, later fully tricked out with backing singers and a brass section (in *One Born Every Minute*, SP229, August 1993).[48] This is something that would have been unthinkable with Green River, Blood Circus, Nirvana, TAD and the label's other 'pure' foundational bands – guitar, bass, drums – in its earliest years.

Epilogue: Lame fest

BUT IN MID-1989, the time of Das Damen's Singles Club release, there was still one obvious avenue through which to expand the audience for the original 'Seattle rock'. Sub Pop had put together a strong label identity and branding, and built an armoury of marketing techniques. They had, too, an expectant fan base in many American towns and had amassed roughly thirty vinyl releases, and all kinds of coloured variants, to sell to it. What was still in its infancy was the network that would stretch to other world markets far beyond the borders of the United States. In early 1988 Sub Pop had licensed their first Fluid album from the German independent label Glitterhouse, likewise founded as a fanzine in 1981. This now became a relationship that went the other way, with Sub Pop feeding Glitterhouse its newest releases, including singles, to sell into the European market. Similar arrangements would follow in 1989 with Tupelo and Blast First in the UK and Waterfront in Australia. In all cases, the Sub Pop logo, or at the very least the name, sat alongside that of the regional label on record or sleeve.

Since, however, part of Sub Pop's appeal was staked on the close identity between its recordings and its live shows, it became a shrewd move to support these world releases with a label tour outside the U.S. Famously, this was eventually undertaken from October to December 1989, when, for the first time, Mudhoney, TAD and Nirvana would embark on exhaustive trips around western Europe, including dates in the UK, the Netherlands, West Germany, Belgium, Hungary, Austria, Italy, Denmark and France ('Worth Going! Worth Kissing! Worth F***king!!' ran the title on the curious Glitterhouse-issue flyer for these shows).

In retrospect, these three bands seem like obvious choices; it does not now seem that it could have been any other way. They ticked all the boxes. Their recordings to date, all of them made with Jack Endino at Reciprocal, had appeared almost exclusively with Sub Pop, and, if it mattered, they could be proven as regional representatives of the Northwest (unlike, for example, Denver's the Fluid). However hard it is to define their place in a 'Sub Pop sound', they also had more audibly in common with one another than with, say, other well-established label bands like the Walkabouts, with their folksy Americana fiddles and harmonicas and hands playing high on guitar necks.[49] And, whatever the slight psychedelic weirdness of names like Nirvana and Mudhoney, at least they weren't called Cat Butt.

These three bands were also renowned for playing the most chaotic and unpredictable shows. 'Did that band absolutely rock the house?', as Bruce Pavitt liked to ask when vetting a new artist for the label, and it is easy to forget that these three had been carefully cultivated to do exactly that – at least when compared to the likes of Blood Circus, who were derided for having 'no edge whatsoever' onstage (as Nirvana put it scathingly in 1990); *they* now began to feel like the 'bastard stepson of Sub Pop'.[50] Mudhoney, obviously chosen as the label's flagship band, had already been extensively road-tested across the U.S. and in Europe in late 1988 and early 1989. Nirvana and TAD, too, had been toured for a year or more in countless small venues up and down the West Coast and elsewhere, not least in Seattle itself. 'Sub Pop Sundays' had run at the city's Vogue Theater since late 1987 and functioned not only as propaganda but as a kind of 'test screening' for bands. As part of one of these Sundays, Nirvana first played publicly under that name early in 1988, and it is telling that Cobain looked back on it later that year with some negativity: 'It just didn't seem like a real show. We felt like we were being judged; it was like everyone should've had score cards.'[51]

Perhaps the most crucial thing these bands shared was their ability to serve the label by acting out a colourful array of 'loser' qualities, across their live shows, their songs, their recordings and their interviews. It is these qualities, in fact, that are the focuses of the next three chapters of this book, band by band. This was what really set them apart for Sub Pop from the likes of Blood Circus, however 'primitive rock 'n' roll' such bands were in other ways. It is also, I think, what Pavitt points towards when he identifies Nirvana, TAD and Mudhoney as the 'really authentic garage rock 'n' roll bands' that could hardly fail to 'get in the face' of the European (particularly British) media.[52] To return to and extend Thurston Moore's view above:

> Sub Pop turned the tables a little bit: We're geeks, we're record collectors, we're losers, we're pathetic. People like Mark Arm [of Mudhoney] and Kurt Cobain and Tad, these guys embodied this in such a great way. They were not your typical good-looking punk-rock stars. They were kinda skinny, nose-picking nerds. Except for Tad, who was a fat, burger-burping geek. They were also lovable, and you sort of wanted to be part of that gang.[53]

This is perfect because it captures both the revulsion and the appeal, *and* makes that combination a key part of label identity for itself and its fans. In turn it serves as a useful reminder that the biggest show for these three bands to date, on the eve of the European tour, drew directly on the loser language that Sub Pop had been busily coining since 1987. This was the so-called 'Lame Fest' of June 1989, the first of numerous 'Lame'-branded label events held across the world into the early 1990s (the final British tour date of December 1989 would be likewise named the 'Lame Fest UK').

One of the original Lame Fest flyers promised 'Seattle's lamest bands in a one night orgy of sweat and insanity!', which gives an idea of what these bands were expected to deliver in performance. Equally telling was the merchandise T-shirt for the event. 'Sub Pop Sells Out!' it proclaimed on the back, and this was true in at least two senses. The label had demonstrated its cultural capital by quite literally selling out Seattle's Moore Theater, with its unusually massive capacity for this kind of alternative rock show. Audience estimates range from something like 1,000–1,500 people right up to as many as 2,300.[54] In so doing it had also emphasized precisely what was truly 'lame' about its operations. At the Moore, Sub Pop had 'sold out' beyond the small venues of the northwestern scene and made clear what was obvious anyway: its intentions to seek mass acclaim and maximum profit through this parade of chaotic losers, as pathetic and hilarious as they were spectacular.

The few minutes of surviving footage of the first Seattle Lame Fest are indicative. Mudhoney stop and start, repeatedly interrupted by a running battle with security personnel attempting to stop the crowd surging onto the stage. 'We're all a bunch of wimpy faggots – remember that!' shouts Mark Arm to a massive roar of approval, turning standard hate-language on its head: 'Welcome to Lame Fest '89, home of the wimpy faggot!'[55] Nirvana jam badly on the 1950s rock standard 'Louie Louie' before breaking directly into 'Blew', the first track on their soon-to-be-released LP, as if demonstrating how limply retro they were. Kurt Cobain ends the set by running back and forth across the stage whirling his guitar round his head by its strap. He is not engaging with the crowd, particularly, and so the effect is something like a toddler at a wedding reception, especially when he dives headlong into the drum kit and Chad Channing carries on drumming on his backside. The crowd goes wild. Paul de Barros's notorious review in the *Seattle Times* complains of the 'perverse, reverse notion that grungy, foul-mouthed, self-despising meatheads who grind out undifferentiated noise and swing around their long hair are good – and "honest" – by virtue of their not being "rock stars"'.[56]

Needless to add, all this was perfect publicity for Sub Pop and grunge, in terms of what was both familiar and different about them. For de Barros, it was sad that Sub Pop's 'primitivism' defined these rock bands through the 'reverse of someone else's market position' rather than through music. But, of course, it was precisely that market position that *made* the music and the event and gave it its special appeal – as the review concedes when it goes on to half-praise the 'young, enthusiastic and clearly intelligent crowd' that the show had attracted, and defined the prevailing atmosphere at the Moore as 'certainly folksy, friendly and nothing like a commercial rock show'.[57]

Pavitt and Poneman must also have been delighted when, a week later, another *Seattle Times* correspondent recalled Sub Pop's 'wild "Lamefest"' against the more 'staid, traditional' showcase of a competitor indie label, Green Monkey.[58] If these kinds of comments seemed to confirm their dominance in Seattle, then they would now expend the energy outwards internationally. Bringing together the uniquely 'lame' trio of Mudhoney, TAD and Nirvana, and taking them straight to Europe, demonstrated the label's pursuit of coverage, of using any and all avenues to push itself to the front of consciousness, towards a project that, though voiced ironically in terms of 'world domination' and so on, increasingly appeared to be just that.

5

Here Comes Sickness: Mudhoney

TO UNDERSTAND MUDHONEY and their importance for Sub
Pop, you can't start with Mudhoney. You need to go back, I think,
to one of several places where it all began for the label. This was June
1987 and its very first single-artist release, Green River's EP *Dry as
a Bone* (SP11). Spinning the disc is a formative experience. In the
beginning a heavily overdriven guitar looms out of nowhere, its
clumsy and disjointed licks echoing into emptiness. Is this someone
practising or something? It certainly sounds like it – at least until
the guitar settles into a cliché blues riff, a sub-Muddy Waters kind
of shuffle, and is joined by a second guitar that duels against it,
shrieking out in a higher register. At about the same moment a sultry
kazoo-like voice arrives, too, relocating the central aural reference
point to what seems a pouting parody of Mick Jagger, or perhaps
Iggy Pop making fun of Mick Jagger. No less full of cliché, this voice
sings a clumsy patter to 'baby', goading her into coming over to his
place because he wants to watch her 'unwind' ('Unwind', by the way,
is the title of this opening song).

Then – a change. Very faintly at first, drums and bass enter the
picture, not at all in rhythmic accompaniment to the opening electric shuffle but, growing quickly louder and louder, driving an express
train across and through it, sweeping away all the solo licks of the
opening and leaving only a flat trail of debris that points to the next
part of the song. Hands glide down fretboards, and a new voice
appears in the middle of Jack Endino's mix, obsessively repeating
a mantra: 'I can I can I can.' And finally the whole thing explodes

in an unholy harmony of men's voices, one of which is a scream, telling you exactly what these men 'can' do, against a striding new riff of which any 1970s hard rock band would be proud. What they can do is three simple words: 'fuck your mind'.

It really is a hair-raising opening. There is something specifically grunge in the music it brings together, and its intensity on record remains unmatched by most other Sub Pop bands of the time. It also cues up some of Green River's best playing later in the song. Nonetheless I think we do need to talk about several uncomfortable things in 'Unwind'. The rudeness of its awakening, for one: it doesn't so much pay homage to the blues, or rock 'n' roll guitar's roots in the blues, as stage their obliteration in the service of a ratty hard rock song; one wonders what the Lester Bangs of 'The White Noise Supremacists' would make of it. The lyrics of the main song should also raise an eyebrow. You know when people say 'I'd like to keep an open mind,' but what they really mean is 'I don't want to think about it'? This is exactly the subtle deception that the song takes aim at. As the lyrics of 'Unwind' make clear, an 'open' mind is the same thing as an 'empty' mind, the same thing as being 'barely alive'. And as they also say, an empty mind can be sown with seed (the sex connotation is very obvious) and can be made to think whatever 'I' want. It is not only 'baby's' body the singer demands, but her mind too. Indeed, the 'I can' mantra coming through the middle of the mix mimics this theft: it emerges from the head between the headphones, from the private space reserved for the open mind. The song may invite baby to 'unwind'; nonetheless it becomes increasingly clear that the word is meant not in the usual sense of 'relax', but instead in the more unsettling one of 'unravel'.

So if there is something that is sad shuffling sex-pest lounge lizard ('come on over to my place' and so on) about this very first Sub Pop song, there is also something disturbing – even psychopathic

– about it. And this, it turns out, is highly appropriate. The theme of serial killers swirled around Green River for the three or so years of their existence. In fact, the band name echoes the nickname of Gary Ridgway, the 'Green River Killer', murderer of something like fifty women in Washington State across the 1980s and still at large when the band were playing and recording. Several of the songs on their first EP, *Come on Down* (Homestead, 1985), imagine these murders from their (then still unidentified) perpetrator's point of view. 'PCC' on *Dry as a Bone* revisits the topic of conscience-free killing. In short, the idea of the psychopath was part of the cultural mythology that Green River used to draw in and titillate and provoke their audiences. The band's fan club was called the 'Tasque Force', a reference to the sheriff's department formed specifically to catch the killer; apparently at least one Green River show in Seattle saw a protest against the tastelessness of the band's name – even when they were supporting bands with names like Dead Kennedys and Crucifucks.[1]

I begin with Green River in this chapter because, in important ways, Green River and Sub Pop were more or less the same thing in those very early days, working together to further shared fortunes. Bruce Pavitt had done some of the distribution of Green River's self-released first single *Together We'll Never* (1986), sending it out with copies of his first vinyl compilation *Sub Pop 100*. (Since the single was on green vinyl, it was possibly also here that he got the idea to release Sub Pop's first official singles on coloured vinyl.) After that, the members of Green River had largely funded the recording, manufacture and promotion of their first Sub Pop EP, *Dry as a Bone*, and, up until the release of their LP *Rehab Doll* (SP15, May 1988), served alongside Soundgarden as one of the label's showcase bands. What then happened has become one of the foundational grunge fables. In late 1987 Green River split to form two new bands, reproducing the apparent cultural schism in Seattle between the 'independent stance of punk' and the accessibility of 'straight-ahead 1970s hard rock'.[2] Mudhoney – or so the fable continues – took away the 'punk' in the form of Green River's singer Mark Arm and one of its former guitarists, Steve Turner, and quickly became the new Sub Pop flagship. Mother Love Bone took the 'hard rock' from Green River's other members and went straight to a major, its remnants eventually becoming Pearl Jam. 'It was Hanoi Rocks vs. Iggy Pop,' as Michael Azerrad sums it up, 'the difference between putting on makeup and playing tricky guitar licks or donning pegged jeans and high-tops and baring your soul, between major-label dreams and indie cred'.[3]

I think it is important, however, to pause for a moment to think about how blunt this binary is. The way Azerrad tells it, it seems a simple matter of 'authenticity' versus 'fakeness', 'cred' versus 'dreams', as if Arm and Turner, Green River's 'punk' contingent, remained true to themselves and their music while the others went off to don feather boas and make-up and play on massive stadium soundstages to hordes of screaming fans for millions of dollars. But let's be frank: Sub Pop's Mudhoney were also putting on an act. It was just that they performed something different. Theirs was the Green River legacy of sickness, absorbed directly through Arm and Turner. As Mudhoney, they built an extensive vocabulary of sickness in their music and lyrics, starting with their most famous song, 'Touch Me I'm Sick'. But beyond that they performed sickness in almost everything they did both on- and offstage, and this was their central contribution to Sub Pop's loser project in its formative years.

Reaching back into the Green River days, sometimes this sickness would emerge in their songs as psychopathic and sociopathic, formed around the consciousless desire to hurt – further tales of the 'barely repressed sexual aggression' that Steve Waksman finds throughout Mark Arm's entire songwriting career.[4] Equally often, it could be a more puerile physical sickness. Most of the talk around early Mudhoney revolved around endless anecdotes of injuries, pratfalls and drunken vomits on the stage, usually involving the band, its hangers-on and the crowd.[5] This made their act as amusing as it was disturbing, a kind of ill-coordinated, perhaps deliberately parodic, comedy, delivered by songs, interviews and their accompanying antics, with the ever-present sex aggression sublimated into a raging innuendo in almost every verbal and visual gesture. Double-entendres are everywhere: Green River had begun with *Come on Down*, *Dry as a Bone* and *Rehab Doll*, and song titles like 'Swallow My Pride'. Mudhoney would continue, famously, with *Superfuzz Bigmuff* and 'In 'n' Out of Grace'. The name 'Mudhoney' itself, indeed, comes from a film of 1965 by the notorious 'nudie-cutie' director Russ Meyer, and its adoption suggests that the band and its label were leaning on Meyer's limitless ability to squeeze crude sex references into every conceivable space. The disc label on Mudhoney's 1989 LP (SP44; more soberly called *Mudhoney*) has a snapshot of someone in ripped jeans doing a headstand on top of a surging gig crowd. I noticed the other day that the spindle hole is perfectly positioned so that, when you place the record on the turntable, the spindle sticks through the crotch of the jeans like a metal penis. The attention to detail is almost unbelievable.

It was also through Green River and Mudhoney that the term 'grunge' first came into focus as a musical genre. Along with many others of the time, Arm himself had used it as casual description: in a fanzine letter of 1981 he described his own high-school art-noise band, Mr Epp and the Calculations, as 'Pure grunge! Pure noise! Pure shit!', and in so doing implied ('pure') that there was something real and valuable there, gold in all Mr Epp's chaotic sonic mess.[6] It was with the Sub Pop slogans for Green River, however, that grunge became a sound, a mental-moral illness and a mark of alternative distinction for young fans: 'ultra-loose GRUNGE', as label advertising put it, 'that destroyed the morals of a generation'.[7] From here Mudhoney could inherit the title of the 'masters of disease and grunge', their first EP containing 'Six epic songs of sickness . . . LOUD ballads of love and dirt', their first LP with 'love songs destined to soil a generation'.[8] In Mudhoney, and in Sub Pop's tireless promotional efforts on their behalf, and all kinds of spin-off projects involving Arm and Turner, grunge became the new musical sickness that could be catching.

Sick Music

By far Mudhoney's most famous song, 'Touch Me I'm Sick' has often been touted as one of the overtures of the grunge era, or at least the most essential statement of the new Seattle genre's identity and sound. The song has also proven controversial as to what it is really about, and this is hardly surprising bearing in mind its lyrics, which seem to reveal someone clumsily goading a girl into catching a fatal disease from him, perhaps so that they can die together. Mark Yarm expresses a standard view when he calls the song 'scabrously funny', all a big, ugly laugh at the expense of someone, not least the band themselves.[9] Michael Azerrad turns the joke specifically on the fans when he points out that the song was issued by Sub Pop in August 1988 on 'turd-brown' collectors' vinyl and the disc label (and later the sleeve) had a grim greyscale image of a toilet on it, apparently Bruce Pavitt's own, shot from below the bowl as if seen by someone slithering towards it on hands and knees.[10] Are you seriously buying this crap?

Catherine Creswell, on the other hand, widens this focus by pointing out that 'Touch Me I'm Sick' appeared at a moment when the HIV/AIDS pandemic was still rapidly growing in the United States, and public understanding, despite some attempts at federal intervention, was still at a bare minimum.[11] From this point of view, Mudhoney and Sub Pop were exploiting a situation comparable to, and in many ways worse than, the one Green River had drawn on with the Green River Killer: something deadly, unexplained, unsolved and frightening that might devastate a community, however small or out-of-the-way (Gina Arnold, looking back, considers it simply 'luck' that more independent artists and fans did not die of AIDS-related illnesses).[12] And while Arm has said repeatedly that he had no intention of alluding to HIV and AIDS in his lyrics, this denial can hardly stretch to cover Sub Pop's publicity campaign. Their 1990 advertising line for the single named it the 'undisputed anthem for the AIDS generation.'[13]

The key point about the song, then, is that it tries hard to play several ways at the same time, the sickly comic layered up on top of the deadly serious and vice versa. This is the art of Mudhoney's grunge, which, just like Sub Pop's, points in several directions at once and commits to none ('What does the word "crack" mean to you?' asks the A-side run-out groove of the original vinyl single, as if underlining the point). Clearly the song falls just short as a brutal jibe about the HIV/AIDS pandemic, which is actually mentioned nowhere in its lyrics, in contrast to the work of certain other Sub Pop bands, like Dwarves (who sang 'Gimme AIDS' in 1990) and Soundgarden ('HIV Baby' for the Singles Club in the same year).[14] On the other hand, 'Touch Me I'm Sick' has always been more than a shit novelty laugh on brown vinyl in a toilet sleeve. In its vicious ultimatum – the girl can either 'come with me' or 'die alone' – it draws on much the same sexual aggression as Green River's 'Unwind', except that the sentiment is now couched in a much snappier and more winning form. Steve Turner's graunching opening riff leads into a verse capped off by the title refrain; this in turn leads to a chorus that is literally a chorus, since the rest of the band join in the singing; this chorus leads into a guitar solo just as it should; perfect. Creswell is surely right, then, to liken 'Touch Me I'm Sick' to those 'rock 'n' roll seduction songs' of earlier times that are satisfying precisely because they 'celebrate the allure of the form itself'.[15] It is a seduction song turned inside out, as it were, leading to death, not consummation.

Mark Arm's vocals are similarly complicated. He may sound just like Iggy Pop, as Dawn Anderson pointed out for *Backlash* in 1988, but wasn't Iggy himself also doing some kind of parody – of big 'rock' singing, of 'good' singing?[16] Take 'Penetration' on *Raw Power* (1973), for example, in which he is barely able to finish the sentences, so much does he stretch out the quality of each syllable; it sounds less like someone singing a rock song about penetration and more like someone comically imitating someone singing a rock song about penetration. Something like this is also true of Arm's 'Touch Me I'm Sick', with its flagrant disregard for vowel sounds and continuous recourse to seductive rock-god vocal posturing ('Come owwwwn!'). Even so, it isn't only a matter of imitation. Arm's lethargic kazoo voice in Green River's 'Unwind' has here become something far more sinister than even Iggy could muster. It is goading, sneering, self-hating and hateful, feeding off the two pelvis-thrusting downbeats that drive the song's curious momentum, and obviously attuned to the remarkable quality of Turner's guitar sound. This sound was often what really gripped critics, in fact. As Tim Cronin found on hearing the band live in 1989, there was something superlatively disgusting about the Mudhoney sound as led by Arm's voice and Turner's guitar, something that was clearly derivative of numerous influences and yet required a new vocabulary to capture its power: 'When Mudhoney has all the cheese and distortion working they get the meanest sound I've ever heard, nastier than the Swans or

Slayer in their respective heydays. It's this all-encompassing distorto-squelch that goes beyond guitar mud bands and stomps anything in any genre.'[17]

Sicker Music

It goes without saying that 'Touch Me I'm Sick' has become a touchstone of the grunge era, the flagship Sub Pop song of the flag-ship Sub Pop band. Predictably enough, Mudhoney immediately named it one of their 'grungiest' efforts, securing the crucial link to the new genre term; it sold out quickly in original press and re-presses, was awarded Rock Single of the Year for 1988 by *Village Voice* and, according to Michael Azerrad, 'single-handedly ignited a press furor over the whole garage-grunge scene'.[18] Nowadays it is cer-tain to come up immediately in books on grunge, and the magnetic title phrase has clung to the top of any number of retrospectives, whether straight up or in parody. The title of Sub Pop's Australian-release label compilation of 1989 made it 'Fuck Me I'm Rich', for example, while in 1992, as part of the platinum-selling *Singles* film soundtrack, Matt Dillon performed it as 'Touch Me I'm Dick'. The phrase's catchiness also seems to get at something of the era's live-wire energy and clumsy bodily antics. Sub Pop's official label video for the song, probably made in about 1992, cuts rapidly between all kinds of live-action head-banging, guitar-wheeling, stage-diving, crowd-surging, fretboard-thrusting antics, as well as several uncon-vincing mid-air splits and a backwards salmon bend, long-blond-hair-to-heels, that Arm borrowed from Iggy Pop and yet somehow managed to make his own.

As an overpowering symbol in all these ways, the song is some-times, too, where the talk about Mudhoney begins and ends – and that is misleading because, whatever its attractions, it isn't fully representative of their early output. There were, I think, equally sickly Mudhoney songs that get far more directly to the heart of what Sub Pop valued them so highly for in their early days. These songs revisit all the same themes as 'Touch Me I'm Sick': the physical disease that might also be mental, that might also be a permanent condition of misery; the comedy of the social outsider and predator – the 'creep', the 'jerk', the 'stray dog' – that is obviously also deeply threatening, particularly towards lone women; the moments of rock parody that carry their own allure but somehow don't add up to a full 'spoof'. Yet they are far more radical musically and, as a direct consequence, much less satisfying; they don't translate to live-antics crowd-surging videos so well. These songs experiment, in fact, with a kind of musical minimalism that was learned from hardcore punk, as well as from the 1960s garage rock to which Mudhoney are often compared. Tommy Ramone spoke of deliberately taking the big rock sound of the 1970s into a 'psychotic world' and narrowing it into 'a straight line of energy': 'In an era of progressive rock, with its complexities and counterpoints, we had a perspective of nonmusicality and intelligence that takes over for musicianship.'[19] A generation of post-Ramones hardcore bands took their cue from this kind of statement. But in Mudhoney's grunge it became all the more of an obsession, a full-blown psychosis with striking creative results.

A prototype was the flip side of the first single, 'Sweet Young Thing Ain't Sweet No More'. This is the 'other' early Mudhoney song, the anti-classic that gets nothing like the same level of attention in all the commentary on the band. As with 'Touch Me I'm Sick', it contains a number of references backwards. The song title echoes artefacts of 1960s chart-pop culture, such as the Monkees' song 'Sweet Young Thing' (1966), as well as those of 'psychedelic' garage bands of the same era: in 1967 the Chocolate Watchband recorded a 'Sweet Young Thing' of their own. Whether citing mainstream or underground, though, Mudhoney's point is clear. Just as Green River, in their song 'Swallow My Pride', had once announced (following Blue Öyster Cult) that 'this ain't the summer of love', so this 'sweet young thing' ain't 'sweet no more'. Innocence, if it ever existed at all, has definitely been lost by the late 1980s.

Appropriately, then, the sound of Mudhoney's 'Sweet Young Thing' is anything but a stereotypically 1960s jangle. Everything heads immediately downwards in this song. Turner's 'distorto-squelch' is as revolting as it is in 'Touch Me I'm Sick', and Arm's slide guitar exerts a heavy drag on the tuned-down initial riff as it enters. All that comes afterwards rattles and echoes with a slow reverb effect, including (unusually) the drums, which try desperately to animate the song and give it some forward momentum. The overall effect is close to comatose, and works well to reflect the murderous afternoon hangover of Arm's lyrics, and the image of the 'sweet young thing' collapsed over the toilet bowl while the 'midday sun' beats down through the window and 'Mama's little pills' skitter across the tiled bathroom floor (this was presumably, by the way, the inspiration for the toilet label and picture sleeve of the original single).

Mudhoney's 'Sweet Young Thing' is, in other words, very definitely not one of rock's 'seduction songs', alluring in its form. After about a minute, it seems to be headed for a chorus or solo but gets stuck on one note for bass and guitars, all hands jammed high on fretboards, sounding more like a screaming headache tinnitus than a convincing musical bridge. This creates a cruelly oppressive atmosphere, which begins to gouge bleeding chunks out of the American dream as each verse follows from the last, with no musical relief from a chorus or middle eight. There is no sympathy here. The child of the title must be 'handled' like an animal, not 'raised' or 'brought up', and Mama can't cope (hence the pills). And then the song's last line, which, typically Mudhoney, is both comic 1950s in its sitcom cliché but also horrific in the violence it foresees, in part because of Arm's writhing scream as he delivers it and Dan Peters's hammering drums underneath: 'Just you wait till your father gets home!' The girl may be bad but her father is worse.

In one way, Mudhoney show their debt to hardcore here and particularly to Black Flag's vision of the ultraviolence that lies so close beneath the surface of the hypocritical American 'family man'. No doubt they were also inspired by some of the sludge metal songs of the Melvins, an influence that was handed back when the Melvins themselves covered the song at an even slower tempo and had it released in an identical toilet sleeve, parody Sub Pop branding, and a hundred different vinyl colours.[20] In other ways, however, Mudhoney go far beyond sources like these, slowly building an intensely claustrophobic scenario that amplifies the sinister aspect lying behind pop's 'Sweet Young Thing' cliché and, with sexual aggression barely repressed, forces it to lose its innocence.

Crucially, they also made this musical style into a general principle. Across much of their early music, notably the EP and two LPs as released by Sub Pop from 1988 to 1991, Matt Lukin's bass line is king, an absolute dictator: the guitars and vocals march to its tune, closely mimicking its contours at every step, just as they do in 'Sweet Young Thing Ain't Sweet No More'. This means both that there are few tunes to sing – compare the early 'melodic' Nirvana – and that the songs' structures typically hurtle verse-by-verse, without chorus breaks, towards a final screamed parting shot from the singer, a catastrophic breakdown conclusion. The brilliantly sociopathic 'No One Has' on the first EP, *Superfuzz Bigmuff*, is a case in point. The tuned-down bass riff that opens this song may be frantic, but Arm's monotone voice both mimics it and cuts across it at half speed, spending some lines of the verse in its nasal middle span and heaving upwards to a scream for the others. There is no chorus, instead a simple repetition only of this verse; the release from it is limited to a few short breaks led by the slide guitar, which sounds just for a moment as if it will push into chorus territory, or at the very least change the key or the register or something. It doesn't: instead, locked to its repeating bass line, the song moves inevitably towards the closing statement of its title at the end, joined by doom-chiming guitars and a final verse in which Arm bellows against the bass for what 'no one has' in desperate fragments of monotone. This, I think, is the best of this Mudhoney style. Whatever it is that the lyrics are seeking, the singer and the song obviously don't find it. Nor will the listener. Arm's final scream overshoots everything else in its straight line of energy and is left hanging alone in the air at the end.

There are lots of other examples. Like 'No One Has', many of them go at an alarming pace, the vocals hugging their bass lines so tightly that there is almost no room to breathe. Take 'Chain That Door' on the first Sub Pop record, 'Flat Out Fucked' on the second, 'Let It Slide' and 'Thorn' on the third, the B-side 'Baby Help Me Forget'. The slower numbers are always most powerful, though, because their claustrophobia is given more time to build. 'Mudride' on *Superfuzz Bigmuff* again references 1960s garage through its distinctly psyche-delic atmosphere. Vibrating as if from sympathetic strings, the guitars home in on a monotone at the beginning and sit there for much of six minutes while Peters's drums shudder like a tabla underneath. There is no inner peace here, however. Perhaps the drums shudder at Arm's lyrics: the singer is busy digging a grave and doesn't care who he is about to hurt, himself included. The chorus, in a weird parody of the slogans of mass advertising, offers a 'ticket for two on a one-way ride'. Possibly the adjective 'grungedelic', first applied to Sub Pop labelmates Cat Butt, is the best way to describe the effect.[21]

The Rose

That Sub Pop was equally invested in this flip side of Mudhoney is obvious from the 1989 sampler compilation *Sub Pop 200*, for which the band provided a cover of 'The Rose'. Remember the Bette Midler version of this song, originally written by Amanda McBroom? It plays over the end credits of the film of the same name, released in 1979. At the beginning of Midler's version are solo, high-register piano chords only, heavily reverbed – a standard film signifier of lonely, pained reflection. Midler starts defining love through metaphor, verse by verse, and this inspires the song gradually to thicken, as if gaining in confidence, first with backing vocals and the deeper bass of the piano. This verse build is all the song is, in fact. There is no chorus, and instead the third verse breaks almost gospel, only to return to the solo piano chords at its end, a cutback sweetly timed to coincide with the song's closing image. This is of 'you', love's disheartened seed, waiting to grow and blossom into 'the rose' when springtime comes.

'The Rose' is, in other words, a classic of the piano ballad literature, a famous diva standard that has been respected as such by the countless subsequent interpreters – LeAnn Rimes, Bonnie Tyler, Elaine Paige, Katherine Jenkins, Keala Settle and many more – who maintain its generic features or modify them only slightly. This reputation is certainly part of what recommended it to Mudhoney (as well as to Arm's former band, the 'supreme noise makers' Mr Epp and the Calculations, who had played it as part of their live set early in the 1980s).[22] Of course, there is no piano, no choir and no singing string section in the grunge version for *Sub Pop 200*. But, just as in 'Sweet Young Thing' and many of the other early songs, there is the same gradual verse-by-verse build without chorus break, making it an ideal target for what Everett True rightly called a 'gruelling, *intense*' cover version.[23] Generically speaking, Mudhoney split the difference here between their deliberately dire sludge rock, satirical noise art and the piano ballad of mass-culture movies.

Lukin's distorted bass line enters first, playing a version of Midler's tender vocal melody exactly where it shouldn't be: down low, and compressed into the pitches of Mudhoney's metal scale. The drums and howling guitars then enter, as do Mark Arm's vocals, all of them mimicking the bass line almost exactly – at least, insofar as Mudhoney's ways of tuning and playing could mimic anything exactly. Aside from the martial drums, the only real driver for Mudhoney's version is, as usual, Arm's voice, which leaves the bass line briefly to turn into a heaving scream on words that emphasize the damage of love: 'razor', 'hunger', 'dying'. A break in the middle, entirely of Mudhoney's invention, is the only relief, Arm speaking a kind of proverb about friendship in a falsetto voice. And then a short guitar solo from Turner, again closely built on the bass line, before Arm's voice comes back in for the last verse and a memorable scream on the final image, the transformation into 'the rose'.

Obviously parody is again part of the point here, perhaps the clearest one of all in Mudhoney. If a parody works on two levels at once – an implied original in the background and a transgression of it in the foreground – then the listener is encouraged to recognize the backdrop from the very beginning, albeit in a roundabout way. Before Lukin's bass enters, the sounds of lapping waves can be heard, presumably a reference to Midler's latest hit film *Beaches* (1988), or perhaps the seaside setting of so many romcoms of the period. This cues everything following to be turned upside down compared to its model, almost to the point that, as one early critic put it, it becomes 'unrecognizable'.[24] 'The Rose' becomes something primitive, desperate, dirty, heavy and offensive to its target in this Mudhoney version, inverting the original song's sweetness and its belief in growth from emptiness, blossom from ugliness, and hope from despair. It may begin with the serene sounds of the ocean, but honey gets immediately dragged through the mud, and in the middle Arm's corny proverb of no particular origin (something you would find nowadays on proverbs.com) rounds off the sense of utter contempt for the sensational diva, for her song, and for all those whose spines tingle as they listen to it at the end of the movie.

As such, this is not just a simple musical 'attack' (as Arm whispers just before the guitar solo), much less a novelty parody in the manner of Weird Al. Rather, Mudhoney and *Sub Pop 200* use Midler as a means of bolstering their own grunge identity and holding on tight to their loser authenticity. Speaking to Everett True in 1989, this is what Arm said about 'The Rose':

> I liked the way its lyrics were so ridiculous. That song is indicative of an attitude that had a real hold over America in the Seventies – that 'Yes, you are a shining star' idea. Think about it – there are billions and billions of people in this world and they're all gonna die. Is there anything anyone can do? That's as political as I get.[25]

As nihilistic as this is, it is a clear position statement. Life isn't like this – there is no rose, or seed, or shining star – so here's a real take, ground out for the eighties against the seventies. In that sense Mudhoney's version claims to be the most honest of all, pointing to a truth behind the sentimental clichés on which the original song depends, and silencing Midler's pitch-perfect expression of them with Arm's brutal foghorn.

To say Mudhoney's 'Rose' became a Sub Pop anthem would be to go too far, at least when compared to what became the real crowd-pleasers like 'Touch Me I'm Sick'. Still, it gets at something fundamental to the message that Sub Pop marketed, something that remained deeply ingrained in its artists even long after they left the label. It is certainly interesting to note that, in August 1992, when a beleaguered and press-hassled Kurt Cobain was wheeled to the microphone on the Reading Festival stage (by Everett True, no less), he stood up, sang the first line of 'The Rose' – and collapsed backwards in a mockery of Midler's famous death scene from the film. Like some anti-diva reborn, Gandalf the White, he then took up his guitar and launched into the first song of Nirvana's headline set. Mudhoney, who had just played, must have been on his mind.

I Wanna Be Your Dog

One thing is certain: 'alternative' rock is as pompous as the regular kind. There is an elitism within it just as much as an elitism that patrols its boundaries. I have heard more than one alternative rocker complain that Mudhoney were unjustly famous because actually, a bit like the Monkees whom they mocked, they too were total fakes, a band that couldn't play its instruments properly. Of course, fuel was added to this fire by Mudhoney's tendency to come over all Sex Pistols in interviews. 'Notes and chords mean nothing to me. It's the attitude that counts', said Steve Turner in March 1989, and again, in February 1992, 'I don't really admire skill', even as he skilfully played blistering anti-solo after anti-solo.[26] Nor did Sub Pop press releases give much evidence to the contrary. There is one for the band's third record that picks out a review from *Rockpool* magazine in bold type: 'Mudhoney, four guys with nothing to say about their music, but plenty to say about their bodily functions.'[27]

The scorn towards Mudhoney, however, tends to deflect attention away from the point that this is just what they and Sub Pop intended. Crudeness and simplicity and rawness and sickness are a choice as much as anything else, a deliberate aesthetic chosen because it communicates something. Mudhoney became extremely well practised at it, more so than any other early Sub Pop band. As the guitarist from labelmates Blood Circus put it on first watching Turner perform his anti-solos: 'these are guys that are very very good at sounding bad'; they were everything that Blood Circus had practised hard to avoid becoming.[28] Arm's approach to slide guitar is a case in point. In many ways it seems like an insult to blues playing. But still it becomes absolutely integral to the Mudhoney grunge sound from 'Touch Me I'm Sick' onwards, cropping up at every stomach-churning break in the songs, bowels to water, all moral fibre thrown overboard. Mudhoney: not so much a case of bodily functions *instead* of music as bodily functions *as* music, often in the service of a grim selfishness and self-hatred that they loved to riff on in interview. 'We say fuck the kids! Except the kids who are buying our records. Then they are fucking themselves', Mark Arm told Everett True in 1989.[29]

However much all this was grounded in punk and hardcore, it was still a risky business. Sub Pop must take the credit for making Mudhoney as legitimate as they were ridiculous. Pavitt has said, in turn, that the label 'would not have happened without Mudhoney'.[30] This was in part achieved through pressure of releases. In the period from 1988 to 1991, when the band moved from Sub Pop to sign with Reprise, they had more music out than any other Sub Pop artist: one EP, two LPs, six singles, countless appearances on label compilations and guest appearances for other labels. They also had gatefolds, posters and an extensive array of coloured vinyl collectables earlier than any other band: the 'Touch Me I'm Sick' single appeared in countless colours including one affectionately named 'puke green'. There were spin-off projects, too, including the 'supergroup' the

Monkeywrench, featuring Arm and Turner, also Turner's Sad and Lonelys, and Arm's solo cover (SP87, November 1990) of Bob Dylan's song 'Masters of War' (originally from *The Freewheelin' Bob Dylan*, 1963). This seems like a parody again, not least because the picture sleeve of the single presents the singer as 'The Freewheelin' Mark Arm'. But it might be better to understand it as yet another attempt to raise the generational stakes, as in 'Sweet Young Thing Ain't Sweet No More'. Dylan's front-cover lovers walk arm-in-arm in full colour. Arm's are pictured in a nuclear-winter black-and-white and

Mudhoney pose for their new releases of late 1989.

are wearing gas masks, as if the Gulf War were more of a threat to existence than the Cold War.

Sub Pop stood, too, behind Mudhoney's early and extensive U.S. tours – across the country and then down the West Coast with Sonic Youth in the last three months of 1988, and again down the same coast in early 1989. Even before this, they had visited Germany with Pavitt and Poneman as part of an independent-label showcase for the first 'Berlin Independence Days' music seminar of August 1988, the point being to make a connection between musical and political independence. Theirs, it would seem, was a triumphant free West in which artists had the leisure to be unpolitical, to snark at official culture, and sing songs about catching diseases if they wished; the tour video shows Arm wearing a label 'LOSER' T-shirt with the Sub Pop logo on the back.[31] They would return about every six months: in March 1989 with Sonic Youth and again in late 1989 with Nirvana and TAD as the Berlin Wall finally fell. ('[T]hose poor Eastern people have been isolated for so long they don't even have a clue. They like Bon Jovi and stuff like that,' reflected Nirvana's Krist Novoselic on this momentous political event, underlining exactly what the Berlin Independence Days had been created to say).[32]

As much of this tourbook suggests, it was largely through the connection to Sonic Youth that the early Mudhoney turned heads in the U.S. and Europe. This was a link dating back some years, apparently directly mediated by Bruce Pavitt. Michael Azerrad has Sonic Youth playing at Pavitt's Fallout Records store in Seattle, presumably at some point in 1984, and then using Green River as support act in Seattle in January 1985.[33] Alec Foege, meanwhile, places Pavitt in New York City in early 1987, wandering around with the members of Sonic Youth and thinking of the greater 'creative and destructive' things he might achieve by switching coasts from west to east.[34] Ultimately he didn't, but it was this continuous link that led to the recording, at Sonic Youth's suggestion, of the split single *Touch Me I'm Sick/Halloween* (SP26) with Mudhoney. This became the second issue of the Sub Pop Singles Club in December 1988, each band covering one of the other's songs. It was also a statement release for Sub Pop's European expansion, appearing in numerous 12″ variants with the label's British and German partners, Blast First and Glitterhouse.

Certainly there was much to be gained by Sonic Youth in this split single. For all that they were well established by this time, and for all the critical acclaim heaped on records like *Daydream Nation* (1988), Sonic Youth were children of the 1950s, not the 1960s like the crazily energetic Mudhoney and the other new Sub Pop bands. Their band name was destined to sound increasingly ironic. Some contemporary accounts, indeed, particularly those written by British critics, present a suspicion of Sonic Youth's flagging influence as symbolic of a larger demise of American rock. In 1990 Roy Wilkinson remarked in *Sounds* that Sonic Youth's celebrated 'daydream nation' of 1988 was looking increasingly like a 'punky reservation' on shrinking territory, cut off from the rest of the world and too 'leftfield' in its 'avant guitar' style to be of much relevance to anyone. He cites the founder of Factory Records, Tony Wilson, as declaring the U.S. independent music dead, and instead encouraging the swinging of the spotlight over to Manchester in the UK, an indie rock scene now with its own stereotypes (the 'dreamy, creamy, steamy' sound, according to Nirvana; the 'microphone just above the head' and the 'pat-on-the-bum mateyness', as Thurston Moore disparaged it).[35] A split single with Sub Pop, Mudhoney, and the gathering fame of the Seattle sound, then, might benefit Sonic Youth in terms of relevance, particularly when, sent to Europe by Sub Pop, Mudhoney's onstage antics would draw headlines and drown out more subtle critique. The 'riot' that closed the show at the London School of

Oriental and African Studies in May 1989 is only the most famous instance of this.[36]

There was clearly much in the Sonic Youth single, too, for Mudhoney and Sub Pop. Whatever the suspicions of the older band's failing attractions, their willingness to record for Sub Pop cemented a 'critical connection' that kept the label financially afloat in its early phase.[37] Moreover, having an astute and respected artist like Kim Gordon sing 'Touch Me I'm Sick' deflected attention away from the nasty misogyny that could easily be read out of its lyrics and those of other Mudhoney songs. In the original, remember, a man goads a woman into catching a disease from him to save her from 'dying alone'. Swapping out Arm for Gordon meant loading the scales on the lyrics' possibly ironic side, an emphasis far safer.[38]

As for the choice of 'Halloween' (originally released in 1985), Matt Lukin, the Mudhoney bassist, suspected that Sonic Youth had put forward the suggestion as a 'joke'. 'I think they thought we wouldn't be able to play it – it's such a quiet, non-Mudhoney type song.'[39] Actually, the idea of *anyone* being able to cover this particular song is remarkable. The original is so completely mid-1980s Sonic Youth in its raked strings, detuned guitars, gong-chiming and, most of all, Gordon's urging whispered hyper-erotic vocal delivery, all but stream-of-consciousness spoken-word, teetering somewhere between fear and desire. (For a reminder of how experimental Sonic Youth's rock was at this time, compare their 'Halloween' to the Dead Kennedys' punk costume song of the same title from a few years before.)

If anyone could cover Sonic Youth's 'Halloween', though, Mudhoney could. The song is made for the radical style they had themselves been developing over the previous year. Like 'Mudride' and 'Sweet Young Thing Ain't Sweet No More', 'Halloween' is another slow number with an endlessly repeated riff, screaming guitar noise, and drums skittering away underneath. True, Mudhoney add a much heavier rock chug to the original, an effect that both loses all the mystery and makes the song far longer (and in some ways far more boring) by snapping it into a stricter rhythmic framework. Also, Arm's voice is clearly far more suited to covering Bob Dylan's fog-horn than Gordon's muted vocals. The anger of his delivery gradually rises, just as it does in Mudhoney's own songs, and he can't get away from a laddish smirk when he sings the word 'come' and an Iggy-like rock twang on 'along'. In other words, the erotic edge of Gordon's delivery – the thing that makes the original in the first place – is pretty much lost.

In fact, some of these features might make the Mudhoney version seem more another anti-diva parody in the 'sick' style, not so differ-ent from their hot take on Bette Midler's 'The Rose': the experimental and elusive Sonic Youth 'stuff[ed] up' by a 'Blue Cheer type of riff', as Turner put it in 1989.[40] But I don't think anyone would say it is that, or only that. There is a categorical difference here. Mudhoney and Sub Pop were far too invested in Sonic Youth to offer a straight-forward parody, and this is made clearest of all by the end of the cover itself, which, after a bit more chugging, turns into three omi-nous descending bass notes repeated over and over again. These form the basis for an outgoing fade-out thrash with one of Turner's most audacious anti-solos and a remarkable drumming display from Peters – a denial once and for all that this was a band that couldn't play its instruments and didn't have any truck with technical skill anyway.

These aren't just any old three notes, though. 3-2-1: they come from another place, the Stooges' debut single 'I Wanna Be Your Dog' (1969). This was a song already strongly associated with Sonic Youth from their 1983 LP *Confusion Is Sex*, where the feedback-instrumental 'Freezer Burn' turns abruptly into a blistering live version of the Stooges song sung by Gordon, with guitar fireworks to rival Turner's.

From there, 'I Wanna Be Your Dog' had become something of an anthem for Sonic Youth, and had in fact served as a regular encore for tours with Mudhoney in 1988 and 1989. Mudhoney, though the supporting act and junior partner, would return to the stage with Sonic Youth (and seemingly any other supporting act, and indeed anyone else who could get up there past the bouncers) for a group improvisation on the song.[41]

The use of the song to round off the Mudhoney cover of 'Halloween' on record, then, seems to issue an affectionate artist-to-artist reference, as well as a neat reminder of how important the live shows became in cementing the link between these bands (and how important it was to Sub Pop to remind the listener of that). Perhaps most telling of all, though, is something else, namely that Arm *doesn't* sing the words over the top. Aside from a bit of moaning in the background, he leaves it solely as an instrumental. This appears a trivial detail, but without his Iggy impression, the reference to 'I Wanna Be Your Dog' can't seem so much about parody – as Arm's earlier noise band Mr Epp might have had it, with their 'I Wanna Wash Your Dog'.[42] Nor can it be about smut, the standard Mudhoney smirk on innuendos. Rather, it makes the quotation a matter of authority, a statement of common influence, as if Mudhoney were deliberately leading down through Sonic Youth's own rock roots back to the Stooges, placing themselves as the latest transformation of 'the comic and the cataclysmic' impulse that Roy Wilkinson once heard as the key to Sonic Youth's brand of musical fusion.[43]

At the same time, to hear Mudhoney playing a Sonic Youth anthem like this was indirectly to reinforce Sub Pop's authority. Bruce Pavitt and the early Sub Pop had been in the vanguard of releasing Sonic Youth's *Confusion Is Sex*-era music in the United States: as its insert proudly states, the compilation *Sub Pop 100* (1986) featured their song 'Kill Yr Idols' at a time when it was otherwise available only on German import. In that case, the three descending notes of 'I Wanna Be Your Dog' surely carry out a lot of complicated symbolic work at the end of this cover version, far more than their simple contour at first suggests. They might be said to crystallize the whole Sub Pop identity, in fact, advancing the label as an alternative rock authority, with the experimental Sonic Youth at its beginnings, the Stooges deep in its background, and the grunge Mudhoney, in all their sinister comedy, as its leading edge.

6

TAD: Heavier than Heaven

SUB POP MADE a monster out of Tad.

In reality he was Thomas Andrew Doyle, a nice guy with a caring mother and a college arts degree from one state over. In early 1988 he had come to Seattle to make his life more about his music, and less about the menial jobs he had been doing. This CV was too cliché, though. Out of it Sub Pop made someone who sounded like a cross between Godzilla and a supervillain: 'Tad, the heaviest MAN in the world, moved to Seattle from Boise, Idaho, and proceeded to take over the whole scene. Tad plays all the instruments himself. For fans of Killdozer, Big Black.'[1] And a year or so later, with a pun on their biggest single to date: 'How heavy thou art! Yes, it's Tad the butcher from Boise, back with a full band and the heaviest groove since the Melvins said hi to Killdozer. Crush me I'm sick!'[2]

The operative word in both these descriptions was 'heavy', a flagship term that had interested Bruce Pavitt ever since the days of the *Subterranean Pop* fanzine, especially in his descriptions of the new 'Seattle sound' of the *Deep Six* compilation (1986). 'Heavy' was perfect for Tad. For one thing, it captured the themes of his lyrics, which envisioned all kinds of gruesome horror and hell (something they had in common with some 'heavy' metal). For another, 'heavy' gave Tad a brutal lineage back into noise rock, as the presence of the name-checked bands – Melvins, Killdozer, Big Black – suggests.

By mid-1989 Tad had also assembled his own brand of 'heavy'. Once a percussionist (with the Boise band H-Hour), he now stepped to the front of the stage as guitarist and singer, backed by a huge

stack of amps and a new band, named TAD in his honour, that became
notorious for the blunt-force sonic trauma it unleashed in its performances. According to Charles Cross's account of an early TAD
show, the 'sound was literally so heavy that I felt like I was having
a heart attack or something . . . it made your chest cavity actually
beat'.[3] This was a danger cued by the many introductory remarks
that Tad would make to his crowds of 'college yuppie types' (as he
liked to bait them), moments before striking his first power chord,
furious eyes staring straight out from behind grizzled hair.[4] 'We're
here to destroy your hearing,' he says on one occasion.[5] On another
he produces what is perhaps the ultimate piece of early Sub Pop
stage banter, caught somewhere between raw threat and its own
parody: 'Don't be shy, don't piss me off, and whatever you do, stand
back, because we are gonna blow your fucking nuts off – if you got
any.'[6]

But 'heavy', of course, got at something else too. Tad, unlike most
of the 'skinny, nose-picking nerds' (as Thurston Moore once called
them) on the early label, weighed 300 pounds (135 kg) or more.[7] It
has proven impossible for critics, then and now, to talk about TAD
without joking about the frontman's size, and this was clearly just
what Pavitt and Poneman realized when they first encountered him
in Seattle in 1988. As much as he was a scarily imposing mountain
of rude masculinity, their 'heaviest MAN in the world' was an immediately appealing figure of fun, someone of excess and exaggeration
in every dimension. Stories of drug and alcohol binges flood the
literature about him, as do anecdotes about his size (tales of stage-
diving antics, for example), and of his remarkable stage presence
and ability to absorb the heckling of his crowds. In November 1989
Roy Wilkinson wrote of the terrace chants of 'You fat bastard'
that Tad met with in London and admired his stand-up comedian's skill in transforming them into 'attacks on the self' that were

more 'aggressively pre-emptive than pathetic'.[8] And in a pre-show interview with *Ugly American* fanzine, Tad spoke of the way he had learned to tailor his shtick to the crowd in front of him:

UGLY AMERICAN: Are you gonna do the 'Fuck U' thing tonight?
TAD: I don't think so. Sometimes that really turns people off. It works with kids cuz they're like 'Fuck You' anyway, they can take a joke. Older people, they take it personally. I made a real ass out of myself in Boston, I was really harsh on the crowd.[9]

If Tad was the epitome of the Sub Pop loser, in other words, he was a loser fully in control of that image as a stage persona, and that was part of what made him an important early 'figurehead' of the label, the 'charismatic clown act' who could hardly fail to amuse a crowd.[10]

TAD play to the camera at the Students' Union of the School of Oriental and African Studies, London, October 1989.

The other part was that the man and his music were an easy package to sell. As Poneman once put it in full marketing mode: 'Heavy dude/heavy music. *Connect the dots.*'[11] The connection was made everywhere by Sub Pop: a pair of run-off grooves from TAD's single *Loser* (SP55, 1989) reads, 'The show ain't over/ till the fat man Rocks.' It was also made by critics. Experiencing this music for the first time in December 1989, *Melody Maker*'s Simon Price was moved to invent the new subgenre of 'Hamburger Metal':

> Riffs that can pinch more than an inch, huge stop-start slabs of sound, each with a coda of tremeloed guitar as Seventies as tassle-fringed leathers and Harley Davidsons, every intervening line featuring what Sir William Rees-Mogg calls 'The Oedipal noun'. By the end the walls are dripping with cholesterol.[12]

Tad and TAD, then, were in many ways the cleverest thing Sub Pop had done to date. In general, Tad was very obviously a 'three-hundred pound marketing tool' for the label and its grunge, as *Ugly American* put it.[13] But more specifically he and his 'heavy' music embodied several different kinds of fusion. Punk attitude merged with metal riffing was only one aspect of this; there was also the collision of Tad's brand of 'scary' (to use the word of Jack Endino) with his unique comedy, more knowingly comic even than the gaffe-prone drunken stage antics of Mudhoney.[14] In fact, it was the interplay of these two characteristics – the terrifying and the funny – that was essential to Tad's appeal. The violent and relentless musical experience prevented the Tad persona degrading into a mere comedy caricature; the Tad persona, meanwhile, made the music, industrially bleak in some of its inheritances, appeal to a far wider audience (some of those 'college yuppies' looking for a good scare) than it might have otherwise.

The whole thing, as another British critic called it on that first European tour, was the 'heavier than heaven' style, and TAD sprang rapidly into life around it in late 1988 as one of Sub Pop's most favoured bands, into whose image and promotion the label poured considerable effort and expense. It is worth remembering that they granted TAD – not Nirvana, not Mudhoney – the opening track of the lavish label sampler *Sub Pop 200*, the controversially misogynistic 'Sex God Missy'. And they obviously spent out on the first TAD LP, given a title that is the ultimate in 'heavy' masculinity: *God's Balls*. Staring back from the front sleeve is Charles Peterson's handsome black-and-white portrait of the man himself, a larger-than-life Tad in forced perspective against the camera – no blurry drag-shutter here. Inside the first 2,000 copies was an impressive gatefold, opening on to a double-LP-size image of the band playing live. One gatefold sleeve contained the disc itself; the other had a massive poster for the wall of your bedroom and, in a few copies only, a fanzine (rebranded, of course, a 'manzine') dedicated to Tad.

The presentation and added extras of *God's Balls* underlines the point. Tad and TAD were supposed to have a certain star quality. But the scary-comic routine had its limits and wore thin, particularly once Nirvana, originally TAD's opening act, began to show what they could do. After that, TAD could never really have made it. They were poorly managed, bounced from boutique label to boutique label, and eventually turned back to Jack Endino to record a kind of 'heavy' self-caricature with a Spinal Tap title, *Infrared Riding Hood* (East-West, 1995), many copies of which were never distributed for sale. These failures can also be attributed to the fact that Tad, though an 'alternative' celebrity, was still held to the 'industry standards for rock stars' (in Clark Humphrey's words), and was inevitably found wanting.[15] He didn't have what Nirvana or Soundgarden had, the angelic face of Cobain or the rippling physique of Cornell, or the suicide solution of either. Just as damning, he and his band didn't have the musical gold that might have lit up those Adonis images of beauty and tragedy. Too heavy for heaven, TAD found nowhere else to go but down.

For a few months in late 1988 and early 1989, though, the band were the better bet for Sub Pop, the 'consistent' performer when compared to some of their labelmates, as Poneman later said.[16] This alone merits them a closer look and listen than their usual lonely place at the end of the grunge roll call of stardom ('Nirvana, Pearl Jam, Alice in Chains, Soundgarden, Mudhoney, TAD') allows. It places them, in fact, in the vanguard of the Sub Pop project as it expanded, and therefore as an indicator of what grunge was in its formative days.

Roots

Listening across the first two records that TAD rapidly made for Sub Pop, the LP *God's Balls* (SP27, March 1989) and the EP *Salt Lick* (SP49, February 1990), one tight connection between them is obvious. This is the horror-movie material from which almost all the lyrics and song titles are made. You can get a hint of this even from looking at the cover image of *Salt Lick*, a custom montage prepared by Michael Lavine. The right way up, it depicts some kind of massive monster truck bursting forwards out of the frame, as if thrown towards the viewer by the explosion underneath it – a common design effect for Sub Pop. Turned upside down, at least four screaming faces can be seen in the flames. This is the band, I presume, in full live flow, but the drag-shutter-like effect makes them look like made-up, melted-face, mutants of the B-movie variety.

Consistent with this atmosphere, 'Wood Goblins', 'Axe to Grind' and 'Hibernation' are some of the song titles on *Salt Lick*, the last one's lyrics detailing the terror moment of suicide by suffocation inside a sealed car ('Rev up, carbon monoxide!'). *God's Balls* adds 'Boiler Room', 'Cyanide Bath', 'Satan's Chainsaw', 'Hollow Man', a remix of 'Sex God Missy' from *Sub Pop 200*, and, in a reference to the trophies that Wisconsin serial killer Ed Gein took from his victims, 'Nipple Belt'. As these titles imply, violence, morbid fear, torture, suicide and sex slavery are typical themes for TAD. Sometimes these are directed towards the first person, but it is also common for the lyrics to situate a lone woman, often as prey for an implicitly male predator, and occasionally ('Axe to Grind', 'Daisy') in her own crazed, ultraviolent moment of sudden freedom. 'Helot', also on *God's Balls*, brings several of these themes together in a single song and, unusually for the intensely personal genre of grunge, resituates them in ancient history. The song is a reimagining of the eruption of Vesuvius in AD 79, as experienced by a tyrannical master and the slave who attempts to carry him to safety. The master can't see or breathe, and white-hot ash fills his lungs; but he clearly gets off on the horrible and masterful power of the erupting volcano, which is described to the slave in a curiously sexual way.

'Well, it just happens that the most interesting things in life just happen to be negative, and like, freaky and weird and dangerous and stuff,' says Kurt Danielson, the band's bass player.[17] Maybe so: but it is equally clear that TAD must have listened to a lot of 1970s horror metal and watched a lot of trash TV and movies before they wrote these songs, particularly in those traditions of horror that make women the principal victims. 'Helot' was apparently inspired by a documentary Tad saw about Pompeii and the remains of a chained (female) slave. He also cites Jack Nicholson as one of his favourite actors, and talks vividly of *The Shining* (as well as *Psycho* and *The Texas Chainsaw Massacre*) in describing the backgrounds for the scenarios of his lyrics.[18]

Michael Lavine's montage print for the front of TAD's *Salt Lick* EP (SP49, February 1990), including the band's handwritten 'YES!'

Perhaps his music was also inspired by Jack Nicholson's role in *The Shining*. It is, after all, almost always violent, obsessive and delusional, and it often puts hatchets through doors. Take the very first Sub Pop 7″ single from mid-1988, on which, yet to form his new band, Tad himself played all the instruments, apparently having walked straight off the street into Endino's Reciprocal Recording. Both of its songs emerge from a howling shroud of guitar feedback that dissipates throughout their verses, and neither really has a chorus or refrain or guitar solo to speak of. 'Ritual Device', as its title

implies, is little more than a chanting on a couple of notes, punctuated by the occasional noun-change and a prehistoric shrieking, like
a swooping pterodactyl or something. Where a chorus or guitar solo
might fall is, instead, an instrumental in which almost all guitar
effects are suddenly cut, allowing the vicious attack of the percussion
to come through: a drum solo, in effect, one that thunders but never
clears the air. And if this reflects Tad's training as a percussionist, the
vocals show his new emphasis on creating a distinctive singing style:
always gravelly, a kind of desperate *Deliverance* drawl.

All this makes for an urgent, brutal and relentless experience,
a music that seems pushed right to the edge of existence – much
like its singer, who, since he has both a 'pain in his arm' and a 'pain
in his chest' seems to be on the verge of the very heart attack that
Charles Cross feared at the live show. Or, to quote one of Everett
True's glowing reviews from 1990, 'the suffocating density of Tad's
sound emanates from the man himself, his anguish and his turmoil.
And, because of it, Tad [the band] play the fiercest, most unsettling,
one-dimensional trash you're ever likely to encounter.'[19]

With a particular focus on the band's creative process, Tad has
labelled the essence of this bleak music with a single word: 'root'.[20]
Note that he doesn't mean 'root' in the conventional harmonic sense
of music theorists, that is, the 'root' pitch on which a chord is built.
To do so wouldn't be very informative at all, indeed, since many of
TAD's songs – as the band's lead guitarist Gary Thorstensen once
complained – are in the key of E, and so the harmonic root is almost
always E.[21] What Tad means is a *rhythmic* 'root', a short one- or two-
bar rhythmic pattern that is set down from the beginning and from
which the entire song is constructed. Typically this pattern is at first
little more than a gentle toying with the overall beat, but always,
halfway through or at the end, it thrashes heavily against it, smashing
and stabbing at the offbeat and the nearby frets of the guitars, and

setting bodies in motion everywhere. The early 'Ritual Device' is a prime example of this. A challenge: after the anticipatory whining feedback, try listening to its opening rhythmic 'root' without moving. You could look to almost any of the songs across *God's Balls* and *Salt Lick* for a similar impetus.

These basic, obsessively repeated rhythmic patterns, and the band's technical skill in playing them, are one key reason why critics have always tended to hear TAD's music as a variety of metal. They are also a consequence of the way it was written and recorded, whether by Tad alone or later with the entire band. For the first single in 1988, drums were laid down first, and everything else was overdubbed on top; once the rest of the band was on board, the main musical idea was to 'hammer just a riff . . . and have a groove to it too' (in Tad's words; Sub Pop advertising picked up on this idea of the 'heaviest groove').[22] Last of all, Tad's vocals were added, which he talks about not in the usual sense as lyrics or melody, but as yet another layer of rhythmic energy, something else in support of 'the background and backbone of the music'.[23]

This approach was clearly very effective. It generated song after song, all cast in a distinctive sound that was 'heavy' in keeping with the lyrics, 'heavy' in its relationship to the lowest, thickest open strings of the guitars (which, incidentally, is why all the songs are in E), 'heavy' as the 'heaviest MAN in the world', and fittingly 'heavy' for Sub Pop's developing sense of a 'Seattle sound'. It also provided an exaggerated 'heavy metal' spectacle for the live shows. Flanking Tad's frontman antics, Danielson (bass) and Thorstensen (lead) would enter what Poneman once described as a kind of headbanging 'seizure'.[24] Sometimes they would go up and down together, in perfect synchronization; sometimes one would come up while the other went down. They could do this for song after song after song until the end of the set.

If there was something comic about this display, something from the Status Quo playbook of rock choreography, perhaps that wasn't completely out of character with the loser stand-up that Tad would do between songs. More of a danger, I think, was that the whole root-led headbanging thing could become mechanical and monotonous – and, the biggest problem of all in a three-minute rock song, simply boring. Perhaps this was why TAD also came to specialize in tense build-up sections, in which the rhythmic root would keep on going while Thorstensen's tremolo lead edged slowly up the guitar neck, fret by fret, as if on the approach to inevitable catastrophe. I wouldn't call these guitar 'solos' as such: the guitars are always about background horror atmosphere in TAD, rather than technical or melodic display that might overshadow the charismatic frontman. Instead they seem a clear musical metaphor for gathering horror, the agonizing approach to the death moment that the lyrics obsess over. A key part of 'Helot' is like this, which I suppose has something to do with the erupting volcano ('can't run from hell' is the song's last line). So are several bridging sections of the single 'Loser', on the road to nowhere. 'Cooking with Gas' heads downwards but has the same effect. And the chorus of TAD's most notorious song of all, the copyright-infringement disaster 'Jack Pepsi', does something similar, except that it is Tad's voice that edges upwards and upwards against the screaming guitars, increasingly frantic at the point of death. The lyrics describe, in the first person, the experience of a truck falling through the frozen surface of a lake, and the desperate attempt to escape as the water rushes in.

The most striking example of this tremolo technique is 'Satan's Chainsaw' on the first LP, *God's Balls*. This is a song about a woman with an erotic attachment to a chainsaw, which might be a guitar, which might be a penis. So far so TAD; in her *Backlash* review, Veronika Kalmar called it 'an amusing little ditty that'll charm the listener right out to the woodshed'.[25] But the song is also different from all the rest: it is in a different key, for one thing, and begins with this bright little offbeat string-bending riff, all hands for once high up on guitar necks. Just for a second this turns the TAD groove into a kind of funk rock, something early 1990s rather than late '80s, more stage-strutting Chili Peppers or Rage Against the Machine than the stereotype of grunge. The band's offbeat grunts and percussive shouts add to this impression while also underlining the raw masculinity symbolized by the title's chainsaw.

In the home stretch of the song, however, the groove is lost when the riff, now confined to Danielson's bass, is built upon as a rhythmic root alone, topped off with a sinister tremolo note in Thorstensen's guitar that somehow manages to sound like both the revving chainsaw blade *and* the growing fear of its approach. This note gradually goes up and up the fretboard while the band chant something or other in the background – a huddled merge of ominous men's voices, out of which bursts Tad's distinctive one, full scream, something about the lone woman running towards the 'smell of gasoline'.

It's a killer moment, because the 'root' here, established in the first seconds of the song, comes back full circle, eventually with the funky little riff and all, except that now its last three notes are fixated on the three-syllable word 'gasoline' – as if this were the song's punchline, the only thing it wanted to say, and the thing it was obsessing about all along. There is ultimately nothing cute or bright about it. This is what TAD could do at their heaviest, when they fully meshed their musical structures and their playing into their horrorshow lyrics, creating something more powerful than all these components alone. Perhaps it is also one of those moments that Everett True identified when he heard the live show in early 1990: the massive performer who 'constantly throws himself against the limits of his psychotic sound; furiously, unrelentingly battering at his guitar', playing the songs that 'bludgeon you into thinking that they've surpassed their structures'.[26]

Industrial Music

Actually, that's it – the smell of gasoline. That's what was made to rise off this music and this band, that's what they were always tainted with. There are all kinds of descriptions and depictions to this end. To the American press, Danielson said that their aim was to 'sound like one big, loud, unoiled machine that was about to explode', and to the British press Tad repeated almost the same thing: 'We're like a big metallic grinding machine that sounds as though it's going to blow up and fall apart at any moment. It needs oil real bad, but it never gets it.'[27] Cartoonist Peter Bagge drew a monster truck driven by a bulging, plaid-wearing Tad for the back of the *Loser* single sleeve in 1989, and this was carried over onto Sub Pop's tour posters and promotional stickers. One logo design, now found in the archive of MOPOP in Seattle, simply states the following, the perfect summary: TAD DIESEL POWER.

This image is particularly fitting for the second record, the EP *Salt Lick*, which seems a clanking piece of machinery opposite the lavish curves and baubles of *God's Balls*. For a start, *Salt Lick* had no gatefold, no poster, no manzine, no coloured vinyl collectors' variant, and only six songs against the ten of the LP. But more importantly, Sub Pop sent the band to record it in Chicago with Big Black's Steve Albini, a producer whom Pavitt had admired since his early fanzine days, and who was already well established for his 'lo-fi' noise approach. The result could be called 'mechanical' in several senses. Most of the songs on *Salt Lick* begin or end abruptly, as if the equipment had been turned on or off at the wrong moment by an amateur, and there are few studio effects. At the same time, Steve

Wied's drums boom and the guitars suck in air like jet engines: the listener becomes keenly aware of the spatial confines of the studio, as if really there in the room among the machinery, confronted by its violent sound. Albini lives up to his reputation, in other words, for the impression of 'documentary' honesty, directness and several different types of authenticity, and this was something carried forward by label and band in advertising the record.[28] Poneman says that the aim was to capture the 'way that the TAD band actually sounded live', while Danielson likens the sessions to the 'recording of a car accident, nothing rehearsed ... it was just a collision, and it was on tape', a two-day explosion in which 'the songs came out of us one after the other, as if we were human artillery.'[29]

All this makes me wonder whether the term 'industrial' is the best way of capturing what both label and band really wanted TAD to be. A recent Sub Pop press note, on the re-release of *God's Balls* (2016), makes several gestures in this direction. It claims that TAD made a 'clang' like Einstürzende Neubauten, one of the foundational industrial rock bands of the 1980s, and reinforces this by pointing out that in the studio, somewhat like the German band, TAD 'employed a variety of unusual instruments – an empty gas tank from a car, a hacksaw, a large brass tube from a microwave transmitter, CB radio mics, a cello bow used on cymbals to emulate guitar feedback – to thunderous effect.'[30] Tad himself has made comparable remarks. In an early interview he speaks of the search for 'metallic, loud, obscure, industrial noise' that guided him from his former band, H-Hour, towards the founding of his new one, TAD.[31] And in another recent Sub Pop press release, he identifies a nowadays little-known British rock band, Head of David, as having exerted a strong influence on TAD, and contrives to use the term 'industrial' twice in different senses:

> They [Head of David] forged together industrial/tribal
> machine-like drum motifs that seemed embedded with the
> industrial landscapes of Birmingham. Overcast skies, damp,
> cold, weathered factories, and the noise of the area had been
> hammered into their recordings. We learned that Steve Albini
> had captured this intensely hideous sonic beauty, this morass
> of belligerent filth.[32]

This is an especially interesting statement, not least because it points to the fluid interchange of American and British music in the formation of post-punk genres like industrial rock; these were always two-way streets, whatever the later attempts to direct one-way traffic. Since 1986 Head of David had been releasing their music on Paul Smith's Blast First, a British indie that had at first existed only as a conduit for Sonic Youth's early recordings to appear in the UK, but had then become the home of new noise signings and licensees from both sides of the Atlantic, including Steve Albini's Big Black. Presumably this is where they got the idea that Albini would produce Head of David's second LP, *Dustbowl* (1988). In turn, as Tad says, it was one factor that recommended Albini to Sub Pop and TAD for the recording of *Salt Lick* in Chicago.

Even so, the TAD–Head of David 'industrial' connection is easily pushed too far. I commented above on the obsessive *Shining* monochrome of TAD's music, but by comparison, it is Head of David that is really the one-track mind. In fact, their endless repetition of simple bass and vocal patterns – in the context of six-minute songs, changing time signatures, heavy reverb and knowingly poetic lyrics quite unlike TAD's – has attracted the labels 'experimental' and 'ambient' in addition to 'industrial' (listen to 'White Bastard' on the first LP, for example, or 'Dog Day Sunrise' on the second). Stephen Burroughs's vocals, meanwhile, are all ghoulish and handsome and echoey, tuning into a New Romantic style that seemed to span everything in the British 1980s from Bauhaus to the Fall to Duran Duran. One thing they are never is the direct and confrontational backwoods drawl of Tad.

These differences add up to what are sharply contrasted packages, almost opposites, in fact, despite the lines of influence that Tad himself now draws. If Head of David play 'ambient' metal, then TAD's three-minute horror songs seem more like 'character' metal. Or, if the meander of Head of David's music makes theirs a 'stoner' metal, then TAD's more focused and regular song structures must best be described as 'amphetamine' (though not 'speed') metal. Or, better, a visual metaphor. The cover of Head of David's *Dustbowl* depicts beautiful greyscale sand dunes with military vehicles moving away from the viewer. It is certainly ominous, but also serene in a post-apocalyptic way. TAD's *Salt Lick*, as I said above, has a flaming monster truck bursting directly out of the frame at the viewer, with the band's faces melting in horror underneath.

What comes out of this comparison is that TAD's achievement was to make a heavy horror caricature out of the industrial, and Sub Pop was only too happy to sell it for them, in songs perfectly measured to a vinyl 7" (on which Head of David could never have fitted; they released no 7" singles). This point can be underlined by listening to the opening track from TAD's first LP *God's Balls*, 'Behemoth', one of their best-known early numbers and a song as much about 'hook' as 'root', with the jangling chord alternations and the whole-band 'motherfucker!' shouts of its chorus. 'Behemoth' might begin with a thirty-second 'industrial' collage of pre-recorded sounds – something briefly reminiscent, perhaps, of Einstürzende Neubauten or the Butthole Surfers, or any number of studio-experimental artists that preceded them. But in TAD's hands it is used towards a typically B-movie end, namely that of palm-sweating horror. An opening heartbeat pulse, gradually getting louder, is silenced by a strange muzak chime-prompt, evoking something very like the moment of cold terror when you must leave a message on someone's answerphone. A few discarded guitar and drum tracks then brutally enter the mix against the pulse, but these are turned down low almost into silence, left eerily with their percussive impact alone and almost no tone and resonance. They are joined by demonic laughter, moaning, the sound of serrated metal skittering across metal, and a weird harmonized vocalizing, making for a kind of prologue in hell before the unoiled infernal machine clanks into motion.

One cute prank effect of this little studio collage intro might be to make you turn your volume dial right up, blowing out your windows and your eardrums when the song really begins a few seconds later. But the more obvious effect is that it heightens the sense of anticipation for vicious sound that was always important to TAD, the band whose 'vision', as Danielson recently put it, whether recording with Endino or Albini, was 'always to make the heaviest music possible'.[33] It also underlines the authority of Tad himself, since it is his piercing pterodactyl scream that abruptly silences the collage, and later the choruses that repeat throughout the song.

Most importantly of all, the collage helps to confuse the question of what the 'Behemoth' is: who, actually, the band is calling a 'motherfucker' in the hook-heavy chorus of the song. In many ways it is a classic hard rock confrontation number, and the band sometimes liked to wax lyrical about the fight with an ancient enemy, something 'biblical . . . big and powerful, intimidating'.[34] Some sources stress TAD's whiteness, making the song specifically about racial confrontation and tracing the lyrics back to an anecdote about a violent encounter with 'Samoan' and 'black' guys looking for 'frat boys to beat up'.[35] Taken alone, however, the song's words leave it as a vivid post-traumatic account of an anonymous attack on the street, terrifying not because of its physical threat but because of the horrific cracking, ringing, slamming *sound* the behemoth makes as it strikes. As Dawn Anderson pointed out in 1989, this lyrical focus on violent sound also makes a neat connection to the band, already notorious for a terrifying sound that, live, might well cause your ribcage to collapse onto your internal organs.[36]

This means that the opening sound collage, in collaboration with the song itself, makes the obvious point as loudly as possible. TAD itself is the Behemoth, and more specifically the 300-pound Tad himself standing at its front hammering the guitar he dwarfs. And this was just as Sub Pop intended. The free poster that was included with early copies of *God's Balls* is big, two LP sleeves wide by three high. It shows Tad's face smushed right up against the lens of Charles Peterson's camera, holding in his hand what I suppose is actually the back of a guitar neck. Yet because of his full-hand grip it could equally be the handle of a knife poised to stab the viewer through the paper. Needless to add, the poster has the word 'BEHEMOTH' in massive letters at the bottom.

Digging

The Behemoth, 'industrial' music, the unoiled machine; hamburger metal, Steve Albini; the smell of gasoline, DIESEL POWER, the woodshed, caricature, 'root'. As useful as these are for getting at what TAD and Tad were about, still none of them quite captures what Sub Pop really meant when, in 1988, the label billed the act's linchpin as 'the heaviest MAN in the world'. They are fragments of a bigger picture, a master image of rock loser masculinity, easily identified through the barrage of contemporary publicity shots of Tad and his band wearing trucker hats and standing next to hay bales and farm machinery and livestock, or out in the woods wielding chainsaws. What they all reinforce is the mythic image of the working man, as drawn from typical film and TV representations of the 'bad' working classes, peopled by characters both comic and disturbing: the violent farmhand or idle 'redneck', the backwoods primitive, the plaid-wearing lumberjack monster, in TAD's case making music that 'my simple mind and throbbing prostate can easily assimilate' (as *Ugly American* put it in late 1989).[37]

That Sub Pop's Bruce Pavitt had long been interested in these caricatures and their potential in music commerce is obvious; he had absorbed a fascination in them from hardcore punk (and elsewhere in rock 'n' roll), and moved to deploy them full in the knowledge that grunge's developing audience was as much college-going, lily-white middle-class 'Generation X' as anything else, standing ready to be terrified and titillated by exactly these kinds of 'bad' working-man characters.[38] Simultaneously this fascination fed into his belief in a decentralized, popular network of new American alternative rock acts. See the way, for example, that he writes about the Madison, Wisconsin band Killdozer in the *Sub Pop* column of February 1987, just prior to the creation of TAD. '[T]hey've matured and grown into a monster: [their EP] *Burl* is HEAVY rootsy dirge with lyrics rooted in the populist mythology of country and blues'.[39] And again a year later, on Killdozer's fourth record:

> Killdozer, featuring the tiny frame and raspy throat of Michael Gerald, is an ALL AMERICAN KIND OF BAND. Despite their cult following amongst elite fans of 'noise', Killdozer is populist, small town, and working class. Michael sings songs about real men: *meat packers, golden glove boxers, and grain elevator operators*. His men play cards and pound beers and knock heads.[40]

This working theme continued into the earliest acquisitions that Pavitt and Poneman made for the Sub Pop label, bands who, in their lyrics, are sometimes found pounding beers and knocking heads, and, more specifically, digging, an activity that unites serial killers and labourers. Blood Circus, as elsewhere, are probably the key precursor here. They dig a lot. But in their B-side 'Six Foot Under' (SP13, June 1988), note also that it is actually 'my daddy' who is the real heavy-smoking, hard-drinking 'working man' of the railways whose grave has now been dug. This seems an important distinction, one also made in some Green River and Mudhoney lyrics. The Sub Pop generation of losers are not so much the working men of rock 'n' roll's past as their indolent offspring – degenerate, even worse, even more useless. The run-out groove on Nirvana's first single, a suggestion barked out by Krist Novoselic's Yugoslavian father, makes the same generational point and became useful to the band as a slogan: 'Why don't you trade those guitars for shovels?'[41]

Occasionally Pavitt would emphasize the ideological side of this working-man focus, harking back to his original fanzine's claim that it was documenting a real musical movement – a piece of authentic folklore – extending across unknown swathes of the American landscape. As he put it to Michael Azerrad, with reference to the rising fame of Nirvana: 'It really started to fit in with this TAD thing . . . the whole real genuine working class – I hate to use the phrase "white trash" – something not contrived that had a more grass-roots or populist feel.'[42] But as Sub Pop liked to make equally obvious, it *was* contrived for sales to heavy rock fans, 'college yuppies', the easily scared, and the timid British who had no such thing at home, typically by pulling on some thread from the background of one or more band members and then handing this over to the label's press advocates. This could be a relatively subtle process, such as when Everett True wrote plausibly of Aberdeen's Nirvana that, 'if they weren't doing this, [they] would be working in a supermarket or lumber yard, or fixing cars.'[43] Or it could be more awkward, such as when True called Mudhoney 'laconic, wry, intelligent, and working class', a claim that jarred against the middle-class backgrounds and college orientations of at least two of them.[44] (Indeed, Steve Turner, the Mudhoney guitarist, provides the strongest Sub Pop example of music as leisurely middle-class whimsy. Disappointed with his band's new LP in 1989, he all but returned to college to complete his anthropology degree.[45])

Or, as with TAD and Tad, the working-class persona could be exaggerated to the point of ridiculous, and fully absorbed by the band into its onstage act and its music. With his Idaho college music degree, Tad probably had the most formal musical training of any of the Sub Pop artists of this time; it is worth noting that, the first time he turned up to record with Jack Endino in Seattle, it was with synthesizers and drum machines, not guitars (arguably the legacy of this can be heard on the machine-like drumming of the early track 'Ritual Device').[46] In this sense he was hardly the rural working man he was made out to be. On the other hand, he was able and willing to do a good and sustained impression of it, one better than most others on the label. He has said that he grew up in Idaho surrounded by 'redneck attitudes and demeanors' and, among numerous jour-neyman jobs, had worked on the 'offal table' in a meat-packing plant in his early days in Seattle ('I can dismember a carcass in maybe 40 minutes,' he told Dawn Anderson in 1990; there is no particular reason to doubt this).[47] Indeed, this is the persona in which he chose to write his early solo songs. In the lyrics of 'Ritual Device', recorded even before he was a Sub Pop artist, he has to 'work in his sleep', 'grow some food', 'tame the beast' and, more digging, 'move some earth'.

It is easy to see how this recommended itself to Pavitt and his new label, who issued the song on a vinyl single with Tad's grizzled and glowering face staring back from the label, and the following text superimposed: 'Hi my name is TAD recorded in Seattle by Jack Endino This side is called Daisy The other side is called Ritual Device Photo taken at Woolworth's I play everything'.[48] All the s's and h's are written backwards in this message, as are some other letters, and there is no punctuation: Tad is presented as a kind of musical idiot-genius, as well as a weird, perhaps lovable, character. The message on the side B run-off groove, meanwhile, is both another play on his offal-table job and an unnerving horror-movie strapline. No comedy backwards letters here, instead the hidden phrase is written in an elegant cursive such as one might imagine the devil himself to have: 'Sharp knives make the butcher sing'.

This typical TAD triangulation of work, horror and comedy certainly left its mark on the *God's Balls* LP, the band's first big statement. The credits on the back falsely list washboard, bongos, dobro, a Homelite chainsaw and a 50-pound sledgehammer as its contributing instruments, while Roy Wilkinson, reviewing it for *Sounds* in May 1989, suggested that they had 'settled on the woodcutter personae as part of their furious lampoon of macho, deer-killin' hillbilly barbarism' (and added, surely to Pavitt's satisfaction, that Killdozer had 'never created a musical beast as ferociously plausible as Tad's').[49] It was with *Salt Lick*, though, that the same triangulation also began to shift, suddenly skewing sharply away from the comic. Picking up on the cues of 'Ritual Device', its songs are dark in the extreme, even beyond the horror scenarios of the first record. They teem with references to personal poverty and toil so desperate that it pushes the working man to a fury of violence, addiction and suicide.[50]

It must have been this, I think, that ultimately dictated the choice of Albini as the record's producer. Already well known as the 'working man' of the recording studio (often dressed in overalls as his 'uniform'), he made the band live the life they were trying to create on record for a few days: they slept on the floor at his house, consumed only 'grilled meat and beer', and were subject to unpredictable 'redneck' pranks (such as when Albini woke Danielson up by nuzzling his cheek with the barrel of a shotgun).[51] Albini also introduced a work regimen designed to elicit the right tone. He had a two-take rule for the instrumental parts, meaning that unrehearsed and half-formed material made it onto tape. For the vocals, he drove Tad similarly hard and hoarse, discouraging anything that might sound like conventional singing as part of a larger drive to avoid prettifying or 'feminizing' the songs. (Tad had already had this idea: compare his statement 'I don't sing – faggots sing', apparently growled at Roy Wilkinson in 1989.[52])

Some of the results of this regimen are unsurprisingly intense. 'Cooking with Gas', a song recorded in the same sessions, is one prime example. The song may begin with a long drawn-out 'Well . . .' in an echo of a blues stereotype, or of the derivative 1950s openings of Buddy Holly or Elvis or Gene Vincent. But there is no tender 'since my baby left me' or 'be bop a lula' to continue it. Instead it turns into one of the most surprising vocals you will ever hear, mostly improvised off the song's title and a few other lines about a working man not just down on his luck, but pushed so close to the edge that he has arrived at the moment of incinerating himself and everything else.

Tad loses almost all his vocal bearings here, worked to the limits by Albini, who manages to latch onto, and bring powerfully forwards, the desperation evident even in the first single some eighteen months before. Sometimes the principal line 'cooking with gas' is tightly in sync with the booming instrumental root that its rhythm comes from, and sometimes it slurs wildly out of it – only to snap violently back at the grim moment of decision ('I've had enough!') that precedes the end of the song.

High on the Hog

Perhaps the most telling result of these Albini sessions is a recording of only about two and a half minutes, a little song that eventually became the second track on the *Salt Lick* EP. Due to a mishearing of the refrain lyric, it is probably better known now as a Nirvana bootleg under the name 'Alcohol'. One night in November 1989 in the north Italian town of Mezzago, during the first Sub Pop European tour, Tad was momentarily indisposed: Danielson asks the crowd to 'pray for Tad . . . he has a bad case of haemorrhoids and boils . . . and also the flu.'[53] With the headbanging Danielson and Thorstensen at his sides, Kurt Cobain stepped up to the microphone to sing it and a few other TAD songs instead, and someone caught it on tape.

The song was actually called 'High on the Hog', and it distils everything about TAD at their Sub Pop height, giving a simultaneous glimpse of the class, gender, race and generation emphases of what for a moment was their product. Like their better-known 'Wood Goblins', the song's main riff sounds like it has been sawn off Henry Mancini's 'Peter Gunn' theme (1958), made famous again by the *Blues Brothers* movie (1980) and the B-52s' 1979 song 'Planet Claire' (on which, incidentally, Nirvana liked to jam pre-show on this European tour).[54] For TAD, the result is a tightly claustrophobic one-bar riff and a few jet-engine power chords that open out into it. This, repeated over and over, is really all the song is, aside from a two-chord verse energized by Danielson's offbeat low-strung bass and leading straight back in to the heavy-heeled, thigh-slapping stomp of the refrain.

This musical simplicity, extreme even for TAD, already hints that the band are aiming at something other than their standard 'beefy, epic-scale riffage of metal' (as Mark Deming once called it).[55] The lyrics serve to confirm the same impression. In his *Salt Lick* review for *Backlash*, Phil West dubbed the song 'grunge-and-western', and that seems about right: the lyrics move in stereotypical folk fashion, verse by verse, through the singer's reflections on his father, mother, girl and dog, each one punctuated by the two-line title refrain that overpowers everything else (as Cobain's vocal demonstrates in Mezzago, it is actually very difficult for one person to sing it live because refrain and verse overlap).[56] These verses have a surprising amount of emotional range, shifting from moments of comic delicacy (the mother taught him how to sew and how to read) through violent abuse (the father taught him how to bleed) and cowardice (the dog who taught him to 'run from the gun'). On record, Tad's vocal, captured with alarming nuance by Albini, traverses all this territory from a guttural growl towards the scream of the refrain, belying the monotone nature of the actual tune.

In short, 'High on the Hog' seems like a deliberate attempt to create a 'grunge folksong' or perhaps 'white-trash blues', a musical fulfilment of one Sub Pop ideal of the loser, strung out somewhere between comedian and outcast on society's fringes, singing a desperate swansong. But if this is a blues, it is ultimately upside down in mood, tapping directly into the label's simultaneous focus on hedonism, abandon and excess. The title 'High on the Hog' (as well as being another butchery term) is a celebration of high living, not suicidal desperation like 'Cooking with Gas'. Drinking and smoking, as his girl taught him, are the only things that this working man needs to know, not (according to the first verse) holding a spade as his father would like to have taught him. Again, the spade, the digging and the father. This is not the working man of rock's past, but the next generation, the idle Sub Pop offspring of the working man, singing a high-on-the-hog blues the wrong way up.

The song is less of a simple stereotype or parody than it at first seems, then, and so in many ways it is a shame that its end resorts to a corny spoken-word section, in which Tad underlines the song's obvious point that his persona is supposed to be 'white trash'. Though Cobain didn't attempt this in Mezzago (playing the pantomime villain was not one of his talents), Tad himself usually did it live, and would mock ('black') disco and (middle-class, 'feminine') fad diets before shrieking for a harmonica solo, presumably as another allusion to folksong or the blues. This, of course, was sarcastic: there are very few solos in TAD's music, and definitely no harmonica in its grunge line-up, just as there isn't a dobro, or a washboard, or the bongos as the back of *God's Balls* claims. There is only Thorstensen's relentless tremolo lead guitar, which edges up and up the fretboard while the rest of the band brutally hammers out the 'Peter Gunn' riff over and over underneath. It is one of those TAD build-up sections at which the band had got so good, twenty seconds of intense 'sonic malevolence' (as Roy Wilkinson called it on hearing them live in 1989), combining an 'instant acceleration to the point of impact with a compelling pattern of tension and release'.[57]

It also perfectly frames the point about TAD and its 300-pound frontman, that they could sit so easily between comedy and violence and horror, and move rapidly between them, 'heavy' in a number of senses all at once. This was what secured their place, I think, in the early Sub Pop grunge limelight, just before the greater appeal and depth of Nirvana began to catch on. As the *Seattle Times* review of the original 1989 Lame Fest put it comparatively: 'Tad had more character [than Nirvana and Mudhoney], mostly by virtue of its tons o' fun lead singer Tad Doyle, whose animalistic growl could melt children.'[58] But if this was so, it was also what began to limit them; their act was inevitably a surface thing, and got old pretty quickly, even with the cachet of Albini to bring out the desperate edge of an alarming record like *Salt Lick*. Symbolically for the band's immediate future, and particularly their relationship with the label that had invented them, the malevolent climb-out at the end of 'High on the

Hog' doesn't go anywhere. It turns back to a few more revolutions of the 'Peter Gunn' riff before collapsing into a cheap laugh from Tad, full Wolf Creek, the maniac in the horror movie. And then finally it turns into a filthy cough, an authentic gesture of failure that Albini lets run even after he has pulled the plug on the instruments.

7
The Nirvana Victim

IN THE LAST chapter I hinted at several different ways in which
TAD gradually became overshadowed and upstaged by Nirvana, now
by far the most famous of all the early Sub Pop bands. This process
began before the first European tour of late 1989, but even so the
show at Mezzago that November seems an appropriately symbolic
moment. The spotlight swung onto Kurt Cobain to sing TAD's set
then and has remained there ever since. 'Heavier than Heaven' – the
slogan coined in Europe for Tad and poking fun, as ever, at his weight
– is now far better known as the title of Charles Cross's 2001 biography of Cobain, where it takes on a tragic resonance that it never
had for its original target. Steve Albini, first engaged by Sub Pop for
TAD's 1990 EP *Salt Lick*, is now far better known for his trademark
'live' sound on Nirvana's *In Utero* (Geffen, September 1993). Likewise, Butch Vig's fame has nothing to do with TAD, on whose third
Sub Pop album *8-Way Santa* (SP89, February 1991) and its single *Jinx*
(SP80, December 1990) he worked. Rather, it grew from his subsequent role for Geffen as producer of the most massive grunge album
of all, Nirvana's *Nevermind* (September 1991).

The overshadowing effect is also true for collectors and collectables. You can still pick up Tad's first single for around $80. Even
the impossibly scarce 'gold' vinyl version, of which there may only
be seventy copies in existence, will set you back little more than a few
hundred dollars. The first Nirvana single (*Love Buzz*, SP23, November
1988) is in quite a different league. There are something like 1,000
hand-numbered copies of this, and a few more unnumbered. It has

entire websites dedicated to it, in which proud collectors register their ownership and write of their trembling hands and sweating palms as they held their copy for the first time. And if it was worth about $30 by a year or so after its release, it has gone up a bit in the intervening period. Recently I saw an apparently genuine copy sell on eBay for £2,655 (around $3,200 in early 2023).[1] That's a lot of money for a thin paper cover housing a 7-inch-diameter piece of plastic; it will be kept silently in storage like any other sacred heirloom. Even the many counterfeits of this first Nirvana single sell for hundreds, far more than almost anything by TAD – which, incidentally, will be genuine, as no one has ever sought to profit from making fakes of their records.

Well – so what? Some artists eclipse others. Some are more celebrated by posterity than others. Some are simply more brilliant than others. I would rather have seen Kiss than Angel; I would prefer a Beatles original to one by the Zombies. It is worth reiterating the point, though, that for a moment in 1988–9 TAD were considered the safer bet for Sub Pop, their frontman the label's charismatic loser 'figurehead', their live show generally superior. That Nirvana were in some ways a 'heavy' live band in the Sub Pop manner is undoubted: Dawn Anderson wrote in mid-1988 that they were 'becoming the kind of band who can turn an entire audience into zombie pod people by their sheer heaviness (this is a compliment)'.[2] Much has been made, similarly, of the 'three guys who sound like nine', and one reviewer confirmed in 1989 that 'Nirvana would sound loud heard over a Walkman at 200 paces.'[3] But the Fluid's Garrett Shavlik, present at some of Nirvana's earliest shows, proclaimed them 'one of the worst live acts ever . . . they were just terrible . . . a chaotic mess – gear falling apart'.[4] And Roy Wilkinson, who heard TAD and Nirvana one after another in London in late 1989, praised TAD's multifaceted 'fusion of levity and aural incision' and by comparison found Nirvana still far too green to headline, hamstrung by their monotonously 'hyperwrought garage sound, every component tensed to breaking point, but all balancing on the same line – plenty of thrust but all in one dimension'.[5] The heaviness of their live show was impressive, but it somehow wasn't cut with the same depth or showmanship as TAD's; it had little release or relief.

As the Sub Pop publicist Nils Bernstein confirms, at that time 'we all thought TAD was going to be the big band', and that makes it briefly interesting to place the original pressing of their *God's Balls* LP (SP27, March 1989) alongside an original of Nirvana's only Sub Pop LP, *Bleach* (SP34, August 1989). Note how the later album seems in many ways a limp imitation.[6] *Bleach* feels and looks so much cheaper, and so much less invested in. It isn't a lavish gatefold, for a start, and within a similar greyscale colour scheme the design falters: the band name is smushed right up against the top when you might expect it to be properly centred, and there is a strange (now iconic) gap between the R and the V in it; the live-action photographic negative on the front isn't a Charles Peterson drag-shutter, though it looks a bit like it. To cap this impression off, there are also unnecessary quotation marks around the album title, as if someone were saying 'Bleach', with crooked fingers in the air, extremely slowly, in a way that seems to exceed even deliberate punk irony.

This negative comparison clearly doesn't extend far beyond the sleeve, however. Occasionally early Nirvana might sound like a cut-price TAD, drawling away at a rhythmic root and a horror scenario for far too long (see the early college airplay hit 'Paper Cuts', later found on *Bleach*). But more often the differences are obvious; actually these close label- and tourmates are awkward to compare directly. Take two songs that have almost the same riff: Nirvana's 'Floyd the Barber' and TAD's 'Boiler Room'. The TAD song is third-person, past tense, a story told about someone else, a trip to the movies.

Whereas, here and elsewhere, Cobain typically prefers to use a kind of fractured first-person, present tense. 'I' and 'you' are really there, and now. As 'Floyd the Barber' demonstrates, he also likes to turn the safe havens of childhood and domesticity into places of danger, a trick largely unknown to TAD. The song's lyrics are populated by characters from the family favourite *The Andy Griffith Show*, beloved of cross-legged children in front of TV sets across the American 1960s. But here these characters are abusive and murderous, and, if I hear it correctly, Cobain uses deliberately infantilized language (it is Floyd's 'peepee' that is pressed up against the protagonist's face) as if to situate the point of view in a specifically childish 'I' who is the victim. If this is intended as comic in its abusive extremes, it is typical that it is not straightforwardly so. 'It's really funny if you've seen the show,' explained Cobain in 1991, adding, 'or there again, maybe it's not funny at all.'[7]

In short, while TAD tend to recount the horror-movie scenarios that inspired them, and so broadly stay within mainstream, if X-rated, boundaries of taste, Cobain descends into more taboo depths, the genuinely scary in place of the conventionally 'scary'. Occasionally this is done with gross and graphic description, but more often, and more powerfully, by allusion and implication. In the Sub Pop single *Sliver* (SP73, September 1990), the grandparents' house visited by the child is for unexplained reasons terrifying. ('But hey, you mustn't get too worried about him – grandpa doesn't abuse him or anything like that,' said Cobain of the song.[8]) 'Polly', written before the Sub Pop era and made famous after it, is a song of rape and torture, ostensibly of a child, in the broken account of their perpetrator. And the fragmented lyrics of 'Sappy', another early song, turn on themes of domestic captivity and self-harm.

It is sometimes tempting to assume, as some biographers have, an autobiographical element in these songs, that they contain fragments of lived experience from what is generally agreed to have been Cobain's terrible childhood, and that this is what gives them this depth. This would be to agree with the critic listening in Newcastle in 1989 who complained that Cobain sang 'almost entirely about himself' for the whole evening.[9] To do so, it seems to me, doesn't give much credit to the vivid songwriting imagination of which Cobain was well aware, and which was further fired up by recording for Sub Pop and touring with the likes of TAD. As he himself once put it, 'when I say "I" in a song, it's not me, 90 percent of the time,' and one implication of this is that he used these songs as vehicles for exploration of the relationship between victim and perpetrator, child and adult, shame and blame, loser and winner, 'I' and 'me' and 'you', often strangely rooted in domestic and small-town situations that serve to accentuate their violence.[10]

The 'hyperwrought' Nirvana, live at the School of Oriental and African Studies, London, October 1989.

This is part, I think, of what gives Nirvana an immediacy and psychological depth that goes beyond TAD's tendency to caricature, and similarly exceeds Mudhoney's intense sociopathic monologues. It is also what allows them their own brand of 'heavy', as well as what has proven their longevity. While the antics of the stumbling drunk, the angry teenager, the sex pest and the rural working man often hang around in the background of their songs, and while their early live shows were famed for their destructive 'fun', still Nirvana remain more elusive, more open to interpretation as an act. In their main releases, if not perhaps their interviews, it is hard to imagine Cobain doing anything so corny as Tad's spoken monologue at the end of 'High on the Hog', or the similar section in the bridge of 'Boiler Room' on *God's Balls*: 'Sweet jizzin' Jesus! Jesus drank corn squeezins and he had sideburns!' His songs always attract more gravity.

Grubby Pop Delights

Still, heaviness and elusiveness were only ever parts of the early Nirvana's alloy. Another part is the term that seems to grate directly against them: 'pop'. The word 'pop' has never been too far distant from descriptions, including self-descriptions, of Nirvana, and has found a strong footing in certain ideas about Cobain. It has become conventional wisdom that he absorbed pop melodies, specifically from 1960s hits, into his songwriting, that some of his favourite artists were chart pop, and that his band liked to lampoon pop-star behaviour whenever they got the chance (see, as an obvious example, Kevin Kerslake's famous 1992 video for 'In Bloom'). The same idea stands behind the indie complaint that Nirvana deliberately 'sold out' in 1990–91, leaving Sub Pop for major-label stardom with the chart-topping, multimillion-selling record *Nevermind*, as expressed here in Ed Sullivan's review for *Ugly American* magazine:

And, oh yeah, the wide-as-the-Arizona-sky pop hooks, hooks
that the Buzzcocks would be proud of. All served up with
that post-Eighties ersatz-punk energy via 70s' hard rock chunk,
lyrics combining volumes of sleepy cynicism with whiny lonely-
boy pathos and the moral truth telling of our desperate times.
Irony, wordplay, and vague flirtations with seaminess. Ta-bump.
'Go forth and multiply . . . inseminate a million markets'.

Not as completely empty as it is boring, *Nevermind* is a
winking reminder of how eternally vapid the human race is.
Nirvana push all the right buttons to make your hips shake but
the only beat I end up hearing is the slap of David Geffen's fat
thighs against their young collective behind.[11]

Nirvana's proximity to pop, for Sullivan, is intertwined with their
very deliberate commercial prostitution, and this is a suspicion that
has followed the band ever since.

It should be noted, however, that the furore around *Nevermind*
was by no means the beginning of this association of Nirvana and
pop. The word is there from the very earliest response to them, even
when they were still the 'Melvins' fan club' (as Dawn Anderson put
it in 1988), little more than a weird northwestern heavy metal band
with no following of their own. Unsurprisingly, the connection
originates with their first single, *Love Buzz* (SP23, November 1988),
which, after all, was a cover of a song by the same band that wrote
'Venus' (made famous by Bananarama in 1986). In early 1989 John
Robb wrote for *Sounds* of the 'grubby pop delights' of this Nirvana
single, while Phil West intended to set Nirvana off from their labelmates when he reported that there would be 'two straight-ahead,
blow-pop tunes' on their forthcoming LP.[12] Around the same time
pop was also regularly cited as a key element in Nirvana's musical
fusion: in mid-1989 Jason Everman, then still the band's second

guitarist, called its music an 'amalgamation of the metal and the pop scenes' in Seattle.[13] (He later reportedly left because he feared the balance had been tipped in the direction of 'jangle pop'.[14]) In fact, this idea of fusion seems to be where the key phrase came from, repeated often enough in interviews to sound like a deliberate guiding concept or unique selling point. To Marlene Goldman, Cobain described the band's music as 'heavy, hard pop', a label echoed in January 1990 by drummer Chad Channing to Matt Emery.[15] And in 1991 Cobain told *Kerrang!* that his band played 'very, very heavy pop . . . like if Cheap Trick were to have a lot of distortion in their guitars'.[16]

A pop sensibility was also attached implicitly to Nirvana's approach to songcraft and construction, often to the detriment of comparable bands on the label. Dawn Anderson wrote of Cobain's signal ability, amidst the 'lead-bottom SubPop sound', to write 'hooks that'll jerk your head around', while, reviewing the LP *Bleach*, Tim Cronin put it more colourfully: he heard Nirvana as one of only a few Sub Pop bands who could 'punch through the bubbling stink'.[17] On the first European tour, Gutter Heijting chose to blame the failings of the live show on the loudspeakers, finding that these had denied the crowd the chance to appreciate the 'subtleties' of Cobain's 'sparkling' songs (TAD's songs, on the other hand, were more 'uniform' and 'definitely PA-proof', whatever the additional appeal of his 'charismatic clown act').[18]

As if picking up directly on this distinctiveness, and attempting to own it, to the German *Amok* magazine Cobain remarked in November 1989 that, if TAD's sound was so heavy it caused an 'earthquake', then Nirvana's unleashed an 'earthquake with flowers that rain down from heaven'.[19] He was joking, but still the joke resonates with Cronin's 'bubbling stink' observation above, and with the clarification Cobain made to Sebastian Zabel only a few days later, deliberately grasping the opportunity to shift the discussion from live to recorded sound: 'We want to make records for listening, not just records for rocking out – where you drop the needle anywhere and always get a hard and fast rock 'n' roll sound.'[20] In turn, this emphasis on the listening experience became part of another commercially oriented practice for which some critics gently teased Nirvana, and which further embedded them in 'pop' behaviour. On the European tour and sometimes elsewhere, the band insisted on playing songs in the same order as they appeared on record: as in, for example, the promotional four-track *Blew* EP (Tupelo/Sub Pop, TUPEP8, December 1989), priming audiences for the experience of the band at home.[21]

Perhaps most striking of all in the early Nirvana's relationship with the term 'pop' is the way they used it as a justification for the band's existence. In interviews of 1991, Cobain confirmed that he considered 'anything that sticks in people's heads' as a 'pop song', a definition stretched wide enough to include, he says specifically, the Butthole Surfers, the Clash, Black Sabbath, the Ramones, the Sex Pistols and even 'fucking Black Flag'.[22] This was defensive, designed to fend off a sense of shame in having deserted the underground with the 'pop' *Nevermind*'s spectacular success; if all the greatest punk and metal and hardcore were somehow pop, that made Nirvana's rise to fame acceptable in the eyes of its critics. But there are hints that he had long thought along these lines anyway, and even that he had come to see pop as part of the answer to the crisis and death of rock in the late 1980s. If rock was bankrupt in its ideology, and an artist could no longer be original, perhaps the best a new band could do was to reconfigure rock as something more like pop's pleasures, spreading its styles across a record in a kind of 'grab bag' or 'compilation tape' arrangement.[23] This connects to the significance of the band name, endlessly discussed in early commentary, and sometimes dismissed as just more wavy-gravy 'retro bullshit'. As the touring band told Italian interviewers in late 1989, one meaning of 'Nirvana' for them was 'simply freedom': freedom from 'categories and labels', the ability to stand apart from 'any style of music'. To want to show 'diversity' in performance and on record, a principle of Nirvana's from the early days onwards, was not at all the same thing, they insisted, as 'selling out'.[24] It was, in fact, a kind of post-rock identity.

Ultimately, I think it was precisely this thinking that placed Nirvana in a strangely antagonistic relationship with Sub Pop. On the one hand, you could say that the band was a dream for Pavitt and Poneman, everything they had wanted since Pavitt's *Subterranean Pop* fanzine of the earliest 1980s. I take it at face value when they write, in what has become a famous early Sub Pop advertising line for *Bleach*, 'They're young, they own their own van, and they're going to make us rich!'[25] Here was a regional northwestern band, with 'working class' pedigree and rock star looks, that was as 'alternative' as it was commercially minded, as 'heavy' as it was 'pop', as ironic as it was sincere, as embarrassing as it was authentic, and as destructive and aggressively masculine as it was increasingly critical of such behaviour. If this was complex fusion territory, it was also extraordinarily rich, as another early press release demonstrates in its attempt to traverse it all in one stride:

> NIRVANA is a heavy pop/punk/dirge combo spawned from the bowels of Seattle, Washington. Although only together for seven months, KURDT (guitar/vocals), CHRIS (bass), CHAD (drums), and JASON (guitar) have blessed this world with a single, an LP entitled 'BLEACH,' and one ripping cut on the *SubPop 200* compilation. NIRVANA sounds like mid-tempo Black Sabbath playing The Knack, Black Flag, and a pinch of the Bay City Rollers.

Selling their bottled sweat and locks of their hair has
proved the biggest money maker so far. Keep an eye out
in the future for dolls, pee-chee folders, lunch boxes, and
bedsheets. ROCK.[26]

The simultaneous problem for Pavitt and Poneman was that
Nirvana, well aware of their potential, typically used it as a way of
distinguishing themselves from Sub Pop and its grunge: of explain-
ing why they were better than any other band on the label, why they
were different from its stereotypes, and why therefore they were
always one foot out of its door. They used pop, in a word, as leverage.
If they were 'pop', this moved them closer to certain early bands on
the label increasingly out of favour (the Fluid, Swallow) and towards
the discrete Seattle 'power pop' scene, fronted by bands like the
Posies, themselves already subject to a Seattle 'feeding frenzy' by
mid-1989 (the Posies signed to Geffen late that year, in a clear anticipation of what Nirvana would later do).[27] Simultaneously 'pop'
moved Nirvana to some extent away from Mudhoney, and certainly
from TAD, whose early songs are almost never described in this way.

As early as August 1988, then, even before their first single had
come out, Nirvana's rejection of the stigma of the 'total heavy grunge
Seattle sound band' already seems an irreverent dig at the label that
would launch them.[28] It would later develop into something more
specific and cutting and self-defining, a line about escaping from 'the
Sub Pop grunge, long haired, retro '70s mold that wasn't very fitting
for us'. Later still, arguably, it fed into Cobain's concerns over the
label's attitude in continuing to stand by acts like Dwarves and the
overt sexism of their lyrics and imagery.[29] In this sense, 'pop', ironically enough, provided a kind of escape route from Sub Pop, a means
of getting away from several stereotypes at once.

Post-Grunge

Undoubtedly, Nirvana's idea of the 'grab bag' record was another swipe at Sub Pop, intended to distinguish the band from some of its contemporaries. This would include foundational label bands such as Blood Circus and their 'big barrage of "rock, rock, rock", just "pow, pow", "next song, next song"' (as Nirvana bassist Krist Novoselic put it early in 1990).[30] It was again part of what they quickly came to understand as their own trajectory, Nirvana's rather than Sub Pop's – a step on the journey towards becoming 'a household name' (like 'Lemon Fresh Pledge', as Novoselic said in 1991).[31] 'We've always tried to accomplish something new with every track and we've always had the idea that each one sounds as though it's been written by a different band,' Cobain told *Melody Maker* in late 1990, on the verge of leaving the Seattle label.[32]

What this implies is that we might even rethink *Bleach*, the Sub Pop LP of 1989. In particular, we should drop the standard notion of it as the $600 album (as its back sleeve proclaims), rough and unplanned and unloved by the band, its lyrics made up on the way to the studio and therefore meaningless. Or else as a teenage, Melvins-fan-club, metal-rage predecessor to the better-known music of a few years later. Or, most of all, as a 'deliberate pandering to the Sub Pop audience', as Nick Soulsby has it.[33] Some of this slander admittedly originates with Cobain himself, for whom a negative retrospective was typical. He was similarly unhappy with *Nevermind* and *In Utero*, and was anyway never one to dwell on the significance or craft of his songs under the prying eyes of his growing mass of interviewers.[34] But for balance, note that this was the same Cobain who was intent on making 'records for listening', who was said by his bandmates to give 'meaning to practically every song', and who later remarked, when Ann Scanlon asked him if the *Bleach* song 'Negative

Creep' was about child abuse, that he was 'glad people ask questions like that because usually no one has any questions about the songs'.[35] *Bleach* also remains Sub Pop's biggest-ever seller, and I don't think this can only be down to *Nevermind* fans buying up an inferior back catalogue. It, too, deserves to be questioned.

One way of doing this is to think of *Bleach* as a statement of intent on Cobain and Nirvana's part, one that both sums up the Sub Pop world view as they had received it and simultaneously attempts to see beyond the label's limitations towards something else. Heard like this, it becomes forty or so minutes of 'heavy pop' that was as much Nirvana-brand as Sub Pop-brand, and that pointed the direction of travel away from the label: not so much pre-grunge, or grunge itself, but already post-grunge.

As Cobain's voice clambers up out of the trail of sludge at the beginning of the heavily downtuned first track 'Blew', this might seem a spurious interpretation. Pavitt apparently requested the ordering that placed this song at the start, and, voice tied closely to bass throughout, it sounds like the stereotypically 'heavy' kind of thing Mudhoney might do (it also, for what it is worth, resembles the beginning of Head of David's first LP, released on Blast First in 1986).[36] The direction of travel is quite different, though. The vocal harmonies in the chorus suggest a lighter style, as does the way the chorus teeters, rhythmically and harmonically, on a pregnant chord, one of those Nirvana 'manic pop thrills' (as Everett True called them) that works better on record than it does live.[37] It is reminiscent, in fact, of the Beatles whom Cobain liked to place as a direct influence on the record, the famous falsetto 'ooo' of Lennon and McCartney exchanged for his characteristic screams of frustration.[38]

A few tracks later, 'About a Girl' is all jangly guitars in a sound that most early Sub Pop bands (except perhaps the folk-rock

Walkabouts) would never have made. Cobain's voice rises uncomfortably to tender heights, answering Novoselic's upwardly mobile and melodic bass line; there is a tambourine, more backing vocals and at least two cute fairy-tale lyrics that make the whole song seem a take on Cinderella, possibly by way of Seattle 'power pop' bands like the Posies. 'Love Buzz', the single, is a cover of a late 1960s chart song that merges the psychedelic into the exoticist, as represented by the 'far-easternness' of the obsessively repeating bass.[39] The 7" version is prefaced by a short tape collage of Cobain's, ending in a foreign-accented announcer's list of what, to a Western audience, would be exotic dance crazes of the 1960s: a 'wild watusi', a 'frug', a 'swingin' hully gully'. The song's 'far-eastern' bass line arrives as if to complete the list.

Extending the impression of the 'grab bag', other tracks on *Bleach* draw more obviously on metal styles. 'Negative Creep' is a missile on one note that nearly quotes a Mudhoney lyric but sounds more like Motörhead. 'Paper Cuts' and 'Sifting', two of Nirvana's longest songs, are slow and expansive in a way that Cobain would later reject as 'too boring' ('I'd rather have a good hook').[40] The latter has a drum intro so splashy that, at least until the guitars come in, it finds the overlap between 1980s hair metal and diva stadium pop. 'Mr Moustache', on the other hand, seems intricate like metal in its relentless energy and frantic moving parts, but points back to no obvious model. Perhaps the influence net just needs to be cast wider. As the *Melody Maker* review of the record put it, the song 'should have been chosen as the theme music for *Batman*'.[41]

Bleach's many guitar solos equally reflect the emphasis on variety. According to Joshua Clover, one of grunge's major innovations as a genre was that it 'reconfigured not just the semantics of the rock song (the lyrical content or the emotional pitch, for example), but the syntactic structure'. This was achieved largely by 'jettisoning traditional guitar heroics', a gesture that symbolizes both 'a rejection of technocratic, masculinist professionalism', and 'a refusal of the solo's egotism in favor of self-abnegation'.[42] He seems to be thinking of those solos on *Nevermind* where Cobain just plays the tune without fuss or embellishment. But the same point works to some extent for the terse, controlled, non-demonstrative guitar solos of quite a few songs on *Bleach*. The solo in 'Scoff', for example, is little more than a three-chord cadence that Cobain leaves to ring out. The one in 'Swap Meet' is a variation on three notes. The 'Floyd the Barber' solo is eight bars of major-chord relief from the minor key and doom rhythm that obsesses the rest of the song.

These can hardly be called unprofessional, though. Nor do any of them take place in anything other than exactly the 'syntactic' positions where any tradition of rock would lead you to expect them. What they are, I think, is one category only of a range of solo styles on the record, each carefully tailored to its song. 'Blew' has a conventional melodic improvisation that leads perfectly back into the chorus, really not so far distanced from George Harrison's efforts for the early Beatles. 'About a Girl', as fits the deliberately naive subject-matter, is tuneful and shapely, up and then down, in a style that Cobain easily recreated for the famous acoustic version in *Nirvana Unplugged*. The 'Sifting' solo is as much an echo of Led Zeppelin as the rest of the song.[43]

The remarkable outro solo in 'Love Buzz', on the other hand, seems as deliberately sloppy as it is indulgent. A minute or so of virtuoso raucousness for the whole band and studio, perhaps it was intended to counterbalance the overt commerciality that Cobain worried about in covering the Shocking Blue number.[44] Numerous tracks of guitar noise are intertwined within it, as is Novoselic's free-ranging bass line, a set of short melodic licks and several vocal interventions in which Cobain seems either to be screaming or imitating ('wah-wah') his own effects pedals. The result is an impression of revelling in the solo space as much as jettisoning its traditional heroics.

Shame and Blame

Having said all this, while *Bleach* is certainly musically various, it is hardly miscellaneous, a 'grab bag' or 'compilation tape' in the most facile sense only. There are numerous things that help to hold it all together. Insofar as he plays on most of its tracks, Chad Channing's drumming style is one link. This has been much maligned, following the later band's lead, for its lightness and technical deficiencies. Jack Endino, recording the first single, complained that Channing was 'barely touching the drums', while Garrett Shavlik of the Fluid, watching the live show, mocked the 'little fella' who had to 'play hard because Krist and Kurt were so loud'.[45] Similarly, Cobain dismissed him as 'more of a jazz drummer' who would 'switch to a heavier thing with us, but still, he couldn't do it natural'.[46]

At the same time, even if it does sometimes exceed his technique, the adventurousness of Channing's playing is obvious, and more than that, it gives *Bleach* an unusual quality fitting for the concept of 'heavy pop' (or 'doom pop', as he calls it).[47] On the one hand, his playing is always exhilarating; if a fill sounds good the first time, he seems to think, do something different the next time anyway (like 'a crazed marching drummer who decided to run away from the parade', in his words).[48] It is also worth noting that Channing came up with the drum parts for the songs on *Nevermind*, and was flattered when Dave Grohl took them up almost exactly.[49] In contrast to Grohl, however, Channing also used a double bass drum pedal with Nirvana, a holdover from his previous band with Jason Everman, the speed metal Stonecrow. This adds a weird depth to the sound of *Bleach*, particularly in songs like 'Blew', 'Negative Creep' and 'Scoff', and quite unlike anything else on Sub Pop at this time. Against all the splashy runaway fills, the bass drum shudders and recoils as Channing hits it at lightning speed in a kind of 'blast' beat, distinct from the two rock-solid tracks on which the Melvins' Dale Crover plays.

The other big continuity on *Bleach* – the most important one of all, something that goes to the heart of Cobain's songwriting – is provided by the personas created in the lyrics. Joshua Clover writes that Nirvana's grunge 'constituted itself by doing a very specific thing with punk's will to confrontation: turning it inward', and so comes to the memorable conclusion (quoting two of its lyrics) that *Bleach*'s place is 'at the corner of *creep* and *shame* . . . the unceasing and un-stable encounter with one's own undesirability, one's own failings'.[50] On closer analysis, however, this sounds a bit one-sided. What Clover doesn't say is that the self-hating loser 'I' of Cobain's songs isn't the only presence in them. Most of them also feature a 'you', typically an authority figure of some kind, someone who is confining the loser, kettling their fury. These figures of authority – sometimes violent, more often merely preachy – spill over out of so many of the songs on *Bleach* and those recorded in the sessions surrounding it. They can easily be listed in a more or less fine-grained way, depend-ing on how closely you listen to the lyrics: parents, lovers, favourite TV characters, the church, teachers, record company execs, moral-ists, vegetarians, trendsetters, gatekeepers, kidnappers, all the world's book-wavers and soul-savers. God. So much so, in fact, that the lines between the actual authorities themselves become blurry and, as Cobain howls in frustration, the focus inevitably falls back on the overwhelmed 'I' itself.

Noting the presence of all these authorities, I would prefer to place *Bleach* a block or so down the street from Clover. That is, at the corner of *shame* and *blame* (the chorus of 'Blew' searches for, but never finds, the word that 'rhymes with shame'). This redraws the terms of the equation relative to many of the other bands on the early Sub Pop label; it is yet another mark of Nirvana's difference from them. In many Sub Pop songs of this time (take TAD's 'Loser' or Mudhoney's 'No One Has' as two good examples), the lyrics depict an 'I' who is wandering and suffering aimlessly, looking for something that can't be found, denied any personal or social significance, and with nothing to lose; this seems to be a permanent state of being, and that is what is important about it. ('It's sort of like the loser is the existential hero of the '90s,' as the TAD bassist put it in 1991.[51]) Cobain's obsession with authority figures, in contrast, tends to focus his song's losers all the more clearly in the present as *victims*.

Cobain has certainly been criticized for his fascination with victimhood. Its intensity has led, for example, to the suspicion that it was what really underlay his defence of women's rights (and implicitly those of other underrepresented and oppressed groups). Insofar as Cobain identified with women at all, suggests Terri Sutton, it was not because they were 'Phairian creatures of great depth, intelligence, and sexiness', but because, like others oppressed, they 'have been and can be prey'.[52] Sometimes in his songs this fascination turns violent: the lyrics of the late single 'Oh, the Guilt' (Touch and Go, 1993) may invoke a strong pathos towards a suffering 'she', but it is also one of Nirvana's most brutal slices of heavy pop, with Dave Grohl's anvil hammerblows and Cobain's screams over the guilt the woman induces; the solo is in danger of tearing the guitar limb from limb. But on *Bleach* there is little that is so uncomfortably directed. Almost every song revolves around 'I' and 'you', as if the real subject were victimhood itself, albeit tied inevitably to the fragile, haunted, suffering male rock star. '[A] grand spectacle (hooray! hooray!)', Sutton writes of the Nirvana live show, 'around men's attempts to express misery, while women clapped from the audience, gagged'.[53] If you can get past that, however, there is something to be marvelled at in the sheer consistency with which Cobain and Nirvana explore the victim, their take on the Sub Pop loser.

There is only one exception to it on the record, in fact, and that is a partial one. This is the B-side song 'Swap Meet', one of those that was only occasionally played live and has rarely been heard since. Unusually for Cobain, it begins as a kind of ballad told from the third-person perspective, and focuses on two people, a 'he' and a 'she'. These characters have their behaviours and possessions, wryly stereotyped according to gender. He loves her but won't show it; she loves him but fears expressing it; he has his cigarettes, she his photograph. The biographical view might be that this has something to do with Cobain's parents, though there is no particular reason to think so. Certainly it seems a satire on small-town life, since Cobain quoted lines from its chorus lyrics directly in joking about what his 'regional' band did for fun in 1989:

> We earn our extra income by creating dazzling art and craft wall hangings, such as pieces of driftwood and seashells glued onto burlap sacks ... We then set up shop at Tacoma's swap meet on Sundays to trade our works for rare turquoise jewelry, which we sell for a sizeable profit.[54]

The striking thing about 'Swap Meet' is that, though it starts out as if a story is about to be woven around these two characters, actually every verse and chorus is the same (save, perhaps, for a few swaps of the above possessions). Though it might resonate with other two-person ballads of urban and suburban life from the pop-rock tradition (the Beatles' 'Ob La Di, Ob La Da' springs weirdly to mind), it is certainly no song of easy-going contentment. Instead it goes nowhere. Its last verse is its first, and the final words of the chorus are given a heavy punchline by the stop-start rhythms of the band and Channing's solos skittering all the way to the bottom of the kit. Once all their possessions are stripped away, what these two characters keep closest to their hearts is one thing alone: bitterness.

Perhaps, unlike 'Floyd the Barber', Cobain couldn't be bothered to tell the rest of this story, or perhaps he didn't have time to write more than one verse in the haste of making up lyrics. Even so, 'Swap Meet' is very effective just as it is. It becomes clear that these two are also victims in the most basic and binary way, that is, of one another. Bitterness is all their relationship, perhaps any relationship, thrives on and it is what lies at its core. Channing's drums arrive at the beginning to give Cobain's ballad a 'leg-up to heaven's back window' (as *Melody Maker* put it).[55] But they also knock it out flat cold at the end. This might be *Bleach*'s bleakest moment of all.

Manic Pop Thrill

Perhaps it is the two songs surrounding 'Swap Meet' on *Bleach*, ultimately, that stand out above all the rest as models of Nirvana's 'heavy pop'. Again, these were songs made to be listened to; they were rarely played live, and have latterly been overshadowed by those of the A-side, in particular the fame of 'About a Girl'. Nonetheless, both bring to clear focus what early Nirvana were all about, and help in understanding just how effectively Cobain and the band created their musical victims.

The first, 'Scoff', obviously centres on a loser, though also present is someone with a room who sees the loser as lazy, juvenile and unworthy; patronizes them (hence the song's title, I suppose); and above all won't give back their alcohol (I paraphrase). As in 'Swap Meet', these lyrics don't change between verses. Instead, what drives the song and its victim is the musical design. This includes a 'prechorus', a channel from verse to chorus, musically distinctive enough to be its own section; Walter Everett has written that it was 'seemingly invented in 1964', and while I presume this was meant tongue-in-cheek, the remark does serve to place the prechorus as a structural element common in the pop-rock tradition from the British Invasion onwards.[56] Possibly that is where Cobain got it from, and certainly it became a hallmark of his songwriting. It is also another stamp of his difference as a Sub Pop songwriter. Prechoruses are absent from the first two TAD albums, likewise from Mudhoney's early material, likewise from almost anything on the label in the late 1980s, many bands tending to butt verse and chorus up against one another without prechorus in a far more schematic way.

The prechorus in 'Scoff', the bit about giving back the alcohol, achieves several things simultaneously. It thickens out the verse harmony with a new continuous picking from Cobain's guitar, while Channing's ride playing now fills out the final-beat stop rhythm hammered from the beginning of the song. Obviously a musical momentum is quickly building, matching the vocals' increasingly desperate demands; this energy is spent by the explosion into the chorus (a typical Nirvana trick; compare the more famous 'In Bloom'), marked by Channing's exuberant low fills, and, at its end, the double bass drum in a 'blast beat' underpinning the return of the original riff. That this riff is now played at a much higher fret on the guitar (and in fact progresses the song to a different key) is important, because it shows exactly what is powerful about this music – that it has moved somewhere from its beginning, literally dragging Cobain's voice upwards with it. An arrow goes through the song from beginning to end, stringing out and intensifying the loser's angst and simultaneously turning it into a remarkable 'manic pop thrill' (as Everett True might say), something unreachable by TAD or Mudhoney.

The song 'Mr Moustache', on the other hand, begins with the thrill in-built already. Its revolving 'Batman' motion, near-impossible for the band to play live, is checked only by force, with the hard stops in its own prechorus. No room is left for a guitar solo at all. Where a solo might fall is instead a gut-wrenching scream that emerges slowly from the last word of the final chorus and lasts something like a mammoth twelve seconds. (Actually, listening very closely, you can hear that it is two screams stitched together by Endino to extend the falsetto part; in an early version with nonsense words, Cobain takes a breath between the two parts of the scream to much less impressive effect.[57])

Following a standard line, Chuck Crisafulli wonders if 'Mr Moustache' is addressed to Cobain's lifelong nemesis, the swaggering small-town mustachioed macho man (and stereotyped hard rock fan). Or, as in later songs like 'Very Ape', if Cobain is here adopting the character so as to mock it.[58] The lyrics, however, don't support either interpretation and are instead better seen, I think, as *Bleach*'s most intense expression of frustration, of being trapped as a victim, of confusion and fury at faddy visionary lifestyle preachiness – at being made to feel inadequate, unclean, guilty. This explains, I think, the allusions to biblical grammar (several lines riff on 'lead us not into temptation' and similar phrases) as well as the elaborate length of the closing scream, and ultimately underlines the point that this scream is what *Bleach* as an album is all about.

Catherine Creswell has written of depression as the central mood that Cobain performed later on, through the fragmentation and clichés of his lyrics ('Polly', 'Stay Away') and the meaningless slurring of one word into a similar-sounding one ('Smells Like Teen

Spirit').[59] It would be wrong to say that this depressive mode is entirely absent from *Bleach*: 'Blew', after all, is used unusually as an adjective, and the prechorus lyrics of 'Scoff' meld sonically into the chorus lyrics, obscuring both. But aren't Cobain's screams the most impressive part of his vocal armoury on this record, far more so than they are on *Nevermind* or *In Utero*? On *Bleach* they range from the 'terrifying screams, hoarse, agonized, godlike screams' that Medwin Pregill noted in 1991, to short falsetto yelps.[60] A kind of solo in themselves, they duel for supremacy with the solo guitar's outrageous string bends in 'Negative Creep'. And most of all they dynamically merge the parts of song after song, a channel for the energy of one section into the next.

For all that they are the extremities of frustration and fury, these screams seem simultaneously calculated as the most extended moments of structural satisfaction, of musical *pleasure* for the listener. The contradiction is, I think, key to the power of early Nirvana, as the ending of 'Mr Moustache' demonstrates. As the extended final chorus of the song concludes, bass and drums cut out suddenly, Channing's hands shooting out to silence the shimmering cymbals. This makes space for Cobain's scream to build against the solo guitar riff alone: for five seconds, all the song's energy is focused into this one rising gesture, as if a musical spotlight had been thrown on to the screaming victim alone, before the rest of the band comes back in.

There are lots of these screams in miniature on *Bleach*, such as just before the conclusion of 'Blew', the end of the 'School' bridge and the transition between prechorus and chorus in 'Paper Cuts'. They were something that the early Nirvana specialized in. But the longest and most impressive is in 'Mr Moustache'. As the band returns underneath, the ever-surprising Channing splashes the cymbals on the *second* beat of the arrival bar, a tiny detail that throws the song's irrepressible momentum forwards onto the front foot again (the end of the song, the same old riff at half speed, is bound to disappoint). I thought grunge was supposed to be sloppy, rough, uncoordinated, ill-adjusted? The scream in 'Mr Moustache' has something of the circus trick about it, the high-wire act, the flying trapeze hand-off. Nirvana's 'heavy pop', in the perfect choreography of its most extreme moments of victimhood, goes far beyond grunge.

Grunge Lite

'They're young, they own their own van, and they're going to make us rich!' Perhaps this was an exaggeration after all. Even so, the sale of Nirvana to Geffen late in 1990 is usually credited with saving Sub Pop from financial collapse at a time when the cultural capital amassed by the label far exceeded the business acumen that might have turned a stabilizing profit. The tales of Sub Pop's approach to accountancy around this time are sobering. Numerous employees were laid off. Pavitt's friend Rich Jensen, charged with tidying up the label's bookkeeping in mid-1991, recalls 'a little disorderly room full of paper' ('The first thing I did was figure out which pieces of paper had dollar signs on them, and put those in a stack').[61] Yet the royalties clause they brokered on Nirvana's *Nevermind*, and the additional notoriety that the new record brought to *Bleach* and the label that had released it, meant that the money would soon be there to stave off collapse.[62]

This line of argument can nonetheless be taken too far. For one thing, it feeds off the standard narrative of Cobain as martyr and saviour, a role that both terrorized and delighted him ('Dive in me!' as he proclaimed in the Sub Pop single of September 1990), and is all too easily exaggerated. In turn this tends to minimize the role of other artists in 'saving' Sub Pop, most of all Mudhoney, who had been cultivated as the cash cow ever since the early success of 'Touch Me I'm Sick', and whose close personal relationships with Pavitt and Poneman fostered a loyalty that lasted longer than Nirvana's (Mudhoney's third Sub Pop record sold 50,000 copies in the U.S. alone, which, while not on Geffen's Nirvana scale, certainly helped avert collapse).[63] The Nirvana-as-saviour line also overlooks Sub Pop's own ability to leverage themselves out of financial trouble, if not through careful accountancy, then through grand gestures, with attempts from 1990 onwards to strike deals with major labels – either to tap into much bigger distribution networks for their own products, or to confer 'indie' credibility on major label releases by running their distribution themselves.[64] It ignores, too, the label's repeated attempts in the early 1990s to reach out to markets in which their products had not yet much appeared. The 'alternative' magazine *Sassy*, aimed at teenage girls, springs to mind, and its giveaway green vinyl single featuring Sub Pop artists (SP171, October 1992).

Perhaps it would be better to say that Nirvana remained in the background for Sub Pop, as aggravation, or provocation, at a time when it became clear to Pavitt and Poneman that to survive their label 'gotta diversify' (to quote Grant Alden in early 1990, interviewing Novoselic and Channing).[65] The *Sassy* collaboration, for example, might well have been inspired by Cobain and Courtney Love, who had featured in the same magazine earlier in the same year. The titles of several compilations from the same time, too, resonate with Nirvana in a way that mocks their success even as it feeds off their now famous phrases. I think of the double 7" *Never Mind the Molluscs* (SP198, March 1993), a compilation of Canadian bands; and before that, early 1992's *Smells Like Smoked Sausages* (SP140; curiously, there is an earlier Ian Tilton snapshot of Cobain that shows him holding up the very same can of processed sausages as the cover image of this release).

It might even be claimed that, when Poneman characterized Nirvana's direction of travel, he was really laying out a new purpose for his label: 'Their latest stuff is more song-oriented than riff-oriented . . . What they're doing right now is definitely pop, but there was such a, if you'll excuse the cliché, potpourri of different sounds on the last album, that you could point to several different sounds as their "real" style.'[66] The next thing anyone knew, after all, Mudhoney took up a Farfisa keyboard. And the 'heavy' TAD's next Sub Pop LP (*8-Way Santa*, SP89, February 1991) was certainly far more of a potpourri than their first two records, *Salt Lick* and *God's Balls*. The first single, 'Jinx', comes complete with Nirvana-like pre-chorus; the verse of the penultimate song, '3-D Witch Hunt', is a buoyant 'jangle pop', TAD meets the Smiths or something. Later there is a demure guitar solo. It is hard to believe that 'About a Girl' does not hang around somewhere behind this: see also 'Plague Years' on the same record.

I think in the same way of the recordings of some of the bigger signings drawn to Sub Pop from 1990 onwards, bands like Los Angeles's L7. Their self-titled debut LP (Epitaph, 1988) is mostly identikit punk; one song ends with a vomit. The Sub Pop EP *Smell the Magic* (SP79, August 1990) inspired something both more varied and more coherent. Beginning with its title, it is still crude and crass: the first pressing was on a veined purple vinyl like spam or thrombosis, and, on the hit single 'Shove' (SP58, January 1990), Suzi Gardner's astonishingly abrasive vocals could 'dissolve multiple layers of scum off a public restroom's porcelain', as someone once said of Blood Circus.[67] The rhymes in the lyrics remain corny; L7 were always more grunge than politically charged northwestern riot grrrl.[68] But what is really arresting about the new Sub Pop L7 is the way in which the fuzzed-out guitars of Gardner and Donita Sparks blaze a melodic path through song after song inspired by different vintages of rock. This approach is announced at the start of 'Shove', in which the 'authentic' equipment buzzing and pedal-footling is silenced by the song's main fuzz melody-riff, which plays against a mirror image of itself on its repetitions and returns winningly at the end in striking counterpoint with the vocals. It impressively shapes off the whole thing as a song, in other words, not just as a riff. Song seems the operative word.

Thirty years on, the challenge has become to listen to some of these artists, and the many more obscure ones that recorded for

L7 pose for early Sub Pop publicity, September 1989.

Sub Pop in the wake of Nirvana's rise to fame, without implicitly dismissing them in jest, and without resorting to turns of phrase like Everett True's 'grunge lite' (a term that retains more than a little suspicion of 'pop' incursion into the original 'heavy' concept).[69] Perhaps the European sampler *Sub Pop Employee of the Month: Lutz R. Mastmeyer* (SPIII/287, 1993) isn't a bad place to start listening again. Delivered with typically self-effacing humour, True's liner notes propose that 'Sub Pop has a far broader variation of sound than ever before.' They riff on the point with a series of wordplays on grunge, calculated to remind the listener of the label's baseline as well as the possibilities emerging from it, fusions out of the original fusion:

'Grave' – a cross between grunge and rave (Pigeonhed)
'Grope' – a cross between grunge and dope (Pond)
'Grench' – a cross between grunge and the French (Les Thugs)[70]

The compilation's track list moves from these artists to Velocity Girl to Eric's Trip and Six Finger Satellite, as well as reclaiming the Walkabouts, an original Sub Pop band that had never proven a good fit with the 'Seattle sound'. Also present are Big Chief's 'One Born Every Minute' (with brass, scratching, and backing vocals) and the Japanese women's garage band Supersnazz ('Uncle Wiggly', from their 1993 Sub Pop debut *Superstupid!*). The result is remarkably lively, in some ways reminiscent of the early fanzine compilations and *Sub Pop 100*, and yet too grounded in the label's history to be a miscellany.

Compilations like *Lutz R. Mastmeyer*, however, were indirect results only of the Nirvana Effect. Perhaps the most intense engagement with Nirvana of any Sub Pop artist after *Bleach* was demonstrated by a home-grown Seattle band, Love Battery. Even the name, actually taken from a Buzzcocks song, reminds me of Cobain's description of the Nirvana concept as an 'earthquake with flowers that rain down from heaven'. Love Battery never really enjoyed the commercial success for which they were made, caught in an awkward moment that the success of labels like Sub Pop and bands like Nirvana had created – between majors and indies, CDs and vinyl. Some of their music is hard to find now, particularly on vinyl. Yet it is worth the effort, I think. Love Battery retained a musical complexity typical of some of the songs on *Bleach*, something increasingly disavowed by Cobain as he moved further towards the definition of his 'pop' as simplicity and repetition, in part to make the songs easier to perform live (the 1990 single 'Sliver' is usually taken as the benchmark).[71]

'Foot', the Love Battery single from November 1991 (SP135), has a kind of Novoselic-and-Channing exuberance in its bass and drums playing, and a Nirvana-like structure in its many stretches of suspense, the lead guitar gurgling or feeding back while waiting for the other instruments to tear in. Ron Rudzitis's vocals, at first buried deep in the mix, gradually emerge with increasing excitement towards the victim screams of the chorus; the lyrics, in their clever Kerouac references, turn out to be as secretly articulate as Cobain's. The song's fluency is nonetheless such that all these allusions remain fairly oblique, at least compared to the surprising final touch, in which the song's instrumental break actually goes so far as to introduce a musical quotation from Nirvana's 'Mr Moustache', the manic Batman riff that carries that whole song along.

This is both amusing and confusing. As ever with Sub Pop, it might in part be a parody for the pleasure of the label's in-crowd listeners, a part-comic, part-bitter memory. Yet, particularly as Rudzitis appears to ask 'What song?' at the beginning of the Nirvana quotation, it is also as if Love Battery are aware of deliberately tapping, like some bar band, into what by late 1991 had become the jukebox classics of Seattle. Grunge had thrived through fusions of other rock styles; the song seems to make the point that it could now allude to its own canon. As the main 'Foot' riff chords re-enter and merge musically with 'Mr Moustache', in fact, the moment is less a parody and more a curious Sub Pop homage, both to the Seattle sound and to the heavy pop that steered a course away from it.

Epilogue: Maximal Listening

IF YOU EVER find yourself in the main terminal at Seattle-Tacoma ('SeaTac') International Airport, you might notice an impressive natural wood and shiny chrome storefront close to the entrance to Concourse C. According to the airport directory, the store within sells 'music, apparel, books, art, and travel items' and is in part intended as a 'Pacific Northwest-centric gift shop' for those on their way to catch flights at the nearby departure gates.[1] One sign above the entrance shows a map of the United States with an oversized Washington State in the top corner. Another sports the slogan 'Spanning the Globe for Profit'. The shop is, of course, the Sub Pop Airport Store.

Opened in 2014, this has met with some criticism, to say the least. An encounter with the store led to the following recent post on Facebook's Pacific Northwest Music Archives:

> I grew up in Pullman [in easternmost Washington State] and lived in Seattle from 88–2000, even did 5 years as a staff engineer at a studio as well as doing live sound for various bands. But when I saw this, I must admit, it made me throw up in my mouth a little . . . Down is up now, apparently . . .[2]

I can understand this. Sub Pop is one of the world's best-known 'independent' record labels and is renowned as one of the original homes of 'alternative' rock: it has a *gift shop* at the *airport*, right next to the duty-free and (at the time of writing) just opposite MAC

Cosmetics and Coach. At the same time the commenter seems to me to capture what has always been at the heart of the Sub Pop project, and what I have been at pains to draw attention to across the chapters of this book. Sub Pop continues to thrive by offering something important, unique and local, even as, with all good humour, it violates it by means of mass commerce.

Responders to the original Facebook post tend to come down on one side or other of this divide. Some find the airport store disgusting, an abuse of everything that Sub Pop is supposed to stand for. Many others see no problem with it. They point out that it is nothing new in principle, a revival only of the Sub Pop Mega Mart that existed downtown as early as the 1990s (and that in 2021 was updated into a new store on 7th Avenue, offering the 'cream of the crap of Sub Pop').[3] They also celebrate it as a fitting symbol – a true people's symbol, perhaps – of Seattle, certainly preferable to the apparently cold corporations also based in the region (Boeing, Microsoft, Starbucks, Amazon) and the usual U.S. airport fare. 'Dammit SubPop store, taking up precious real estate where a Hudson News or a Sbarro's should be,' reads one sardonic post in the thread. Indeed, insofar as the airport store sells the music of local artists, it might be said to be putting money in the pockets of northwesterners and encouraging their work. Quite literally, in one case: several posts suggest that Mark Pickerel, the Screaming Trees drummer, is an employee there.

For many, then, the store isn't at all stomach-churning but rather stomach-settling. Numerous commenters talk in ritual terms about making sure to visit every time they pass through SeaTac, even if they do occasionally complain about the lack of actual recorded media in favour of other merchandise. And counterintuitive as it may seem, there is no reason to assume that this kind of restorative 'local' contact will become any less important as the 'globalized' Internet age advances. As Holly Kruse has argued, the instantaneous ease of sharing music worldwide may not so much erode the importance of locality as reinforce it.[4] The Web makes musical experiences of Seattle possible everywhere, and one prominent mediator in this experience is, and remains, Sub Pop Records.

Something similar goes for the anniversaries observed by the label. In July 2008 Sub Pop celebrated its twentieth anniversary with three days of music events in Seattle, including a party at the city's most iconic landmark, the Space Needle. A flag with the label logo was unfurled up there, and even the mayor of the city got in on the whole loser act, thanking the label for its 'questionable taste in music, generous nature and improbable solvency'.[5] In short, Sub Pop became welcomed and integrated into the city's civic calendar, and became rubber-stamped as an important civic institution, akin to those more obviously global and corporate. This has been reinforced at five-year intervals. The Silver Jubilee of 2013 saw, among other events, Mudhoney play at the top of the Space Needle, lording it over the city in a ceremonial gesture long beloved of rock and pop artists.[6] The music and comedy festival SPF30 followed in August 2018.[7] There will be more in 2023.

I see no evidence that residents and tourists alike have done anything other than welcome these festive additions to the calendar. But just as with the airport store, I can imagine some alternative brows have furrowed over the appearance of the accompanying merchandise, not least the local Elysian Brewing Company's trio of 'Loser', 'Nevermind' and 'Superfuzz' pale ales. (The same would apply to the Georgian 'Touch Me I'm Bock' amber beer, which will surely get to Seattle eventually, if it hasn't already.) Is that really what *Bleach* was written for? Or *God's Balls*? Or *Superfuzz Bigmuff*? What would Kurt say? Then again, alternative rock band tie-ins with alcohol are nothing new, and obviously make a lot of thematic sense (witness the Stolichnaya vodka promotions of the early 1990s).[8] And recall that Cobain said in 1992 that he didn't feel 'in the least bit guilty for commercially exploiting a completely exhausted Rock youth Culture'.[9] Why not a microbrewery, as much as a band, as much as a record label?

Losers – Remastered

Speaking to PBS in 1993, Jonathan Poneman remarked that 'as long as there is a Sub Pop, there will probably always be like this kind of real primitive punk rock type thing happening on the label'.[10] This was certainly true that year: see the label's heavy investment across the 1990s in bands like the Supersuckers (formerly the Black Supersuckers), who took as much from the loser ethos as they did from the hardcore punk of Dwarves (who affectionately styled them 'Dwarves Jr').[11] It has also been borne out over the last thirty years, particularly perhaps in the past decade or so, and drawing on bands both from within the Pacific Northwest and far outside it. There is always something roaring on Sub Pop. I think of METZ, Deaf Wish, So Pitted, Hot Snakes and Pissed Jeans. There is also Bully, who in 2020 released a 7″ cover of Nirvana's 'About a Girl' (SP1376, three vinyl colours). Here Cobain's most radio-friendly 'jangle pop' song is steamrollered into a stereotypical sludge style, as if forcibly reversing not only *Bleach* but also Nirvana's *Unplugged* set and the acoustic version that made the song world famous. Obviously, noisy losers still abound at the label.

This is not to ignore the recordings for Sub Pop of those whose music would hardly fit the 'primitive rock' bill, for example Shabazz Palaces, Spoek Mathambo, THEESatisfaction and clipping. Gillian Gaar is right to draw attention to the place of these artists in the label's recent catalogue.[12] Nor is it to overlook Sub Pop's successful line in recorded comedy, or its forays into the further reaches of 'indie' rock and pop that the early label was itself instrumental in propagating. But it is to say that the 'very aggressive, very raw form of guitar-driven rock 'n' roll' (as Poneman put it to PBS) remains an unshakeable core aspect of Sub Pop's identity, just like the flannel shirts it still sells on its website. More than that, it still underpins the label's reason for existence and its ways of accounting for what is important about the music it inspires – why it should be made and why it should be sold. Matt Korvette of Pissed Jeans writes up Deaf Wish for the Sub Pop website in the following way, notable because it so precisely echoes the language of thirty years before:

> Contrary to the critics who are looking to suss out cultural trends and movements (but have never actually lifted a greasy bass cab onto a stage in order to entertain a couple dozen people), the decision to play loud, distorted, unabashed guitar-rock isn't a strategic move but a higher calling (or curse, depending on one's point of view). Some might say the pursuit of rocking out via deafening amplifiers, crusty drums and a beer-battered PA is a spiritual one, an affliction that either strikes or doesn't. Few groups today embody this sentiment like Melbourne's aptly-named Deaf Wish.[13]

The 'rock is back' versus 'rock is dead' debates will stumble on around bands like this, as Korvette also points out. And just as they did in 1988, Sub Pop will profit by sitting on the fence between these positions and encouraging the rampant noise to take over, the work of people 'afflicted' (or 'cursed' or 'called') by rock and more likely to ask 'a fellow musician what they do for their "real" job . . . than talk shop about publicists, ticket counts, and online promotions.'[14]

The label's vision of a network of 'regional and local bums who refuse to get an honest job' (as Pavitt put it in 1982) lives on.

The potential reach of the loser has undoubtedly developed in the same thirty-year period. I note that, since 2007, Poneman and the label have branched into educational philanthropy, endowing so-called 'Loser Scholarships', meant to assist high-school students attend university, provided that they can show creatively how they are 'unabashedly [themselves] without conforming to any preconceived ideas of "normal"'.[15] Simultaneously, the targets of losership remain the same as ever. All of the artists mentioned above, and many more, have appeared in so-called 'Loser Editions', an initiative launched in 2011 that sees limited-number coloured vinyl versions of new releases available for pre-order direct from the Sub Pop website, with bonus extras ranging from the simple (posters, stickers, band photos) to the extravagant: the Helio Sequence album *Negotiations* (SP910, 2012) came with a CD to be played at the same time as the vinyl as a 'quadrophonic surround companion'.[16] Since 2013 and Soundgarden's *Screaming Life/Fopp*, the phenomenon of the 'Loser Edition' has also revived the classic EPs and LPs of the grunge era, including by Green River, TAD, Afghan Whigs and L7; there are many others still to be revived. These stand alongside deluxe coloured vinyl anniversary editions of Nirvana's *Bleach* and Mudhoney's early Sub Pop records.

This feeds a nostalgia also fuelled by the coffee-table books of Charles Peterson photos, as mentioned in Chapter Three. I imagine Loser Editions are a decent money-spinner, and certainly they fill a gap that eBay cannot: you can get the twentieth-anniversary *Bleach* on white vinyl for $60, where the original white would cost thousands. They also bring those artists back into the current discography, which may be a profitable move when, inevitably, some of them choose to give it another go, newly restyled as 'pioneers' of alternative rock. A glut of new Afghan Whigs releases appeared between about 2014 and 2017, including two new full albums; these were also the years that saw the Loser Editions of their early 1990s records. And, according to a press release, L7 were supposed to contribute a single for the seventh edition of the Singles Club in 2022/3, on the heels of the reappearance of their classic *Smell the Magic* (SP1379; originally SP79, 1990).[17]

There will surely be another Mudhoney record sooner or later, too. They have not so much re-formed as never really gone away, and, following a 1990s hiatus with Reprise, most of their material has appeared on Sub Pop. Mark Arm once said that grunge can never die, just as long as 'there's someone playing it or writing songs in that style'.[18] He has quite literally lived this proposition out, even through grunge's credibility implosion and against the proclamation ('I won't live long!') in his most famous song. Mudhoney persists too, counter to its guitarist Steve Turner's often-repeated remark that the lifespan of a good band was about 'three years'.[19] To listen to their latest, *Digital Garbage* (SP1225, 2018) and *Morning in America* (SP1325, 2019), is to encounter all kinds of raucous Stooges guitars, lurid slide effects and straight-ahead songs led by their bass lines; also Mark Arm is still not finding what he is looking for. All the 1988 trademarks are still there. 'Who doesn't love Mudhoney?' asks Gillian Gaar, and she can pose the question rhetorically because, whatever the modest ebb and flow of their popularity, Sub Pop has carved out a niche for them as its spring-eternal flag-bearing Seattle band.[20] Mudhoney quite literally fulfil the old rock authenticity claim of staying 'true to themselves', simply because they haven't changed that much in 35 years.

Tad, on the other hand, has reinvented himself as Thomas Andrew Doyle, a composer of art music for orchestra. This may come as a surprise. It seems like the last thing that the 'shit-stained rock beast' (as John Robb called him in 1989) would do is write and record an orchestral score and mix it in his home studio. Then again, the charismatic persona up onstage was never the real Thomas Doyle: Sub Pop's 'heaviest MAN in the world' was always a 'three-hundred pound marketing tool'.[21] What *was* real was the neverending search for the heaviest of the heavy, as evident from all the old Endino and Albini 'industrial' stuff, and even far beyond that, in the post-Sub Pop recordings like *Infrared Riding Hood* (EastWest, 1995), which saw the band smashing hammers on metal pipes to brutalize their percussion attack (listen to 'Emotional Cockroach').

It seems entirely consistent, then, that Doyle's *Incineration Ceremony* (SP1249, ash-grey vinyl, 2018) is another forty-minute dive into the depths, now transferred to the most heavy of all music's blunt instruments, the (synthesized) symphony orchestra. The epic metal riffs have found a natural home in the orchestral ostinato, and so, with low brass, reverberating piano and percussion, tremolo strings, and stab chords throughout, the entire universe begins to teeter; the astronomer Carl Sagan's 'Pale Blue Dot' speech, recited at the end, finally brings it down on top of the listener. Titles like 'Silent Incineration' and 'Meditations in Null' suggest that Doyle is aiming somewhere between *The Rite of Spring* and a horror movie soundtrack.

Where these two overlap, of course, is the sacrificing of virgins. Well: you can take Tad out of TAD, but you can't take TAD out of Tad. Or either, indeed, out of Sub Pop.

Sub Pop 1000

In the light of all these legacies of losership, I want to respond finally to one of the most intriguing Sub Pop signals of recent times: the silver jubilee release in April 2013 of yet another compilation, titled *Sub Pop 1000*. This felt significant largely because of what it wasn't. Though a compilation, it wasn't a sampler of then-current Sub Pop artists, of which there have been many over the past decades (see, as one example, 2016's *Make Sub Pop Great Again*). Nor was it tied into a magazine anniversary feature on the label, as with *Mojo's Sub Pop 300!* (2008) and *Sub Pop Silver Jubilee* (2013) and *Uncut's SPF/30* (2018). Nor was it a soundtrack (see the 1996 coloured vinyl boxset for Doug Pray's film *Hype!*), nor did it accompany a book (the CD that came with Charles Peterson's *Screaming Life*). Nor, even, was it a sarcastic retrospective into the era that made the label famous: 1991's CD compilation *The Grunge Years* springs to mind, in its 'limited edition of 500,000'.[22] In fact, as far as I can see, *Sub Pop 1000* had little press and little to help it make an impact. For a label that had made a three-decade art of overselling what was destined to be undersold (to paraphrase what Chris Eckman of the Walkabouts once said), it was provocatively mute.[23]

That said, part of *Sub Pop 1000*'s intention was obviously to turn the heads of collectors, especially those drawn, perhaps nostalgically, to independent labels and stores. It appeared as a special edition of 5,000 copies on the newly instituted 'Record Store Day' in a subtle pale blue swirl vinyl, and, with an accompanying sixteen-page booklet and original sleeve artwork by the narrative artist Nathan Fox, made clear allusions to *Sub Pop 100* and *Sub Pop 200*, in turn placing *Sub Pop 1000* as a kind of runner's-up prize for those who had missed out decades before. In typical style, Poneman capitalized on this in his booklet note, which, under the title 'We *Still* Want Your Money!', wearily and self-consciously revived the same old humour that turns the label and its customers into losers and dupes: 'Yes, I know. I may as well be a carnival barker; inviting you, valued listener, to step-right-up! If Sub Pop has ever had a mission other than to separate you, gullible customer, from your wallet (and the contents therein), it's to inspire nasty, compulsive behavior.'[24]

This house brand of rhetoric was only the most obvious, how-ever, of the ways in which *Sub Pop 1000* invoked its distant ancestors – not only *Sub Pop 100* and *200*, but the fanzine tape compilations that had preceded them thirty years before. Looking closely at the ten artists featured on the compilation, only one or two can be said to have been 'on' the label and its subsidiaries at the time of release. In other words, it is less a traditional sampler, a kind of 'try a track before you buy the album', than about *curating*. But that raises the obvious question: curating what? Not the music of a city or region like *Sub Pop 200*, since the artists here are from all over the world, not just the Pacific Northwest. Nor a network of 'underground' inde-pendents situated across the United States, like *Sub Pop 100* or its tape predecessors. Independence isn't mentioned, actually (Sub Pop itself has been 49 per cent owned by Warner since 1995).

What *Sub Pop 1000* was primarily doing, it seems to me, was again advancing the label's own right to curate, a right reinforced by the historical trawl of Poneman's booklet notes through the impact of the early and now iconic compilations. In featuring these non-label artists on its compilation, Sub Pop is reassuring us that they are of value, even though there is little direct profit to be gained from promoting them. And in so doing the label is underlining once again what was always its lifeline as an independent: their right to tell us what is important, to use these artists to sell their brand through their taste. This is just the same as with the Singles Club, the consumer gamble of which was always that you had to pay in full and in advance without even knowing whose singles you would receive. Poneman continues:

> *Sub Pop 1000* is our gift to you, patient benefactor, for your unwavering devotion in the face of occasionally wavering good taste. Put together as a labor of love, *Sub Pop 1000* carries no

further agenda than to provide a crucial, maximal listening experience for its own sake. By that measure, it succeeds and then some. With artists from disparate parts of the globe, our quest for World Domination appears to be complete – again![25]

The sarcastic tone should not obscure that something important is being said here – in fact, as ever, the sarcasm embeds it and makes it more personal, powerful and authentic. 'Maximal listening experience' is the key phrase. It suggests that, by placing your trust in Sub Pop and merging your taste with theirs, you can afford to do nothing other than listen, listen without agenda and 'for its own sake' (an expression that recalls Pavitt's art-for-art's-sake fanzine slogans of independent music from thirty years before). Or, to use what is a cliché, but one that crops up again and again around Sub Pop then as now, you are invited to listen in as the 'music speak[s] for itself.'[26]

A Victory for Polio

This, if anything, has proven one key slab of the path to success and repeated 'World Domination'. But it is worth asking one final question: what is this music that 'speaks for itself'? The answer from *Sub Pop 1000* is pretty clear. Ultimately what screams the loudest on the record is once again a back-to-basics 'primitive' rock. This is something else that Poneman is hinting at with his word 'maximal': no compromise, no rules, all dials pinning, the Sub Pop knobs turned to the max. The opening track of the compilation begins, indeed, from the biggest grunge cliché of all, now as redoubled and exaggerated as it could be. 'Kidult', by the Italian trio His Electro Blue Voice, starts with a quiet, throbbing, suspenseful low bass, until – surprise, or not – the full attack of metal guitars, drums and electronics tears in. It is a visceral musical gesture that unites His Electro Blue Voice with

Nirvana, TAD and countless others of the late 1980s, as well as their inspirations, not least Pavitt's (and Cobain's) beloved Wipers. 'There is an *incredible honesty* conveyed by these guys,' wrote Pavitt in *Subterranean Pop* #1 in 1981, reviewing Wipers' *Is This Real?*. 'When the guitar finally rips in, you *feel it*.'[27] The same claim seems to echo through His Electro Blue Voice in 2013.

True, *Sub Pop 1000* is cushioned with other numbers that indicate the label's later development, for example by the Argentinian electronic composer Chancha Via Circuito or the synthpop duo Peaking Lights. The primal rock seems somehow irrepressible, though, and keeps welling up and breaking through. The cello of Lori Goldston (most famous as Nirvana's cellist, and one of the only women artists on *Sub Pop 1000*) bears an unmistakeable resemblance to a grunge anti-solo. Protomartyr ambush with a two-fret riff. And, most obviously of all, there is Iron Lung's 'A Victory for Polio'. This is eighty seconds of hardcore punk (or its even more hardcore variant, 'power violence') that seems to regress not so much to *Sub Pop 100* and *200* as to long before those collections, towards some of the early 1980s regional compilations that preceded the label (Seattle's *What Syndrome?* springs to mind, as does Boston's *Bands that Could Be God*). At the end of the first side of the vinyl, this track comes across as a triumphant resurgence of something virulent that should have died out long ago – a victory for polio indeed. It goes back to a place that the label had never been, towards a pinpoint of rawest masculine aggression, before men's victimized suffering with Nirvana, before TAD's charismatic horror stageshow, before Mudhoney's slovenly loser antics.

The song's ferocity is so extreme as to be almost comic, in fact, and, when the singer screams the title at double-speed at the end and drops the mic, one obvious response may be a weary smile at how stereotypical some hardcore gestures became. Yet Iron Lung's presence on the record is something more serious, intended specifically, it seems, as a piece of patronage, consistent with the elder-statesman role that Poneman (and Pavitt, although no longer part of Sub Pop) nowadays likes to play.[28] After all, Iron Lung's story is one that could come from the early American indie rock landscape from which Sub Pop grew. Iron Lung is not just a two-man hardcore band: it is a band that moved from Reno to Seattle and in 2007 became a small record label under the same name. Since then, it has built up a considerable catalogue of several hundred releases at a breakneck rate of twenty or so per year. Not all of these are available on the major streaming services and so retain, to some extent, the cachet of the 'alternative'.

The most obvious model for Iron Lung might be SST Records, a similar story of a band intertwined with a label. This rings true from Iron Lung's focus on punk, hardcore punk, DIY ethics, aggressive iconoclasm, transgressive symbolism and, as ever, the general veneration of the holy Black Flag. Yet Sub Pop also looms as a big influence, particularly in the limited-edition coloured vinyl singles and coloured tapes (some of them already quite valuable to collectors), consistent sleeve and image design, run-out groove messages and a wealth of merchandise: badges, stickers, even a turntable slip mat are all adorned with the label logo (a line drawing of an iron lung, no less). Similarly regulative is the same belief in the better and 'heavier' sound of 7" singles as primary medium, and in raucous black-and-white live photos, some of them drag-shutter in style. The humour is, too, very reminiscent of Sub Pop. It is self-effacing, grandeur-deluded, and emphasizing a tongue-in-cheek overselling of the brand, curiously at odds with the repeated insistence that 'making money [is] never a concern'.[29] Recently I noted the launch of the 'Disease Filter II', a label-branded coronavirus face mask.[30]

Most importantly, the Iron Lung website does a comparable job to fanzines like the original *Subterranean Pop*, in that it serves as the hub of a network for small labels whose releases it curates in the context of 'classics' (Wire's 1977 LP *Pink Flag* is a standing item), as well as through direct sales and sampler mixtapes. As they do this, Iron Lung's founders, Jensen Ward and Jon Kortland, make it clear that the genre of their own band is not intended as the limits of the label's operations. 'There can only be so much power violence in the world, right?', says Ward, and specifies that the label strategy is best understood as a non-strategy: it is simply 'to release good music that we have had a direct connection to, that most other people in the world may not get a chance to enjoy'.[31]

This innocent-sounding recourse to universal good taste and underground brilliance is another reminder of the early Sub Pop, as is the Iron Lung label slogan, found everywhere on its outlets, 'WE KNOW WHAT WE LIKE AND WHAT WE DON'T LIKE' (compare Poneman's often repeated summary of the Sub Pop acquisition strategy: 'It's just the music that we like').[32] It is important to remember, then, that rock is fundamentally assumed in both cases. We like rock; we *believe* in rock; we are devoted to rock; and, certainly, it seems pretty clear, the heavier and more hardcore the better. Genres outside rock are considered largely surplus to requirements, as they were for the early Sub Pop. (At the time of writing, I note that while there is a 'Soul/Funk/World' category on the Iron Lung website, it is restricted to one LP, James Brown's soundtrack for *Black Caesar*.)

But there is something else still about Iron Lung. As much as Sub Pop might aim to patronize it, the small label is also a direct competitor to the bigger, older one. There are several instances, in fact, of bands preferring to release their music with Iron Lung rather than Sub Pop. His Electro Blue Voice might be one of them, having moved to the former from the latter for their most recent LP. The Australian band Total Control is certainly another, staying with Iron Lung to release their second LP, *Typical System* (2014), after the commercial success of their first, *Henge Beat* (2011), and in doing so rejecting Sub Pop and other bigger labels. Again, this is not to do with an identity of genre – Total Control are more likely to be described as 'genre-smashing' than as 'power violence'[33] – but instead is a matter of something more personal, as frontman Daniel Stewart explains:

> We want everyone in the world to hear our music, but we don't really think we need to do much more to get there. We don't think we should take shortcuts, and we've seen the way other bands operate when they do take those shortcuts, to try to enhance their popularity, and it just seems they're often very miserable in the position they are in. Someone is telling them how to operate and where to go, and they're answerable to those people because those people are experts in popularity. I think we're experts in writing songs and playing them and having a good, strong, loving dynamic, so that's what we focus on.[34]

'Trust' is the crucial word that comes up, as in Stewart's summary: 'It makes sense to put out a record with people you trust ... I think things could get really fucked if we went outside of that.'[35]

In these circumstances, Sub Pop begins to appear like a major of old, and moves into something like the cold, faceless 'corporate' position. The world-famous grunge label with a shiny storefront at the Seattle airport loses out to the dude (Ward) who works in a video store and says: 'I kind of do this loser teenager job and also play in rock bands and put out records.'[36] The corporate-indie opposition is clearly out of date: Iron Lung considers Sub Pop to be an indie, just a big one with 'money and a pretty heavy catalog to back them up, and everybody knows them and they're popular and everybody loves them'.[37] Yet the dynamic is just the same as the one that Bruce Pavitt mobilized, sold and profited from across the 1980s in his fanzine and his label. The oppositional engine of rock rolls on. Sub Pop may offer its services as one of the doyens of indie rock; it may now offer a small boutique label, Hardly Art, as indie subsidiary to soften the image of the corporate ogre. And its advocates may point out the limits of what the generation beneath might be able to achieve through DIY websites like Bandcamp, and why established labels that provide a 'considerable amount of work and upfront investment' still matter.[38]

Yet as it does all this, Sub Pop inevitably also provokes that generation through the same friction – part admiration, part disdain – that produced it and its grunge loser men in the first place. That is one of its ongoing legacies. Steve Waksman once wrote of the eternal 'uneasiness' of rock as a form of mass culture, and pointed out that 'the desire for belonging in rock has continually been set against the longing to be set apart.'[39] That's it – that's it, the quality that still marks all this noise, the motor that drives it onwards.

REFERENCES

Preface: If Only They Knew

1 These terms from Clark Humphrey, *Loser: The Real Seattle Music Story* [1995] (Seattle, WA, 2016), p. vi, also iv.
2 I refer to Greg Prato, *Grunge Is Dead: The Oral History of Seattle Rock Music* (Toronto, 2009); and Mark Yarm, *Everybody Loves Our Town: A History of Grunge* (London, 2011).
3 I take this from the Conflict Records sampler *Bands that Could Be God* (1984).
4 See the PBS documentary *Remarkable People Making a Difference in the Northwest: At Home with Sub Pop* (prod. Jean Walkinshaw, 1993), 14:00.
5 Stephen Tow, *The Strangest Tribe: How a Group of Seattle Rock Bands Invented Grunge* (Seattle, WA, 2011), p. 149.
6 Jonathan Evison, 'Defining the "Seattle Sound" Once and for All', liner notes for the deluxe reissue of Green River's EP *Dry as a Bone* (Sub Pop, SP1261, January 2019).

Introduction: Big Dumb Rock

1 From an interview in *Rockerilla*, originally published in Italian, available at www.livenirvana.com, accessed 1 May 2022. My translation.
2 Gina Arnold, *On the Road to Nirvana* (London, 1998), p. 140.
3 Everett True, *Live through This: American Rock Music in the Nineties* (London, 2001), p. 103.
4 This is a paraphrase of Keir Keightley's description of rock: see his 'Reconsidering Rock', in *The Cambridge Companion to Pop and Rock*, ed. Simon Frith, Will Straw and John Street (Cambridge, 2001), p. 122.
5 See the reverse of the Sub Pop compilation *Fuck Me I'm Rich* (Waterfront Records, DAMP 104, 1989).
6 As told to Bernd Bohrmann in Heidelberg, November 1989, in 'TAD Nirvana', *Amok*, available at www.livenirvana.com, accessed 1 May 2022. My translation.
7 See the 1989 interview from the *Matt Lukin's Legs* fanzine, available at www.livenirvana.com, accessed 1 May 2022.

8 The full original in Italian, from Chiesa's fanzine *Rockerilla*, can be found at www.livenirvana.com; this is the basis of my quotations and translation here. The interview is also reproduced and translated in Nick Soulsby, ed., *Cobain on Cobain: Interviews and Encounters* (London, 2016), pp. 41–8, though there it is abridged.

9 See the Bob Gulla interview with Nirvana from cdnow.com, 18–28 May 1999, available at www.livenirvana.com, accessed 1 May 2022.

10 Kurt Cobain, liner notes, *Incesticide* (Geffen/Sub Pop, DGCD-24504, 1992).

11 True, *Live through This*, p. 103.

12 See, as sample reviews, Roy Wilkinson, 'Soundgarden: Sonic Bloom Boys', *Sounds*, 11 February 1989, p. 18; Push, 'Mudhoney/Soundgarden: School of African and Oriental Studies, London', *Melody Maker*, 20 May 1989, p. 28; and Everett True, 'Sub Pop, Sub Normal, Subversion: Mudhoney', *Melody Maker*, 11 March 1989, p. 28. Also the descriptions in Phil West's May 1989 article 'Hair Swinging Neanderthals' for the University of Washington's *Daily*, reproduced in Soulsby, *Cobain on Cobain*, p. 4. Also for the Italian magazine *Il Mucchio Selvaggio* in 1989, www.livenirvana.com, accessed 1 May 2022, and in Tim Cronin's review of Nirvana's *Bleach* in *Ugly American*, 4 (Winter 1989), at www.uglyamericanzine.com, accessed 1 May 2022.

13 Michael Cox, 'Swallow (Tupelo/Sub Pop Import)', *Backlash* (April 1989), p. 9.

14 The quoted phrase is Keith Cameron's, describing Nirvana and Mudhoney in 'Screaming Trees: Fulham Greyhound', *Sounds*, 10 March 1990, p. 28.

15 As quoted in Michael Azerrad, 'Introduction', in Charles Peterson, *Screaming Life: A Chronicle of the Seattle Music Scene* (New York, 1995), p. 16.

16 In an interview of April 1990 with Anne Filson and Laura Begley of *Dirt* fanzine, reproduced at www.livenirvana.com, accessed 1 May 2022.

17 As quoted from the Seattle *Rocket* in Clark Humphrey, *Loser: The Real Seattle Music Story* [1995] (Seattle, WA, 2016), p. 130.

18 As quoted in David Fricke, 'Kurt Cobain', *Rolling Stone*, 27 January 1994, p. 37.

19 Kurt Cobain, liner notes, *Incesticide*.

20 Steve Albini, 'Tired of Ugly Fat?', *Matter*, 5 (September 1983), p. 12.

21 See Humphrey, *Loser*, p. 166.

22 See Cobain's interview with Everett True titled 'In My Head I'm So Ugly', *Melody Maker*, 18 July 1992, p. 24.

23 On grunge and the promise of gender equality, see, for example, Catherine Strong, *Grunge: Music and Memory* (Abingdon, 2011), pp. 108–9.

24 Dawn Anderson, 'TAD: Mountain Man or Man Mountain?', *Backlash* (April 1989), p. 7; Veronika Kalmar, 'TAD: God's Balls', *Backlash* (April 1989), p. 9.

25 Kalmar, 'TAD: God's Balls', p. 9.

26 Anderson, 'TAD: Mountain Man or Man Mountain?', p. 7.

27 Everett True, 'Sub Pop. Seattle: Rock City', *Melody Maker*, 18 March 1989, p. 26.

28 The quotations (regarding Nirvana) are from Keith Cameron, 'Nirvana/Melvins/Dwarves/Derelicts: Seattle Motorsports International Garage', *Sounds*, 13 October 1990, p. 28.

29 Cynthia Rose, 'Sub Pop: See Label for Details – An Interview with Bruce Pavitt', *Dazed and Confused* (1994), available at https://rocksbackpages.com, accessed 14 September 2022.

30 True, 'Sub Pop, Sub Normal, Subversion: Mudhoney', p. 28.

31 West, 'Hair Swinging Neanderthals'.

32 Terri Sutton, 'The Soft Boys: The New Man in Rock', in *Trouble Girls: The Rolling Stone Book of Women in Rock*, ed. Barbara O'Dair (New York, 1997), p. 529.

33 As told to Grant Alden in February 1990, see www.livenirvana.com, accessed 1 May 2022.

34 Greil Marcus, *Lipstick Traces: A Secret History of the Twentieth Century* (Cambridge, MA, 1990), p. 57.

35 David Buckley, R.E.M. *Fiction: An Alternative Biography* (London, 2002), p. 5. Emphasis in original.

36 This is cited as appearing in *Guitar World*; I quote it from a Sub Pop press release on Mudhoney for their second full-length record *Every Good Boy Deserves Fudge* (Sub Pop, SP105, 1991).

37 Humphrey, *Loser*, p. iv.

38 Everett True projects a Sub Pop 'movement' via a quotation from Poneman in 'Sub Pop. Seattle: Rock City', p. 26. Mimmo Caccamo picks this up in the interview for 'London Calling' on Radio Onde Furlane in October 1989 at www.livenirvana.com, accessed 1 May 2022. Mat Snow calls the Sub Pop label 'cultish' in 'You, My Son, Are *Weird*', *Q* (November 1993), p. 33.

39 See Caccamo, 'London Calling'.

40 Robert Allen, 'Welcome to Nirvana's Nightmare', *Backlash* (June 1989), p. 12.

41 Everett True, 'Sub Pop: Seattle: Rock City', p. 26.

42 Arnold, *On the Road to Nirvana*, p. 273.

43 Chuck Crisafulli, *Teen Spirit: The Stories behind Every Nirvana Song* (New York, 1996), p. 18.

44 Kurt Cobain, *Journals* (London, 2002), pp. 1–2.

45 As quoted in Keith Cameron, '10 Tours that Changed Music: Burn Baby Burn!', *Q* (March 2002), p. 93.

46 Gina Arnold talks about these other 'scene' success stories in *On the
Road to Nirvana*, pp. 104, 127 and 206; see also True, *Live through
This*, p. 103, citing the cartoonist Peter Bagge on Chicago.

1 Subterranean Pop

1 Bruce Pavitt, 'New Pop Manifesto', *Sub Pop #1* (May 1980), reproduced
in Pavitt, *Sub Pop USA: The Subterranean Pop Music Anthology,
1980–1988* (New York, 2015), p. 15. Emphases are Pavitt's own.

2 From *Sub Pop #8*, ibid., p. 167.

3 See Pavitt's retrospective commentary on the first issue of the fanzine,
in Pavitt, *Sub Pop USA*, p. 8.

4 Clark Humphrey, *Loser: The Real Seattle Music Story* [1995] (Seattle,
WA, 2016), p. 71.

5 The education institutions included an Alternative Learning Process
School in Illinois (with members of what would become the Seattle
band Soundgarden), and Evergreen State College in Olympia.
See Mark Yarm, *Everybody Loves Our Town: A History of Grunge*
(London, 2011), p. 55; and Gillian G. Gaar, *World Domination:
The Sub Pop Records Story* (New York, 2018), pp. 1–6.

6 Here, incidentally, Pavitt appears to link the label 'pig-fuck' to
aggressive and toxic masculinity generally, rather than its later specific
association with certain strands of noise rock.

7 The quotations in this paragraph are all from Pavitt, 'New Pop
Manifesto', pp. 14–15.

8 *Sub Pop #2*, in Pavitt, *Sub Pop USA*, p. 50. Pavitt's capitals.

9 These latter quotations from Pavitt, 'New Pop Manifesto',
pp. 14–15.

10 See, for example, Gaar, *World Domination*, pp. 1–23; and Stephen
Tow, *The Strangest Tribe: How a Group of Seattle Rock Bands Invented
Grunge* (Seattle, WA, 2011), pp. 51–2 and 123.

11 *Sub Pop #2* in Pavitt, *Sub Pop USA*, p. 50; and also the phrase 'great art,
great music' in Pavitt's retrospective account of the fanzine's origins,
Sub Pop USA, p. 7.

12 See Johnson's essay 'Emergency Late-Night Peanut Butter Sandwiches',
in *Sub Pop USA*, p. 44.

13 Pierre Bourdieu, *The Rules of Art: Genesis and Structure of the Literary
Field*, trans. Susan Emanuel (Cambridge, 1996), p. 21. See also 'loser
takes all' on the same page.

14 Pierre Bourdieu, *The Field of Cultural Production: Essay on Art and
Literature*, ed. Randal Johnson (New York, 1993), p. 39.

15 From the front page of *Sub Pop #6*, February 1982, reprinted in Pavitt,
Sub Pop USA, p. 147.

16 Gaar, *World Domination*, p. 4.

17 See Alison Piepmeier, 'Why Zines Matter: Materiality and the
    Creation of Embodied Community', *American Periodicals*, XVIII/2
    (2008), pp. 213–38 (p. 235).

18 Ibid., p. 222.

19 See *Sub Pop* #3, in Pavitt, *Sub Pop USA*, p. 84.

20 Piepmeier, 'Why Zines Matter', p. 222.

21 *Sub Pop* #8, in Pavitt, *Sub Pop USA*, p. 181.

22 *Sub Pop* #4, p. 117, Pavitt's emphasis. See also the front cover of the *Sub
    Pop USA* anthology: 'A decade of punk, hardcore, metal, hip hop,
    electro, soul, art/noise, and rock 'n' roll from the founder of Sub Pop'.
    The claim of diversity is also borne out to some extent by the later *Sub
    Pop* column in Seattle's *Rocket*: see Pavitt's report (on 'black/funk/rap'
    labels in New York City, for example, or his fond accounts of the career
    of Grandmaster Flash and the Furious Five in *Sub Pop* (October 1983),
    in Pavitt, *Sub Pop USA*, p. 223.

23 'New Wave' is Pavitt's own hesitant term in *Sub Pop* #2, in Pavitt, *Sub
    Pop USA*, p. 50.

24 *Sub Pop* #1, ibid., p. 37.

25 See Holly Kruse, *Site and Sound: Understanding Independent Music
    Scenes* (New York, 2003), pp. 115–16. Pete Dale identifies a similar
    preference for 'pop' over 'punk' in British fanzines of the mid-1980s
    in 'Are You Scared to Get Punky? Indie Pop, Fanzines and Punk Rock',
    in *Ripped, Torn and Cut: Pop, Politics and Punk Fanzines from 1976*,
    ed. The Subcultures Network (Manchester, 2018), pp. 170–75.

26 Kruse, *Site and Sound*, pp. 115–16.

27 *Sub Pop* #2, in Pavitt, *Sub Pop USA*, p. 64.

28 See Calvin Johnson's essay '"You're in Charge"', in Pavitt, *Sub Pop USA*,
    p. 135.

29 Pavitt, *Sub Pop USA*, pp. 38, 295 and 313.

30 Ibid., pp. 69 and 17.

31 Ibid., p. 26.

32 *Sub Pop* column (July 1983), ibid., p. 214.

33 On the ideology of American rock criticism, see Kembrew McLeod,
    '*1/2: A Critique of Rock Criticism in North America', *Popular Music*,
    xx/1 (2001), pp. 50–52.

34 See various reviews in Pavitt, *Sub Pop USA*, pp. 68, 40, 54, 27 and 67.

35 See, for example, the 'New Pop Manifesto' pages, ibid., pp. 14–15. Good
    examples of Burns's cartoons are the back page of *Sub Pop* #4 and the
    front page of *Sub Pop* #5, reprinted ibid., pp. 134 and 137 respectively.

36 *Sub Pop* column (July 1983), ibid., p. 214.

37 *Sub Pop* #8, ibid., p. 170.

38 *Sub Pop* #6, ibid., p. 147.

39 *Sub Pop* column in *The Rocket* (November 1984), ibid., p. 261. Steve
    Waksman discusses hardcore localism in *This Ain't the Summer of Love:*

Conflict and Crossover in Heavy Metal and Punk (Berkeley and Los Angeles, CA, 2009), pp. 210–11.

40 *Sub Pop* #6, in Pavitt, *Sub Pop USA*, p. 147.

41 See ibid., in order of citation, *Sub Pop* #5, p. 138 (Pavitt's emphasis); column of July 1983, p. 214; *Sub Pop* #6, p. 150.

42 See the first chapter ('The Birth of the Self-Made Man') of Michael S. Kimmel's *Manhood in America: A Cultural History* (New York, 1996), pp. 13–42.

43 Arnold, *On the Road to Nirvana*, pp. 34, 37, 82 and 115.

44 As quoted in Gareth Murphy, *Cowboys and Indies: The Epic History of the Record Industry* (London, 2015), p. 328; also Martin Aston, 'Go Forth and Grunge', *Q* (October 1992), p. 29.

45 In an interview published on his website at https://brucepavitt.com, accessed 1 May 2022. On the influence of Albini, see also Pavitt, *Sub Pop USA*, p. 377.

46 Steve Albini, 'Tired of Ugly Fat?', *Matter*, 5 (September 1983), p. 12.

47 Steve Albini, 'Tired of Ugly Fat?', *Matter*, 7 (February 1984), p. 13.

48 Arnold, *On the Road to Nirvana*, p. 70.

49 *Sub Pop* #5, in Pavitt, *Sub Pop USA*, p. 143.

50 Michael Hafitz, 'Tape Reporter', *Boston Rock*, 26 (February 1982), p. 31.

51 *Sub Pop* #7, in Pavitt, *Sub Pop USA*, p. 156.

52 *Sub Pop* #9, ibid., pp. 191–9.

53 For this advert, see the *Sub Pop* column for July 1983, ibid., p. 214.

54 *Sub Pop* column for November 1983, in Pavitt, *Sub Pop USA*, p. 226. Also Steve Albini's similar denunciation of MDC in 'Tired of Ugly Fat?', *Matter*, 5 (September 1983), p. 12.

55 See Charles R. Cross, *Heavier than Heaven: The Biography of Kurt Cobain* (London, 2001), p. 104.

56 Kurt Cobain, *Journals* (London, 2002), p. 163. On Wipers see *Sub Pop* column of July 1986, in Pavitt, *Sub Pop USA*, p. 322.

57 *Sub Pop* #1, ibid., p. 15.

58 Quoted in Arnold, *On the Road to Nirvana*, p. 124.

59 Pavitt, *Sub Pop USA*, p. 146.

60 *Sub Pop* #4, ibid., p. 117. 'Flattered' is from Gaar, *World Domination*, p. 9.

61 See Cross's essay in Pavitt, *Sub Pop USA*, p. 202.

62 See Michael Goldberg, 'Rock 'n' Roll Fanzines: A New Underground Press Flourishes', *Rolling Stone*, 29 March 1984, p. 57.

2 Sub Pop Rock City

1 See the back of the vinyl version of *The Blasting Concept* (SST013, 1983).

2 See Kaye's sleeve note on the back of *Nuggets: Original Artyfacts from the First Psychedelic Era, 1965–1968* (Elektra 7E-2006, 1972).

3 Quotation from *Pebbles, Vol. 1* (Mastercharge Records, PBLP-1, 1978).

4 Kaye, sleeve note for *Nuggets*.

5 Bruce Pavitt, *Sub Pop USA* column for May 1984, reproduced in Pavitt, *Sub Pop USA: The Subterranean Pop Music Anthology, 1980–1988* (New York, 2015), p. 244.

6 Some of these compilations' tracks have been re-released on *It Crawled from the Basement: The Green Monkey Records Anthology* (Green Monkey, GM1001, 2009).

7 The Tiny Holes tracks here have recently been re-released on *City of Siege: Olympia* (K Records, KLP271, 2019).

8 *Sub Pop #8* (August 1982), reproduced in Pavitt, *Sub Pop USA*, p. 170.

9 Quotation from the direct-marketing insert for *Seattle Syndrome Two* (Engram, ENG 012, 1982).

10 Peter Blecha, *Sonic Boom: The History of Northwest Rock, from 'Louie Louie' to 'Smells Like Teen Spirit'* (New York, 2009), pp. 248–50.

11 Clark Humphrey, *Loser: The Real Seattle Music Story* [1995] (Seattle, WA, 2016), p. 71.

12 Gina Arnold, *On the Road to Nirvana* (London, 1998), p. 52.

13 Mark Yarm, *Everybody Loves Our Town: A History of Grunge* (London, 2017), pp. 80–81.

14 See, for example, the explanatory article by Patrick MacDonald, 'Heavy Metal in the Suburbs', *Seattle Times*, 12 June 1983, pp. E1 and E6.

15 Yarm, *Everybody Loves Our Town*, pp. 78–9.

16 Steve Waksman, *This Ain't the Summer of Love: Conflict and Crossover in Heavy Metal and Punk* (Berkeley and Los Angeles, CA, 2009), p. 7.

17 See ibid., p. 224 for SST's fusion descriptions of its early 1980s bands. See also Pavitt's 1984 description of the Canadian metal band Voivod as 'meeting head on with hardcore', in *Sub Pop USA* column of December 1984, in Pavitt, *Sub Pop USA*, p. 265.

18 The words of Art Chantry, as recounted in Greg Prato, *Grunge Is Dead: The Oral History of Seattle Rock Music* (Toronto, 2009), p. 13.

19 Prato, *Grunge Is Dead*, p. 73.

20 As quoted in Arnold, *On the Road to Nirvana*, p. 213.

21 Dawn Anderson, 'White Noise: *Deep Six* (C/Z Records)', *The Rocket* (June 1986), p. 25.

22 *Sub Pop USA* column of April 1986, in Pavitt, *Sub Pop USA*, p. 313.

23 *Sub Pop USA* column of January 1985, ibid., p. 268.

24 See, for example, the *Sub Pop USA* column of February 1988, in which Malfunkshun are identified as the 'godfathers of the whole heavy glam scene'; reprinted ibid., p. 377.

25 *Sub Pop USA* column of April 1986, ibid., p. 313.

26 See Waksman, *This Ain't the Summer of Love*, pp. 289–90.

27 Prato, *Grunge Is Dead*, pp. 82–92, supplies numerous recollections of Malfunkshun that reinforce these points.

28 Anderson, 'White Noise', p. 25.

29 Waksman, *This Ain't the Summer of Love*, p. 250.

30 See Hanzsek as quoted in Stephen Tow, *The Strangest Tribe: How a Group of Seattle Rock Bands Invented Grunge* (Seattle, WA, 2011), p. 124; and in Yarm, *Everybody Loves Our Town*, p. 107.

31 As quoted in Yarm, *Everybody Loves Our Town*, p. 127.

32 Booklet for *Sub Pop 200* (SP25, December 1988), inside cover.

33 Dawn Anderson, 'It May Be the Devil and It May Be the Lord . . . But It Sure as Hell Ain't Human', *Backlash* (August–September 1988), p. 8.

34 For 'Mexican Seafood', see the 7″ compilation *Teriyaki Asthma*, v. 1 (C/Z Records, CZ009, 1989).

35 Everett True, 'Sub Pop. Seattle: Rock City', *Melody Maker*, 18 March 1989, pp. 26–7. Also, Tomasso Schultze's interview with Jason Everman in the German fanzine *Trust*, 19 (September 1989), available at www. livenirvana.com, accessed 1 May 2022.

36 See Pavitt, *Sub Pop USA*, pp. 341, 346 and 355, respectively. Emphasis in original.

37 Justin Henderson, *Grunge: Seattle*, rev. edn (Berkeley, CA, 2016), p. 38; Tow, *The Strangest Tribe*, p. 41; Gillian G. Gaar, *World Domination: The Sub Pop Records Story* (New York, 2018), pp. 46–7.

38 John Peel, 'Pop', *The Observer*, 29 January 1989, p. 48.

39 See Dawn Anderson et al., 'The Champs and Chumps of '88'; and Veronika Kalmar, 'Sub Pop 200 (Sub Pop)', *Backlash* (December 1988), pp. 5 and 7.

40 Adam Block, 'Of Grammys, Godheads, and Dry Dreams', *The Advocate* (28 March 1989), p. 47. Emphasis in original.

41 Simon Reynolds, 'Various Artists: *Sub Pop 200*', *Melody Maker*, 25 February 1989, p. 29. Emphases in original.

42 Waksman, *This Ain't the Summer of Love*, pp. 274 and 298.

43 As quoted in Yarm, *Everybody Loves Our Town*, p. 46.

44 Everett True, 'Ten Myths about Grunge, Nirvana and Kurt Cobain', *The Guardian*, 24 August 2011, p. 22.

45 Catherine Strong, *Grunge: Music and Memory* (Abingdon, 2011), p. 110.

46 Jonathan Evison, 'Defining the "Seattle Sound" Once and for All', liner notes for the deluxe reissue of Green River's EP *Dry as a Bone* (Sub Pop, January 2019); Pavitt, as quoted in Michael Azerrad, *Our Band Could Be Your Life: Scenes from the American Indie Underground, 1981–1991* (New York City, 2001), p. 424; Everett True, *Live through This: American Rock Music in the Nineties* (London, 2001), p. 103.

47 Arnold, *On the Road to Nirvana*, pp. 164–5.

48 See Strong, *Grunge: Music and Memory*, p. 109.

49 From a 1988 interview reprinted as 'The Original Girl Trouble: Q&A with Bon Von Wheelie', *Tom Tom Mag* (September 2019), https://tomtommag.com, accessed 1 May 2022.

50 Lester Bangs, 'The White Noise Supremacists', *Village Voice*, 30 April 1979, www.villagevoice.com, accessed 1 May 2022.

51 Ibid.

52 Jim Puccio, 'Seattle Syndrome Two', *Boston Rock*, 38 (March 1983), p. 37.

53 Arnold, *On the Road to Nirvana*, p. 302.

54 Ibid., p. 164.

55 See *Sub Pop* #2, in Pavitt, *Sub Pop USA*, p. 78; also *Sub Pop* #4, ibid., p. 131.

56 On, for example, the back of the label series *Dope-Guns-'N-Fucking in the Streets* (from catalogue number Scale 12, 1988 onwards).

57 As quoted in Prato, *Grunge Is Dead*, p. 98.

58 Arnold, *On the Road to Nirvana*, p. 302.

59 See Rupa Huq, *Beyond Subculture: Pop, Youth and Identity in a Postcolonial World* (Abingdon, 2006), pp. 135–41.

60 Terri Sutton, 'The Soft Boys: The New Man in Rock', in *Trouble Girls: The Rolling Stone Book of Women in Rock*, ed. Barbara O'Dair (New York, 1997), p. 529.

61 Strong, *Grunge: Music and Memory*, p. 107.

62 As quoted in Dawn Anderson, 'TAD: Mountain Man or Man Mountain?', *Backlash* (April 1989), p. 7.

3 Lamestains

1 Jonathan Poneman, liner notes to Blood Circus, *Primal Rock Therapy: Sub Pop Recordings: '88–'89* (CD release, SP177B; November 1992).

2 Everett True, 'Sub Pop. Seattle: Rock City', *Melody Maker*, 18 March 1989, p. 26.

3 Simon Reynolds, 'Various Artists: *Sub Pop 200*', *Melody Maker*, 25 February 1989, p. 29.

4 Everett True, 'Sub Pop, Sub Normal, Subversion: Mudhoney', *Melody Maker*, 11 March 1989, p. 28.

5 As quoted in Veronika Kalmar, 'Blood Circus: My Riff's Bigger', *Backlash* (June–July 1988), p. 5.

6 Everett True, 'Soundgarden: The Mutate Gallery', *Melody Maker*, 10 June 1989, p. 10.

7 John Robb, 'White Noise White Heat', *Sounds*, 21 October 1989, p. 18.

8 True, 'Soundgarden: The Mutate Gallery'.

9 As cited in Kit Boss, 'Young, Loud and Snotty – All Right, Who Are These Local Guys Who Have the Avant-Garde Music Press Swooning? Read On . . .', *Seattle Times*, 24 August 1989, p. F1.

10 Rick Marin, 'Grunge: A Success Story', *New York Times*, 15 November 1992, p. 9. See also the retrospective in Alan Siegel, 'When Grunge was Fake News', *The Ringer*, 8 November 2017, www.theringer.com, accessed 1 May 2022.

11 On 'visual rhyme' in collectorship, see Brenda Danet and Tamar Katriel, 'No Two Alike: Play and Aesthetics in Collecting', in *Interpreting Objects and Collections*, ed. Susan M. Pearce (London, 1994), pp. 227–8.

12 The insert cited here was included in, for example, the Meat Puppets' *Huevos* (sst 150, October 1987).

13 In Johnson's essay '"You're in Charge"', in Pavitt, *Sub Pop USA: The Subterranean Pop Music Anthology, 1980–1988* (New York, 2015), p. 135.

14 See Thomas K. Fitzpatrick, *The Blood Circus* (London, 1975).

15 Quoted in Boss, 'Young, Loud and Snotty'.

16 *Sub Pop USA* columns of September 1987 and January 1988, in *Sub Pop USA: The Subterranean Pop Music Anthology, 1980–1988* (New York, 2015), pp. 364 and 375.

17 Shaw, 'Iron Butterfly: *Scorching Beauty*', *Phonograph Record* (February 1975), available at www.rocksbackpages.com, accessed 1 May 2022.

18 From Part 1 of Dan Sauter's interview with the Blood Circus guitarist Geoff Robinson for the *Music-Life-Radio* podcast, 15 April 2012, www.musicliferadio.com, *c.* 47:00, accessed 1 May 2022.

19 Steve Waksman, *This Ain't the Summer of Love: Conflict and Crossover in Heavy Metal and Punk* (Berkeley and Los Angeles, CA, 2009), p. 250.

20 Michael Azerrad, *Our Band Could Be Your Life: Scenes from the American Indie Underground, 1981–1991* (New York, 2001), p. 421.

21 Quoted in Cynthia Rose, 'Sub Pop: See Label for Details – An Interview with Bruce Pavitt', *Dazed and Confused* (1994), available at www.rocksbackpages.com, accessed 14 September 2022.

22 From 'The CP legend continues' by user Jambosalta, September 2015, review of Charles Peterson, *Touch Me I'm Sick*, www.amazon.co.uk, accessed 1 May 2022.

23 As quoted in Jennifer Maerz, 'Fly off the Wall', *The Stranger*, 23 October 2003, www.thestranger.com, accessed 1 May 2022.

24 As quoted in Arnold, *On the Road to Nirvana*, p. 217.

25 As quoted in Michael Azerrad, 'Introduction', in *Screaming Life: A Chronicle of the Seattle Music Scene* (New York, 1995), p. 20.

26 'Technophallus' is from Steve Waksman, *Instruments of Desire: The Electric Guitar and the Shaping of Musical Experience* (Cambridge, MA, 2001), for example p. 188.

27 Waksman, *This Ain't the Summer of Love*, p. 248.

28 Quoted in Maerz, 'Fly off the Wall'.

29 Pavitt as quoted in Azerrad, 'Introduction', p. 23.

30 Arnold, *On the Road to Nirvana*, p. 214.

31 Clark Humphrey, *Loser: The Real Seattle Music Story* [1995] (Seattle, WA, 2016), p. 166. See also Cobain's interview with Everett True titled 'In My Head I'm So Ugly', *Melody Maker*, 18 July 1992, p. 24.

32 Art Chantry, *Art Chantry Speaks: A Heretic's History of 20th-Century Graphic Design*, ed. Monica René Rochester (New York, 2015), p. 6.

33 Back of original vinyl release of Reverend Horton Heat, *Smoke 'Em if You Got 'Em* (SP96, November 1990).

34 Chantry, *Art Chantry Speaks*, p. 6.

35 Azerrad, 'Introduction', p. 14; and Justin Henderson, *Grunge: Seattle*, rev. edn (Berkeley, CA, 2016), p. 36.

36 David Hepworth, *A Fabulous Creation: How the LP Saved Our Lives* (London, 2019), p. 243.

37 Michael Azerrad, 'Seven Inches of Pleasure', *Rolling Stone*, 4 February 1993, p. 18.

38 Joe Bonomo, 'Number 4', *No Such Thing as Was*, 21 March 2019, www.nosuchthingaswas.com, accessed 1 May 2022.

39 Alison Piepmeier, 'Why Zines Matter: Materiality and the Creation of Embodied Community', *American Periodicals*, XVIII/2 (2008), p. 235.

40 There is endless variation in how these messages are written: while many are hand-etched, some are in capitals, some are in joined-up lower-case, and some are a mixture of both cases; some have quotation marks around them. I have standardized them here, while keeping spelling errors and most punctuation.

41 See Dawn Anderson, 'Signin' on the Dotted Line, and Other Tales of Terror', *Backlash* (March 1991), p. 2.

42 Quoted in Everett True, 'Nirvana: Bleached Wails', *Melody Maker*, 21 October 1989, p. 47.

43 Mimmo Caccamo, 'London Calling' on Radio Onde Furlane, 27 October 1989, available at www.livenirvana.com, accessed 1 May 2022.

4 A Collector's Label

1 See, for example, Dawn Anderson's editorial 'Backwash' for *Backlash* (March 1989), p. 2. Also Jack Endino's T-shirt in the image on the back of the self-titled CD *Endino's Earthworm* (Cruz Records, CRZ CD 021, 1992). The 'Manzine' included with the first five hundred copies of TAD's *God's Balls* gives the label name as 'Sob Pup'.

2 Gillian G. Gaar, *World Domination: The Sub Pop Records Story* (New York, 2018), p. 40; and Gina Arnold, *On the Road to Nirvana* (London, 1998), p. 46.

3 Michael Azerrad, *Our Band Could Be Your Life: Scenes from the American Indie Underground, 1981–1991* (New York, 2001), p. 436.

4 See Steven Wells, 'Espresso Way to Your Skull', *New Musical Express*, 18 July 1992, p. 47.

5 Naomi Klein, *No Logo* (London, 2005), p. 47.

6 From Lena Jordebo's interview with Nirvana for the Swedish radio station P3, 27 October 1989, available at www.livenirvana.com, accessed 1 May 2022.

7 As quoted in Anne Filson and Laura Begley's interview, 'Long Haired Nirvana Guy Shaves Head!', 27 April 1990, for *Dirt* fanzine (1990), available at www.livenirvana.com, accessed 1 May 2022.

8 As quoted in Rupert Frisby's interview 'Apathy in the UK', *Lime Lizard* (April 1991), p. 38.

9 Mimmo Caccamo, 'London Calling' on Radio Onde Furlane, 27 October 1989, available at www.livenirvana.com, accessed 1 May 2022.

10 Grant Alden, 'Sub Plop?', *The Rocket* (August 1991), p. 22.

11 Edwin Pouncey, 'Put Mud in the Music', *New Musical Express*, 27 May 1989, p. 22.

12 John Robb, 'White Noise White Heat', *Sounds*, 21 October 1989, p. 18.

13 See the interview with Grant Alden, February 1990, available at www.livenirvana.com, accessed 1 May 2022.

14 See, for example, Arnold, *On the Road to Nirvana*, p. 47, on Lisa Fancher, the founder of Frontier Records.

15 Here I draw on Will Straw, 'Sizing Up Record Collections', in *Sexing the Groove: Popular Music and Gender*, ed. Sheila Whiteley (London, 1997), pp. 3–16.

16 Ibid., p. 5.

17 Nick Hornby, *High Fidelity* (London, 2000), p. 48.

18 This definition of 'nerdishness' is from Straw, 'Sizing Up Record Collections', p. 8.

19 See two essays on the practice of collecting: Brenda Danet and Tamar Katriel, 'No Two Alike: Play and Aesthetics in Collecting', in *Interpreting Objects and Collections*, ed. Susan M. Pearce (London, 1994), pp. 220–39; and, in the same volume, Russell W. Belk and Melanie Wallendorf, 'Of Mice and Men: Gender Identity in Collecting', pp. 240–53.

20 Tad as interviewed by Ed Sullivan and Rob B., 'Tad/Nirvana/Mudhoney/Sub Pop', *Ugly American*, 4 (Winter 1989), www.uglyamericanzine.com, accessed 1 May 2022. See also Bill Reid, KITS Radio interview with Nirvana, 28 January 1990, available at www.livenirvana.com, accessed 1 May 2022.

21 As quoted in Arnold, *On the Road to Nirvana*, p. 217.

22 David Hepworth, *A Fabulous Creation: How the LP Saved Our Lives* (London, 2019), p. 223.

23 Quotations from ibid., pp. 223–4.

24 Mike McGonigal, 'Colored Vinyl Is For Big, Spoiled Record Babies', *Detroit Metro Times*, 3 February 2015.

25 See, for example, the discussion 'True Colors' in the Discogs blog, 18 April 2019, https://blog.discogs.com, accessed 1 May 2022.

26 Hepworth, *A Fabulous Creation*, p. 223.

27 Quotations from ibid., p. 224.

28 In Bob Gulla's interview with Nirvana from cdnow.com, 18–28 May 1999, available at www.livenirvana.com, accessed 1 May 2022.

29 John Pette at Pette Discographies, describing Poison Idea's *Taken by Surprise* (SP86), www.pettediscographies.com, accessed 1 May 2022.

30 Mark Shafer, 'An Electric Fence', WAIF Radio, 6 October 1989, available at www.livenirvana.com, accessed 1 May 2022.

31 Clark Humphrey, *Loser: The Real Seattle Music Story* [1995] (Seattle, WA, 2016), p. 138.

32 Alden, 'Sub Plop?', p. 21.

33 Michael Azerrad, 'Seven Inches of Pleasure', *Rolling Stone*, 4 February 1993, p. 18.

34 This is conventional wisdom; the Classic 45s website makes an informed argument for it at 'The Joy of 45 Collecting: Why 45s Sound Better than LPs', www.classic45s.com, accessed 1 May 2022.

35 Pete Paphides, 'Seven Inches of Heaven', *The Guardian*, 16 November 2002, Weekend Supplement, p. 54.

36 As quoted in Azerrad, 'Seven Inches of Pleasure'.

37 As quoted in Mark Yarm, *Everybody Loves Our Town: A History of Grunge* (London, 2011), p. 130.

38 See Danet and Tamar, 'No Two Alike', p. 226, on 'instant collectables'. For Sub Pop Singles Club vol. 5, see www.subpop.com, accessed 1 May 2022.

39 As quoted in Yarm, *Everybody Loves Our Town*, p. 128.

40 Poneman attributes this text to Pavitt in Greg Prato, *Grunge Is Dead: The Oral History of Seattle Rock Music* (Toronto, 2009), p. 132.

41 Everett True, 'The Damenbusters', *Melody Maker*, 7 January 1989, p. 30.

42 Inner sleeve of Nirvana/The Melvins, *Here She Comes Now/Venus in Furs* (Communion Comm 23, June 1991).

43 As quoted in Nick Jones, 'Smashing Pumpkins: Fuck Off... We're from CHICAGO!', *Spiral Scratch*, 9–23 January 1992, p. 2.

44 As quoted in Prato, *Grunge Is Dead*, p. 133.

45 See 'Ramones – Carbona Not Glue b/w I Can't Be', www.discogs.com, accessed 1 May 2022.

46 Tad's words, in the interview with *Ugly American*, 4 (Winter 1989).

47 See the Sub Pop podcast Season 3 Episode 1, 'The New Brunswick Connection', 23 May 2017, http://subpop.fm, accessed 1 May 2022.

48 Grant Alden, interview with Nirvana, February 1990, available at www.livenirvana.com, accessed 15 September 2022.

49 For the Walkabouts' own reflections on this mismatch, see Grant Alden, 'The Walkabouts Take On Folk, Psychedelia and the World', *The Rocket* (June 1989), p. 13.

50 See ibid.; see also Dan Sauter's interview with Geoff Robinson for the *Music-Life-Radio* podcast, 15 April 2012, www.musicliferadio.com, Part 2, 26:00, accessed 1 May 2022.

51 Dawn Anderson, 'It May Be the Devil and It May Be the Lord . . . But It Sure as Hell Ain't Human', *Backlash* (August–September 1988), p. 8.

52 As quoted in the PBS documentary *Remarkable People Making a Difference in the Northwest: At Home with Sub Pop* (prod. Jean Walkinshaw, 1993), at 3:40.

53 As quoted in Yarm, *Everybody Loves Our Town*, p. 128.

54 See Steve Turner's estimate in Mike LaVella's interview with Mudhoney in *Maximumrocknroll* (August 1990), available at www.ocf.berkeley.edu, accessed 1 May 2022.

55 See the footage in the deleted scene 'Lame Fest '89: Lame Security' from the Mudhoney documentary *I'm Now: The Story of Mudhoney* (dir. Pease and Short, 2012), www.youtube.com, accessed 1 May 2022.

56 Paul de Barros, 'War Upstages Music at Lamefest '89 Concert', *Seattle Times*, 12 June 1989, p. D5.

57 Ibid.

58 Patrick MacDonald, 'Acts at Backstage to Preview Upcoming Albums', *Seattle Times*, 16 June 1989, p. 8.

5 Here Comes Sickness: Mudhoney

1 See Patrick MacDonald, 'The Dead Kennedys Stay Alive Musically', *Seattle Times*, 19 October 1984, p. 12; and the reminiscence in Mark Yarm, *Everybody Loves Our Town: A History of Grunge* (London, 2011), p. 51.

2 Steve Waksman, *This Ain't the Summer of Love: Conflict and Crossover in Heavy Metal and Punk* (Berkeley and Los Angeles, CA, 2009), p. 251.

3 Michael Azerrad, 'Introduction', in *Screaming Life: A Chronicle of the Seattle Music Scene* (New York, 1995), p. 23.

4 Waksman, *This Ain't the Summer of Love*, p. 294.

5 See, as one example of many, Greg Chapman's account of a Mudhoney and Monster Magnet show in Trenton, New Jersey, in December 1991: 'Mark Arm threw up a couple of times on stage, but I missed it because I was up in th[e] band room drinking the rest of their alcohol. Another night passes by in a drunken blur . . .'. See *Ugly American*, 7 (Winter 1991), www.uglyamericanzine.com, accessed 1 May 2022.

6 In a letter to *Desperate Times*, 1/2 (22 July 1981), reprinted in Maire M. Masco, *Desperate Times: The Summer of 1981: The Complete Reprint of the Seattle Underground Newspaper 'Desperate Times' with Commentary and Indexes* (Tacoma, WA, 2015), p. 43.

7 From the Sub Pop catalogue insert of mid-1988.

8 Sub Pop catalogue inserts of mid-1988 and early 1990 respectively.

9 Yarm, *Everybody Loves Our Town*, p. xiv.

10 Michael Azerrad, *Our Band Could Be Your Life: Scenes from the American Indie Underground, 1981–1991* (New York, 2001), p. 426.

11 See Creswell, '"Touch Me I'm Sick": Contagion as Critique in Punk and Performance Art', in *GenXegesis: Essays on 'Alternative' Youth (Sub) Culture*, ed. John M. Ulrich and Andrea L. Harris (Madison, WI, 2003), p. 86. Also Virginia Berridge, 'AIDS, the Media and Health Policy', in *AIDS: Rights, Risk and Reason*, ed. Peter Aggleton, Peter Davies and Graham Hart (London, 1992), pp. 13–27.

12 Gina Arnold, *On the Road to Nirvana* (London, 1998), p. 163.

13 From the Sub Pop catalogue insert of early 1990.

14 As one example, see Dawn Anderson's mention of the Northwest AIDS Foundation benefit of early 1990, in 'Backwash', *Backlash* (February 1990), p. 4.

15 Creswell, '"Touch Me I'm Sick"', p. 85.

16 See Anderson's 'Scene Drool', *Backlash* (August–September 1988), p. 11.

17 Tim Cronin, 'Sylvia Juncosa, Soundgarden, Mudhoney', *Ugly American*, 3 (1988), www.uglyamericanzine.com, accessed 1 May 2022.

18 See J. R. Higgins, 'Mudhoney: No Nonsense Seattle Supergrunge', *Backlash* (December 1988), p. 1. See also Dave Porter, 'Count Them, Please', *Seattle Times*, 8 January 1989, p. L2; and Michael Azerrad, 'Seven Inches of Pleasure', *Rolling Stone*, 4 February 1993, p. 18.

19 As quoted in Timothy White, 'What Do Joey Ramone's Mum and Dad Think of Their Little Boy? . . .', *Sounds*, 3 February 1979, p. 26.

20 Melvins/Steel Pole Bath Tub, 'Sweet Young Thing Ain't Sweet No More/I Dreamed I Dream' (Boner Records, BR21, 1990).

21 See the back of Cat Butt's first single *64 Funny Cars* (Penultimate, August 1988) and the slogan 'grungedelic fuel injected suicide'.

22 See the Mr Epp and the Calculations live recording *Live As All Get Out!* (Deus Ex Machina, 1983). Also Veronika Kalmar, '*Sub Pop 200* (Sub Pop)', *Backlash* (December 1988), p. 7.

23 Everett True, 'Sub Pop, Sub Normal, Subversion: Mudhoney', *Melody Maker*, 11 March 1989, p. 29. True's emphasis.

24 Patrick MacDonald, 'Mudhoney (Who?) Leapfrogs from Obscurity to Fame', *Seattle Times*, 24 March 1989, p. 8.

25 True, 'Sub Pop, Sub Normal, Subversion: Mudhoney', p. 29.

26 The first quote is from ibid., p. 29. The second is from James Rotondi, 'Steve Turner Turns on the Fuzz Gun', *Guitar Player* (February 1992), p. 98.

27 From a Sub Pop press release on Mudhoney for their second full-length record *Every Good Boy Deserves Fudge* (Sub Pop SP105, 1991).

28 Quote from Dan Sauter's interview with the Blood Circus guitarist Geoff Robinson for the *Music-Life-Radio* podcast, 15 April 2012, www.musicliferadio.com, Part 1, 43:40, accessed 1 May 2022.

29 True, 'Sub Pop, Sub Normal, Subversion: Mudhoney', p. 29.

30 As quoted in Gillian G. Gaar, *World Domination: The Sub Pop Records Story* (New York, 2018), p. 37.

31 On Berlin Independence Days, see John Rockwell, 'Berlin Rocks as Musical Walls Come Down', *New York Times*, 17 November 1993, p. C9.

32 See the interview with Matt Emery, 6 January 1990, transcribed at www.livenirvana.com, accessed 1 May 2022.

33 Azerrad, *Our Band Could Be Your Life*, p. 417.

34 As recalled by Thurston Moore of Sonic Youth in Alec Foege, *Confusion Is Next: The Sonic Youth Story* (London, 1995), p. 215.

35 See Roy Wilkinson, 'A Load of Tony Baloney', *Sounds*, 1 September 1990, p. 16; and the Nirvana interview with 'Joe' in Leeds, 25 October 1990, available at www.livenirvana.com, accessed 1 May 2022.

36 Keith Cameron, *Mudhoney: The Sound and the Fury from Seattle* (London, 2013), p. 117.

37 As quoted in Greg Prato, *Grunge Is Dead: The Oral History of Seattle Rock Music* (Toronto, 2009), p. 137. On Sonic Youth's intellectual side, which jarred against Mudhoney and Sub Pop, see the documentary film *I'm Now: The Story of Mudhoney* (dir. Adam Pease and Ryan Short, 2012), at 44:00.

38 On critical respect for Gordon, see for example Christina Kelly, 'Kim Gordon', in *Trouble Girls: The Rolling Stone Book of Women in Rock*, ed. Barbara O'Dair (New York, 1997), pp. 449–52.

39 As quoted in True, 'Sub Pop, Sub Normal, Subversion: Mudhoney', p. 28.

40 As quoted in Edwin Pouncey, 'Put Mud in the Music', *New Musical Express*, 27 May 1989, p. 22.

41 See also Sonic Youth's first network TV appearance, on the NBC show *Night Music* (1989), as recounted at 'The Sonic Youth Concert Chronology', www.sonicyouth.com, accessed 1 May 2022.

42 See the Mr Epp retrospective *Ridiculing the Apocalypse* (CD; Super Electro Sound Recordings, 1996).

43 Wilkinson, 'A Load of Tony Baloney', p. 16.

6 TAD: Heavier than Heaven

1 From the Sub Pop catalogue insert of mid-1988.

2 Sub Pop catalogue insert of early 1990.

3 See the documentary *TAD: Busted Circuits and Ringing Ears* (dir. Adam Pease and Ryan Short, 2008), at 8:30.

4 Ibid., at 21:20.

5 Ibid., at 7:40.

6 Ibid., at 20:10.

7 As quoted in Mark Yarm, *Everybody Loves Our Town: A History of Grunge* (London, 2011), p. 128.

8 Roy Wilkinson, 'Nirvana/TAD/The Cateran: London SOAS', *Sounds*, 4 November 1989, p. 41.

9 In an interview with Ed Sullivan and Rob B., 'Tad/Nirvana/ Mudhoney/Sub Pop', in *Ugly American*, 4 (Winter 1989), www.uglyamericanzine.com, accessed 1 May 2022.

10 I translate these quotations from Gutter Heijting, 'De bloem van Sub Pop: Nirvana & TAD', *Opscene* (February 1990), available at www.livenirvana.com, accessed 1 May 2022 [Dutch text].

11 Greg Prato, *Grunge Is Dead: The Oral History of Seattle Rock Music* (Toronto, 2009), p. 199. Emphasis in original.

12 Simon Price, 'Opening Time', *Melody Maker*, 9 December 1989, p. 27. Rees-Mogg was a journalist and ex-editor of *The Times*.

13 'TAD/Nirvana/Mudhoney/Sub Pop'.

14 Endino as quoted in Yarm, *Everybody Loves Our Town*, p. 142.

15 Clark Humphrey, *Loser: The Real Seattle Music Story* [1995] (Seattle, WA, 2016), p. 146.

16 As quoted in Keith Cameron, '10 Tours that Changed Music: Burn Baby Burn!', *Q* (March 2002), p. 92.

17 Quoted in Jim Mawdsley, 'The Fat Man Talks', *Boiling Point* (November 1989), available at www.livenirvana.com, accessed 1 May 2022.

18 Heijting, 'De bloem van Sub Pop'.

19 Everett True, 'Screaming Trees/TAD/Nirvana: Pine Street Theatre, Portland, USA', *Melody Maker*, 3 March 1990, p. 20.

20 As quoted in Stephen Tow, *The Strangest Tribe: How a Group of Seattle Rock Bands Invented Grunge* (Seattle, WA, 2011), p. 154.

21 As remembered by Tad in Prato, *Grunge Is Dead*, p. 200.

22 *TAD: Busted Circuits and Ringing Ears*, at 12:25 and 27:40.

23 Tow, *The Strangest Tribe*, p. 154.

24 *TAD: Busted Circuits and Ringing Ears*, at 10:10.

25 Veronika Kalmar, 'TAD: God's Balls', *Backlash* (April 1989), p. 9.

26 True, 'Screaming Trees/TAD/Nirvana: Pine Street Theatre, Portland, USA', p. 20.

27 As quoted in Dawn Anderson, 'TAD: Mountain Man or Man Mountain?', *Backlash* (April 1989), p. 6; and in Edwin Pouncey, 'Balling with God', *New Musical Express*, 2 September 1989, p. 8.

28 See Brian Jones, 'The Power of a Production Myth: PJ Harvey, Steve Albini, and Gendered Notions of Recording Fidelity', *Popular Music & Society*, xlix/3 (2019), pp. 354–5.

29 *TAD: Busted Circuits and Ringing Ears*, from 32:00. Also the interview with the band conducted by Dean Whitmore for the re-release of *Salt Lick* and included on the back of its insert poster (SP1178, 2016).

30 See 'TAD: God's Balls (Deluxe Edition)', *Sub Pop*, 4 November 2016, www.subpop.com, accessed 1 May 2022.

31 Anderson, 'TAD: Mountain Man or Man Mountain?', p. 7.

32 See Tad Doyle's artist statement, *Sub Pop* (2016), www.subpop.com, accessed 1 May 2022.

33 As quoted in Dean Whitmore's interview for the re-release of *Salt Lick* (SP1178, 2016).

34 As quoted in Anderson, 'TAD: Mountain Man or Man Mountain?', p. 7.

35 See the quotation from Kurt Danielson in Yarm, *Everybody Loves Our Town*, p. 142.

36 See Anderson, 'TAD: Mountain Man or Man Mountain?', p. 7.

37 In Ed Sullivan and Rob B., 'Tad/Nirvana/Mudhoney/Sub Pop'.

38 On grunge and 'Generation X', see Catherine Strong, *Grunge: Music and Memory* (Abingdon, 2011), pp. 134–7.

39 Bruce Pavitt, *Sub Pop* column (February 1987), reproduced in Pavitt, *Sub Pop USA: The Subterranean Pop Music Anthology, 1980–1988* (New York, 2015), p. 343. All emphases are Pavitt's own.

40 *Sub Pop* column (March 1988), ibid., p. 380. Pavitt's emphasis.

41 See, as one example of this anecdote, Bob Gulla's interview with Nirvana from cdnow.com, 18–28 May 1999, available at www.livenirvana.com, accessed 1 May 2022.

42 As quoted in Michael Azerrad, *Our Band Could Be Your Life: Scenes from the American Indie Underground, 1981–1991* (New York, 2001), p. 439.

43 Everett True, 'Sub Pop. Seattle: Rock City', *Melody Maker*, 18 March 1989, p. 26.

44 Everett True, 'Sub Pop, Sub Normal, Subversion: Mudhoney', *Melody Maker*, 11 March 1989, p. 28.

45 As recounted in the documentary film *I'm Now: The Story of Mudhoney* (dir. Adam Pease and Ryan Short, 2012), at 52:00.

46 See the interview with Jack Endino conducted by Dean Whitmore for the re-release of *God's Balls* (SP1177, 2016).

47 See Dean Whitmore's interview for the re-release of *Salt Lick*, and Ed Sullivan and Rob B., 'Tad/Nirvana/Mudhoney/Sub Pop'. See also Anderson, 'TAD: Mountain Man or Man Mountain?', p. 6.

48 This text from A-side label of Tad, *Daisy/Ritual Device* (SP19, August 1988). The strip of booth photos from which the label image is taken can be seen in Dawn Anderson, 'Scene Drool', *Backlash* (August–September 1988), p. 11.

49 Roy Wilkinson, 'Tad: *God's Balls* (Sub Pop SP27)', *Sounds*, 6 May 1989, p. 32.

50 Everett True, quoting a review of *Salt Lick* by Push, in 'The Larder They Come: TAD & Nirvana', *Melody Maker*, 17 March 1990, p. 12. Also Phil West, 'TAD: *Salt Lick* (SubPop)', *Backlash* (February 1990), p. 8.

51 See Whitmore, interview for the re-release of *Salt Lick*.

52 Wilkinson, 'Tad: *God's Balls* (Sub Pop SP27)', p. 32.

53 For the video of the live show in Mezzago, see 'Nirvana and Tad – Live at Bloom, Mezzago, Italy', www.youtube.com, accessed 1 May 2022.

54 For an example of this jam, see the beginning of the show at Issy-les-Moulineaux in December 1989, 'Nirvana – Tad Live at Fahrenheit Concerts', www.youtube.com, accessed 1 May 2022.

55 'God's Balls Review by Mark Deming', www.allmusic.com, accessed 1 May 2022.

56 West, 'TAD: *Salt Lick* (SubPop)', p. 8.

57 Wilkinson, 'Nirvana/TAD/The Cateran: London SOAS', p. 40.

58 Paul de Barros, 'War Upstages Music at Lamefest '89 Concert', *Seattle Times*, 12 June 1989, p. D5.

7 The Nirvana Victim

1 For the appraisal of value in 1989, see Nils Bernstein, 'Berlin Is Just a State of Mind', *The Rocket* (December 1989), p. 14.

2 Dawn Anderson, 'It May Be the Devil and It May Be the Lord . . . But It Sure as Hell Ain't Human', *Backlash* (August–September 1988), p. 8.

3 See the chapter title in Greg Prato, *Grunge Is Dead: The Oral History of Seattle Rock Music* (Toronto, 2009), pp. 152–73, itself a quotation from a remark made by Jeff Gilbert. Also Robert Allen, 'Welcome to Nirvana's Nightmare', *Backlash* (June 1989), p. 12.

4 As quoted in Prato, *Grunge Is Dead*, p. 161.

5 Roy Wilkinson, 'Nirvana/TAD/The Cateran: London SOAS', *Sounds* (4 November 1989), p. 41.

6 As quoted in Prato, *Grunge Is Dead*, p. 196.

7 As quoted in Rupert Frisby's interview 'Apathy in the UK', *Lime Lizard* (April 1991), p. 38.

8 See Push, 'Nirvana: Heaven Can't Wait', *Melody Maker* (15 December 1990), p. 39.

9 As quoted in Christopher Sandford, *Kurt Cobain* (London, 1996), p. 132.

10 See Jon Pareles, 'Nirvana, the Band that Hates to Be Loved', *New York Times*, 14 November 1993, Section 2, p. 32.

11 Ed Sullivan, 'Nirvana – *Nevermind*', *Ugly American*, 4 (Winter 1989), www.uglyamericanzine.com, accessed 1 May 2022.

12 John Robb, 'On the Subs Bench', *Sounds* (22 April 1989), p. 19; and Phil West, 'Hair Swinging Neanderthals', *The Daily* [University of Washington], 5 May 1989, available at www.livenirvana.com, accessed 1 May 2022.

13 See Everman's interview with Tomasso Schultze, 'Nirvana', *Trust*, 19 (September 1989), available at www.livenirvana.com, accessed 1 May 2022, my translation.

14 Tim Perlich, 'Guitar Onslaught Nirvana's Promise', *Now* (12 April 1990), p. 25.

15 See Marlene Goldman's interview, 18 July 1989, transcribed at www.livenirvana.com; also Matt Emery's interview, 6 January 1990, transcribed at www.livenirvana.com, accessed 1 May 2022.

16 As quoted in Mike Gitter, 'Revenge of the Nerds', *Kerrang!* (24 August 1991), p. 16.

17 Dawn Anderson, 'Nirvana: Signin' on the Dotted Line, and Other Tales of Terror', *Backlash* (March 1991), p. 1; Tim Cronin, 'Nirvana – Bleach (Sub Pop)', *Ugly American*, 4 (Winter 1989), www. uglyamericanzine.com, accessed 1 May 2022.

18 Gutter Heijting, 'De bloem van Sub Pop: Nirvana & Tad', *Opscene* (February 1990), available at www.livenirvana.com, accessed 1 May 2022 [Dutch text]. My translation.

19 Bernd Bohrmann, 'TAD Nirvana', *Amok* (1989), available at www. livenirvana.com, accessed 1 May 2022 [German text]. My translation.

20 Sebastian Zabel, 'Sweet wie Hönig: Nirvana', *Spex* (December 1989), available at www.livenirvana.com, accessed 1 May 2022 [German text]. My translation.

21 See the interview by Colleen Cronin, Tyler Jarman and Dean Gein for WORT Radio, 7 April 1990, available at www.livenirvana.com, accessed 1 May 2022.

22 As quoted in Michael Deeds, 'Nirvana', *New Route*, 15 (December 1991), p. 18. See also Keith Cameron, 'Nirvana Be in My Gang?', *New Musical Express* (21 September 1991), p. 8.

23 Terms from bassist Krist Novoselic in an interview with Grant Alden in early 1990, transcribed at www.livenirvana.com, accessed 1 May 2022.

24 In the interview for *La Patasgnafara*, 26 November 1989, available at www.livenirvana.com, accessed 1 May 2022 [Italian text]. My translation.

25 From the Sub Pop catalogue insert of early 1990.

26 From part of a 1989 promotional kit posted by Chris Stout on the Pacific Northwest Music Archive Facebook page, 19 December 2020.

27 On the Posies and their imminent (and much-derided) signing to a major label, see 'Lashback' and 'Backwash' in *Backlash* (June 1989), p. 2. 'Feeding frenzy' is J. R. Higgins's term in the live review 'The Posies at the Attic, May 20', *Backlash* (June 1989), p. 11.

28 In the 1988 interview with *Nothing* magazine, available at www.livenirvana.com, accessed 1 May 2022.

29 See the interview with *Sniffin' Rock* fanzine (May 1991), available at www.livenirvana.com, accessed 1 May 2022. Also Cobain's interview with Everett True, 'In My Head I'm So Ugly', *Melody Maker* (18 July 1992), p. 24.

30 In the interview with Grant Alden, early 1990.

31 From an interview with Peter Atkinson, 'Nirvana's Earthly Goal: To Be Wildly Successful', *Record-Journal* (September 1991), available at www.livenirvana.com, accessed 1 May 2022.

32 Push, 'Nirvana: Heaven Can't Wait', p. 39.
33 Nick Soulsby, *Dark Slivers: Seeing Nirvana in the Shards of Incesticide* (London, 2012), p. 44.
34 See Gillian G. Gaar, 'Verse Chorus Verse: The Recording History of Nirvana', *Goldmine* (14 February 1997), available at www.nirvanaclub. com, accessed 14 September 2022.
35 See the Novoselic interview with *Feedback Factory Press* (October 1991), reproduced at www.livenirvana.com, accessed 1 May 2022. Also Ann Scanlon, 'Heaven Can Wait: Nirvana', *Melody Maker* (14 September 1991), p. 37.
36 See Gaar, 'Verse Chorus Verse'.
37 Everett True, 'The Larder They Come: TAD & Nirvana', *Melody Maker* (17 March 1990), p. 13.
38 On Cobain and the Beatles, see Mimmo Caccamo, 'London Calling' on Radio Onde Furlane, 27 October 1989, available at www. livenirvana.com, accessed 1 May 2022.
39 'Far-easternness [*Fernöstliches*]' is Tomasso Schultze's word, in the interview above.
40 Sam King, 'Down on the Bleach', *Sounds* (9 June 1990), p. 21.
41 Push, 'Nirvana: *Bleach* (Tupelo)', *Melody Maker* (19 August 1989), p. 35.
42 Joshua Clover, *1989: Bob Dylan Didn't Have This to Sing about* (Berkeley and Los Angeles, CA, 2009), p. 70 and p. 80.
43 Push, 'Nirvana: *Bleach* (Tupelo)', p. 35.
44 See Robb, 'On the Subs Bench', p. 19.
45 As quoted in Prato, *Grunge Is Dead*, p. 161.
46 See Gaar, 'Verse Chorus Verse', and Anderson, 'Nirvana: Signin' on the Dotted Line', p. 2.
47 As quoted in Krist Novoselic, 'Bleach: Krist Novoselic Interviews Chad Channing', *Seattle Weekly* (27 October 2009), www.seattleweekly. com, accessed 1 May 2022.
48 As quoted ibid.
49 See Prato, *Grunge Is Dead*, p. 279.
50 Clover, *1989*, pp. 76 and 79.
51 As quoted in Grant Alden, 'Tad: A Loser's Meditation on the Art of Noise', *The Rocket* (February 1991), p. 17.
52 Terri Sutton, 'The Soft Boys: The New Man in Rock', in *Trouble Girls: The Rolling Stone Book of Women in Rock*, ed. Barbara O'Dair (New York, 1997), p. 529.
53 Ibid., p. 528.
54 See Joe Preston's 1989 interview from *Matt Lukin's Legs*, available at www.livenirvana.com, accessed 1 May 2022.
55 Push, 'Nirvana: *Bleach* (Tupelo)', p. 35.
56 Walter Everett, *The Foundations of Rock: From 'Blue Suede Shoes' to 'Suite: Judy Blue Eyes'* (Oxford, 2009), p. 146.

57 'Nirvana – Mr. Moustache [Early Studio Demo]', www.youtube.com, accessed 1 May 2022.

58 Chuck Crisafulli, *Teen Spirit: The Stories behind Every Nirvana Song* (New York, 1996), p. 27.

59 Catherine J. Creswell, '"Touch Me I'm Sick": Contagion as Critique in Punk and Performance Art', in *GenXegesis: Essays on 'Alternative' Youth (Sub)Culture*, ed. John M. Ulrich and Andrea L. Harris (Madison, WI, 2003), p. 81.

60 Medwin Pregill, 'Pus Free Pop', *Columbia Spectator* (26 September 1991), p. 9.

61 As quoted in Gillian G. Gaar, *World Domination: The Sub Pop Records Story* (New York, 2018), p. 56.

62 See Steve Waksman, *This Ain't the Summer of Love: Conflict and Crossover in Heavy Metal and Punk* (Berkeley and Los Angeles, CA, 2009), pp. 252–3.

63 Martin Aston, 'Go Forth and Grunge', *Q* (October 1992), p. 29.

64 See Gina Arnold, 'Better Dead than Cool: Punk Philosophers Nirvana', *Option*, 42 (January–February 1992), p. 75; Anderson, 'Nirvana: Signin' on the Dotted Line', p. 1; also Grant Alden, 'Sub Plop?', *The Rocket* (August 1991), pp. 21–4; and Barbara Davies, 'Artist Developments: Dirt on Mudhoney', *Billboard* (21 November 1992), p. 22.

65 From the interview with Alden in early 1990; also Bernstein, 'Berlin Is Just a State of Mind', p. 14.

66 As quoted in Phil West, 'The Heaviest HUB Show in History', *The Daily* [University of Washington], 5 January 1990, p. 7A.

67 Ransom Edison, 'Blood Circus: Primal Rock Therapy', *Backlash* (January 1989), p. 8.

68 See Clover, *1989*, p. 76; and Catherine Strong, *Grunge: Music and Memory* (Abingdon, 2011), pp. 111–12, who also mentions Thurston Moore's label 'foxcore' for L7 and other women's grunge bands.

69 See, as one example, the use of 'grunge lite' in Everett True, *Live through This: American Rock Music in the Nineties* (London, 2001).

70 Everett True (as 'The Reverend True'), booklet essay for *Sub Pop Employee of the Month: Lutz R. Mastmeyer* (SP111/287, 1993).

71 See Susan Rees, 'Is This Bliss?', *Alternative Press*, 44 (January/February 1992), www.altpress.com, accessed 1 May 2022; also Dawn Anderson, 'Nirvana: "Sliver"/"Dive" (SubPop)', *Backlash* (November 1990), p. 13.

Epilogue: Maximal Listening

1 See the write-up at https://exploresea.org, accessed 1 May 2022.

2 Post of 25 August 2021 by Rodney Johnson, at www.facebook.com/hashtag/subpop, accessed 1 May 2022.

3 See 'Announcing Sub Pop on 7th, the New Retail Store from Sub Pop Records in Seattle's South Lake Union Neighborhood', *Sub Pop*, 25 January 2021, www.subpop.com/news, accessed 1 May 2022.

4 See Holly Kruse, 'Local Identity and Independent Music Scenes, Online and Off', *Popular Music and Society*, XXXIII/5 (2010), pp. 625–39.

5 As quoted in Gillian G. Gaar's report 'Swingin' on the Flippity Flop: Sub Pop 20', *Blurt Online*, 22 July 2008, accessed 1 May 2022.

6 See Ann Powers, 'Sub Pop's Silver Jubilee Celebrates 25 Years of Artisanal Music in Seattle', *The Record: Music News from NPR*, 15 July 2013, www.npr.org, accessed 1 May 2022.

7 See 'Sub Pop's 30th Anniversary – SPF 30', https://spf30.subpop.com, accessed 1 May 2022.

8 I refer to the two CD compilation volumes of *Stolar Tracks* (1992–3), described at www.discogs.com, accessed 1 May 2022.

9 Kurt Cobain, liner notes, *Incesticide* (Geffen/Sub Pop, DGCD-24504, 1992).

10 See the PBS documentary *Remarkable People Making a Difference in the Northwest: At Home with Sub Pop* (prod. Jean Walkinshaw, 1993), at 2:30.

11 As Dwarves' Blag Dahlia states, in Greg Prato, *Grunge Is Dead: The Oral History of Seattle Rock Music* (Toronto, 2009), p. 149.

12 Gillian G. Gaar, *World Domination: The Sub Pop Records Story* (New York, 2018), p. 116.

13 Matt Korvette, 'Deaf Wish' [n.d.], www.subpop.com, accessed 1 May 2022.

14 Ibid.

15 On these scholarships, see 'Think You're a Loser? Sub Pop Wants to Send You to College', *The Guardian*, 19 February 2016; see also 'The Sub Pop Loser Scholarship 2022', www.subpop.com, accessed 1 May 2022.

16 See 'Sub Pop Loser Edition FAQ', *Sub Pop*, 5 June 2012, www.subpop. com, accessed via Wayback Machine at https://archive.org/web; and 'The Helio Sequence – Negotiations', www.discogs.com, both accessed 1 May 2022.

17 See 'Sub Pop Singles Club Vol. 7 Is Now Open for Subscriptions', *Sub Pop*, 16 December 2021, www.subpop.com, accessed 1 May 2022.

18 As quoted in Mark Yarm, *Everybody Loves Our Town: A History of Grunge* (London, 2011), p. xv.

19 As quoted in Elizabeth Wurtzel, 'Mudhoney Can't Sell Out', *Musician* (January 1991), available at www.ocf.berkeley.edu, accessed 1 May 2022.

20 Gaar, 'Swingin' on the Flippity Flop: Sub Pop 20'.

21 Ed Sullivan and Rob B., 'Tad/Nirvana/Mudhoney/Sub Pop', in *Ugly American*, 4 (Winter 1989), www.uglyamericanzine.com, accessed 1 May 2022.

22 See *The Grunge Years* (SP112b, 1991).

23 PBS, *Remarkable People Making a Difference in the Northwest: At Home with Sub Pop*, at 14:00.

24 Jonathan Poneman, booklet note for *Sub Pop 1000* (2013).

25 Ibid.

26 This particular instance from the end of Gaar, 'Swingin' on the Flippity Flop: Sub Pop 20'.

27 *Sub Pop* #1 (May 1980), reprinted in Bruce Pavitt, *Sub Pop USA: The Subterranean Pop Music Anthology, 1980–1988* (Brooklyn, NY, 2015), p. 22. Emphasis in the original.

28 See, for example, the report of the audience with Pavitt and Poneman at the Experience Music Project in Gaar, 'Swingin' on the Flippity Flop: Sub Pop 20'.

29 Zachary Lipez, 'Jensen Ward on Iron Lung: Band, Label, and Worldview', *Bandcamp Daily*, 22 November 2016, https://daily.bandcamp.com, accessed 1 May 2022.

30 Apparently no longer available, however, as of 16 September 2022.

31 Rob Bonett, 'Rob Bonett from Useless Children Interviews Iron Lung', *Crawlspace*, 18 January 2013, https://crawlspacemagazine.com, accessed 1 May 2022.

32 As quoted in Gaar, *World Domination*, p. xvii.

33 'Genre-smashing' is Jenn Pelly's term from 'Review: Total Control – Typical System', *Pitchfork*, 26 June 2014, https://pitchfork.com, accessed 1 May 2022.

34 David Glickman, 'Peeled Opened and Shattered', *Impose Magazine* (2015), https://imposemagazine.com, accessed 1 May 2022.

35 Fred Pessaro, 'Don't Waste My Time: An Interview with Daniel Stewart of Total Control', *Vice Magazine*, 19 June 2016, www.vice.com, accessed 1 May 2022.

36 As quoted in Kevin Diers, 'Jensen Ward (Iron Lung, Innumerable Forms, Nasti)', *No Echo*, 29 January 2019, www.noecho.net, accessed 1 May 2022.

37 Lipez, 'Jensen Ward on Iron Lung: Band, Label, and Worldview'.

38 As quoted from the current Sub Pop CEO, Megan Jasper, in Gaar, *World Domination*, p. 138.

39 Steve Waksman, *This Ain't the Summer of Love: Conflict and Crossover in Heavy Metal and Punk* (Berkeley and Los Angeles, CA, 2009), p. 307.

DISCOGRAPHY

The following discography lists important recordings cited, directly and indirectly, in the present book. The Sub Pop ones are the original U.S. releases, with corresponding catalogue numbers (SP). But by no means all are the work of Sub Pop; other labels are indicated. The discography is organized loosely in chronological order, giving months where available, within categories that assume vinyl originals unless otherwise stated. For vinyl singles, both (or all) tracks are listed.

Many of these recordings, of course, have since become available on other media, though it is worth noting that not all of them are currently available on popular music streaming services. In a few cases the only real recourse is to find the original vinyl or tape, or to hope that someone has uploaded a recording of it to sharing platforms like YouTube.

Various Artist Collections

Life Elsewhere (Mr Brown, 1980)
Sub Pop #5 (cassette only; July 1981)
Seattle Syndrome (Engram, 1981)
Sub Pop #7 (cassette only; Spring 1982)
Sub Pop #9 (cassette only; June 1983)
Local Product (cassette only; Green Monkey, 1983)
What Syndrome? (cassette only; Deus Ex Machina, 1983)
Bands that Could Be God (Conflict, 1984)
The Sound of Young Seattle (cassette only; Dust Bunnie, 1984)
Deep Six (C/Z, March 1986)
Sub Pop 100 (SP10, September 1986)
Sub Pop 200 (SP25, December 1988)
Secretions (C/Z, 1988)
Fuck Me I'm Rich (Waterfront/Sub Pop, 1989)
Teriyaki Asthma, vol. I (7"; C/Z, 1989)
Tribute to Alice Cooper (2 × 7"; SP121, June 1991)
Smells Like Smoked Sausages (2 × 7"; SP140, February 1992)
Sassy (for *Sassy* magazine; SP171, October 1992)
Never Mind the Molluscs (2 × 7"; SP198, March 1993)

Sub Pop Employee of the Month: Lutz R. Mastmeyer (SP111/287, 1993)
Sub Pop 1000 (SP1000, April 2013)

EPs and LPs (also referred to as 'mini LPs' and 'mini albums')

Iggy and the Stooges, *Raw Power* (Columbia, February 1973)
Black Flag, *Damaged* (Unicorn/SST, November 1981)
Mr Epp and the Calculations, *Of Course I'm Happy. Why?* (7";
    Pravda, 1982)
The Visible Targets, *The Visible Targets* (Park Avenue, 1982)
Mr Epp and the Calculations, *Live As All Get Out!* (cassette only;
    Deus Ex Machina, 1983)
Sonic Youth, *Confusion Is Sex* (Neutral, 1983)
Green River, *Come on Down* (Homestead, 1985)
Gone, *Gone II – But Never Too Gone!* (SST, November 1986)
Das Damen, *Das Damen* (reissue; SST, 1986)
Head of David, *LP* (Blast First, 1986)
Killdozer, *Burl* (Touch and Go, 1986)
Dinosaur Jr, *You're Living All Over Me* (SST, July 1987)
Green River, *Dry as a Bone* (SP11, July 1987)
Soundgarden, *Screaming Life* (SP12, October 1987)
Green River, *Rehab Doll* (SP15, May 1988)
The Fluid, *Clear Black Paper* (SP16, May 1988)
Girl Trouble, *Hit It or Quit It* (K Records/Sub Pop SP20, September 1988)
Sonic Youth, *Daydream Nation* (Enigma/Blast First, October 1988)
Mudhoney, *Superfuzz Bigmuff* (SP21, November 1988)
L7, *L7* (Epitaph, 1988)
Das Damen, *Marshmellow Conspiracy* (SST, 1988)
Head of David, *Dustbowl* (Blast First, 1988)
Sir Mix-a-Lot, *Swass* (Nastymix, 1988)
Swallow, *Swallow* (Tupelo/Sub Pop SP24, March 1989)
TAD, *God's Balls* (SP27, March 1989)
The Walkabouts, *Cataract* (SP31, March 1989)
The Fluid, *Roadmouth* (SP36, June 1989)
Cat Butt, *Journey to the Center of* (SP41, August 1989)
Nirvana, *Bleach* (SP34, August 1989)
Nirvana, *Blew* (Tupelo, December 1989)
Mother Love Bone, *Shine* (Stardog, 1989)
Mudhoney, *Mudhoney* (SP44, 1989)
The Posies, *Failure* (PopLlama, 1989)
TAD, *Salt Lick* (SP49, February 1990)
Afghan Whigs, *Up in It* (SP60, April 1990)
Mark Lanegan, *The Winding Sheet* (SP61, May 1990)

The Reverend Horton Heat, *Smoke 'Em if You Got 'Em* (SP96, November 1990)

Dwarves, *Blood Guts and Pussy* (SP67, 1990)

L7, *Smell the Magic* (SP79, 1990)

Mudhoney, *Every Good Boy Deserves Fudge* (SP105, July 1991)

TAD, *8-Way Santa* (SP89, 1991)

The Sad and Lonelys, *The Sad and Lonelys* (Super Electro Sound Recordings, 1991)

Blood Circus, *Primal Rock Therapy* (SP22, December 1988; CD reissue as SP177B, November 1992)

Pond, *Pond* (SP186, February 1993)

Velocity Girl, *Copacetic* (SP196, March 1993)

Les Thugs, *As Happy as Possible* (CD; SP228b, October 1993)

Pigeonhed, *Pigeonhed* (CD; SP224b, December 1993)

Supersnazz, *Superstupid!* (SP209, May 1993)

Eric's Trip, *Songs about Chris* (2 × 7"; SP205, April 1993)

TAD, *Infrared Riding Hood* (CD; EastWest, April 1995)

Mr Epp, *Ridiculing the Apocalypse* (CD; Super Electro Sound Recordings, 1996)

Pissed Jeans, *Hope for Men* (SP730, June 2007)

Helio Sequence, *Negotiations* (SP910, September 2012)

METZ, *METZ* (SP1015, October 2012)

Total Control, *Typical System* (Iron Lung, June 2014)

Deaf Wish, *Pain* (SP1141, August 2015)

Afghan Whigs, *In Spades* (SP1150, May 2017)

Thomas Andrew Doyle, *Incineration Ceremony* (SP1249, April 2018)

Mudhoney, *Morning in America* (SP1325, September 2019)

Singles

The Chocolate Watchband, *Sweet Young Thing/Baby Blue* (Uptown, 1967)

The Stooges, *I Wanna Be Your Dog/1969* (Elektra, 1969)

Bette Midler, *The Rose/Stay with Me* (Atlantic, March 1980)

Neo Boys, *Never Comes Down/Give Me the Message/Rich Man's Dream* (Trap, 1980)

Dead Kennedys, *Holiday in Cambodia/Police Truck* (Optional, October 1980)

Minor Threat, *In My Eyes/Out of Step/Guilty of Being White/Steppin' Stone* (Dischord, December 1981)

Green River, *Together We'll Never/Ain't Nothin' to Do* (Tasque Force, 1986)

Soundgarden, *Hunted Down/Nothing to Say* (SP12a, June 1987)

Blood Circus, *Two Way Street/Six Foot Under* (SP13, May 1988)

Swallow, *Trapped/Guts* (SP14, May 1988)

Cat Butt, *64 Funny Cars/Hell's Half Acre* (Penultimate, August 1988)

Mudhoney, *Touch Me I'm Sick/Sweet Young Thing Ain't Sweet No More*
(SP18, August 1988)

TAD, *Daisy/Ritual Device* (SP19, August 1988)

Nirvana, *Love Buzz/Big Cheese* (SP23, November 1988)

Sonic Youth/Mudhoney, *Touch Me I'm Sick/Halloween* (SP26,
December 1988)

TAD/Pussy Galore, *Damaged I/Damaged II* (SP37, June 1989)

Das Damen, *Sad Mile/Making Time* (SP39, July 1989)

Love Battery, *Between the Eyes/Easter* (SP45, October 1989)

Skin Yard, *Start at the Top/Watch* (SP47, October 1989)

Fugazi, *Song #1/Joe #1/Break In* (SP52, December 1989)

L7, *Shove/Packin' a Rod* (SP58, January 1990)

TAD, *Loser/Cooking with Gas* (SP55, January 1990)

Dwarves, *She's Dead/Fuckhead* (SP50, February 1990)

Big Chief, *Chrome Helmet/Blowout Kit* (SP53, March 1990)

The Fluid, *Tin Top Toy/Tomorrow* (SP57, March 1990)

Lubricated Goat, *Meating My Head/20th Century Rake* (SP65,
April 1990)

Babes in Toyland, *House/Arriba* (SP66, May 1990)

Dickless, *I'm a Man/Saddle Tramp* (SP59, May 1990)

Dinosaur Jr, *The Wagon/Better than Gone* (SP61, June 1990)

Thee Headcoats, *Time Will Tell/Davey Crockett (Gabba-Hay!)* (SP71,
June 1990)

Nirvana, *Sliver/Dive* (SP73, September 1990)

Soundgarden, *Room a Thousand Years Wide/H.I.V. Baby* (SP83,
September 1990)

Dwarves, *Drug Store/Detention Girl/Astro Boy/Motherfucker* (SP81,
October 1990)

Mark Arm, *The Freewheelin' Mark Arm* (SP87, November 1990)

The Reverend Horton Heat, *Psychobilly Freakout/Baby You-Know-Who*
(SP96, December 1990)

Smashing Pumpkins, *Tristessa/La Dolly Vita* (SP90, December 1990)

Melvins/Steel Pole Bath Tub, *Sweet Young Thing Ain't Sweet No More/
I Dreamed I Dream* (Boner, 1990)

Melvins, *With Yo' Heart, Not Yo' Hands/Four Letter Woman/Anal Satan*
(Sympathy for the Record Industry, 1990)

The Fluid/Nirvana, *Candy/Molly's Lips* (SP97, January 1991)

Hole, *Dicknail/Burnblack* (SP93, March 1991)

Shonen Knife, *Neon Zebra/Bear Up Bison* (SP108, April 1991)

Nirvana/The Melvins and Buzzo, *Here She Comes Now/Venus in Furs*
(Communion, June 1991)

Love Battery, *Foot/Mr Soul* (SP135, November 1991)

Green Magnet School, *Singed/Slipper* (SP136, December 1991)

Ramones, *Carbona Not Glue/I Can't Be* (Unofficial, with Sub Pop branding and catalogue number SP666, 1991)

The Monkeywrench, *Bottle Up and Go/Cold Cold World/Out of Focus* (SP139, January 1992)

Big Chief, *One Born Every Minute/Lot Lizard* (SP229, August 1993)

Jale, *Cut: Promise/3 Days* (SP235, November 1993)

The Jesus Lizard/Nirvana, *Puss/Oh, the Guilt* (Touch and Go, 1993)

Hardship Post, *Slick Talking Jack/If I . . .* (SP262, November 1994)

Bully, *About a Girl/Turn to Hate* (SP1376, November 2020)

BIBLIOGRAPHY

Albini, Steve, 'Tired of Ugly Fat?', *Matter*, 5 (September 1983), p. 12
—, 'Tired of Ugly Fat?', *Matter*, 7 (February 1984), p. 13
Alden, Grant, 'The Walkabouts Take on Folk, Psychedelia and the World', *The Rocket* (June 1989), p. 13
—, 'Tad: A Loser's Meditation on the Art of Noise', *The Rocket* (February 1991), pp. 17–18
—, 'Sub Plop?', *The Rocket* (August 1991), pp. 21–4
Allen, Robert, 'Welcome to Nirvana's Nightmare', *Backlash* (June 1989), p. 12
Anderson, Dawn, 'White Noise: *Deep Six* (c/z Records)', *The Rocket* (June 1986), p. 25
—, 'It May Be the Devil and It May Be the Lord . . . But It Sure as Hell Ain't Human', *Backlash* (August–September 1988), p. 8
—, 'Scene Drool', *Backlash* (August–September 1988), p. 11
—, 'Backwash', *Backlash* (March 1989), p. 2
—, 'TAD: Mountain Man or Man Mountain?', *Backlash* (April 1989), pp. 6–7
—, 'Backwash', *Backlash* (June 1989), p. 2
—, 'Backwash', *Backlash* (February 1990), p. 4
—, 'Nirvana: "Sliver"/"Dive" (SubPop)', *Backlash* (November 1990), p. 13
—, 'Signin' on the Dotted Line, and Other Tales of Terror', *Backlash* (March 1991), p. 1
—, et al., 'The Champs and Chumps of '88', *Backlash* (December 1988), p. 5
Anderson, Kyle, *Accidental Revolution: The Story of Grunge* (New York, 2007)
Arnold, Gina, 'Better Dead than Cool: Punk Philosophers Nirvana', *Option*, 42 (January/February 1992), pp. 70–75
—, *On the Road to Nirvana* (London, 1998)
Aston, Martin, 'Go Forth and Grunge', *Q* (October 1992), pp. 28–9
Azerrad, Michael, 'Seven Inches of Pleasure', *Rolling Stone*, 4 February 1993, p. 18
—, *Our Band Could Be Your Life: Scenes from the American Indie Underground, 1981–1991* (New York, 2001)
—, *Come as You Are: The Story of Nirvana* (New York, 2001)
—, 'Come as You Are', *Mojo* (August 2008), pp. 92–7

Bangs, Lester, 'The White Noise Supremacists', *Village Voice*, 30 April 1979, available at www.villagevoice.com

Bannister, Matthew, *White Boys, White Noise: Masculinities and 1980s Indie Guitar Rock* (Aldershot, 2006)

Baumgarten, Mark, *Love Rock Revolution: K Records and the Rise of Independent Music* (Seattle, WA, 2012)

Belk, Russell W., and Melanie Wallendorf, 'Of Mice and Men: Gender Identity in Collecting', in *Interpreting Objects and Collections*, ed. Susan M. Pearce (London, 1994), pp. 240–53

Bernstein, Nils, 'Berlin Is Just a State of Mind', *The Rocket* (December 1989), p. 14

Berridge, Virginia, 'AIDS, the Media and Health Policy', in *AIDS: Rights, Risk and Reason*, ed. Peter Aggleton, Peter Davies and Graham Hart (London, 1992), pp. 13–27

Blecha, Peter, *Sonic Boom: The History of Northwest Rock, from 'Louie Louie' to 'Smells Like Teen Spirit'* (New York, 2009)

Block, Adam, 'Of Grammys, Godheads, and Dry Dreams', *The Advocate*, 28 March 1989, p. 47

Bohrmann, Bernd, 'TAD Nirvana', *Amok*, 15 November 1989, available at www.livenirvana.com [German text]

Bonett, Rob, 'Rob Bonett from Useless Children Interviews Iron Lung', *Crawlspace*, 18 January 2013, https://crawlspacemagazine.com

Bonomo, Joe, 'Number 4', *No Such Thing as Was*, 21 March 2019, www.nosuchthingaswas.com

Boss, Kit, 'Young, Loud and Snotty – All Right, Who Are These Local Guys Who Have the Avant-Garde Music Press Swooning? Read On . . .', *Seattle Times*, 24 August 1989, p. F1

Bourdieu, Pierre, *The Rules of Art: Genesis and Structure of the Literary Field*, trans. Susan Emanuel (Cambridge, 1996)

—, *The Field of Cultural Production: Essay on Art and Literature*, ed. Randal Johnson (New York, 1993)

Buckley, David, *R.E.M. Fiction: An Alternative Biography* (London, 2002)

Cameron, Keith, 'Screaming Trees: Fulham Greyhound', *Sounds*, 10 March 1990, p. 28

—, 'Nirvana/Melvins/Dwarves/Derelicts: Seattle Motorsports International Garage', *Sounds*, 13 October 1990, p. 28

—, 'Nirvana Be in My Gang?', *New Musical Express*, 21 September 1991, p. 16

—, 'L's Belles', *New Musical Express*, 28 March 1992, p. 28

—, '10 Tours that Changed Music: Burn Baby Burn!', *Q* (March 2002), pp. 92–3

—, 'Spirit of '88', *Mojo* (August 2008), pp. 80–91

—, *Mudhoney: The Sound and the Fury from Seattle* (London, 2013)

Chantry, Art, *Art Chantry Speaks: A Heretic's History of 20th-Century Graphic Design*, ed. Monica René Rochester (New York, 2015)

Chapman, Greg, 'Mudhoney/Monster Magnet', *Ugly American*, 7 (Winter 1991), available at www.uglyamericanzine.com

Chiesa, Guido, 'Interview with Kurt Cobain', *Rockerilla* (October 1989), available at www.livenirvana.com [Italian text]

Clover, Joshua, *1989: Bob Dylan Didn't Have This to Sing About* (Berkeley and Los Angeles, CA, 2009)

Cobain, Kurt, liner notes, *Incesticide* (Geffen/Sub Pop, DGCD-24504, 1992)

—, *Journals* (London, 2002)

Cohen, Jason, 'Strangely Famous in Greece, the Walkabouts Trace Their American Roots', *Option* (November 1995), available at www.rocksbackpages.com

Cox, Michael, 'Swallow (Tupelo/Sub Pop Import)', *Backlash* (April 1989), p. 9

Creswell, Catherine J., '"Touch Me I'm Sick": Contagion as Critique in Punk and Performance Art', in *GenXegesis: Essays on 'Alternative' Youth (Sub)Culture*, ed. John M. Ulrich and Andrea L. Harris (Madison, WI, 2003), pp. 79–102

Crisafulli, Chuck, *Teen Spirit: The Stories behind Every Nirvana Song* (New York, 1996)

Cronin, Tim, 'Sylvia Juncosa, Soundgarden, Mudhoney', *Ugly American*, 3 (1988), available at www.uglyamericanzine.com

—, 'Nirvana – Bleach (Sub Pop)', *Ugly American*, 4 (Winter 1989), available at www.uglyamericanzine.com

Cross, Charles R., *Heavier than Heaven: The Biography of Kurt Cobain* (London, 2001)

Dale, Pete, 'Are You Scared to Get Punky? Indie Pop, Fanzines and Punk Rock', in *Ripped, Torn and Cut: Pop, Politics and Punk Fanzines from 1976*, ed. The Subcultures Network (Manchester, 2018), pp. 170–88

Danet, Brenda, and Tamar Katriel, 'No Two Alike: Play and Aesthetics in Collecting', in *Interpreting Objects and Collections*, ed. Susan M. Pearce (London, 1994), pp. 220–39

Davies, Barbara, 'Artist Developments: Dirt on Mudhoney', *Billboard*, 21 November 1992, pp. 20 and 22

de Barros, Paul, 'War Upstages Music at Lamefest '89 Concert', *Seattle Times*, 12 June 1989, p. D5

Deeds, Michael, 'Nirvana', *New Route*, 15 (December 1991), pp. 18–19

Diers, Kevin, 'Interview with Jensen Ward', *No Echo*, 29 January 2019, www.noecho.net

Duncombe, Stephen, *Notes from Underground: Zines and the Politics of Alternative Culture* (London, 1997)

Edison, Ransom, 'Blood Circus: Primal Rock Therapy', *Backlash* (January 1989), p. 8

Everett, Walter, *The Foundations of Rock: From 'Blue Suede Shoes' to 'Suite: Judy Blue Eyes'* (Oxford, 2009)

Evison, Jonathan, 'Defining the "Seattle Sound" Once and for All', liner
 notes for the reissue of Green River's EP *Dry as a Bone* (Sub Pop,
 SP1261, January 2019)
faris, marc, '"That Chicago Sound": Playing with (Local) Identity in Under-
 ground Rock', *Popular Music and Society*, XXVII/4 (2004), pp. 429–54
Filson, Anne, and Laura Begley, 'Long Haired Nirvana Guy Shaves Head!
 National Hysteria Ensures, Nirvana Keeps On Going', *Dirt* (1990),
 available at www.livenirvana.com
Fitzpatrick, Thomas K., *The Blood Circus* (London, 1975)
Foege, Alec, *Confusion Is Next: The Sonic Youth Story* (London, 1995)
Fricke, David, 'Kurt Cobain', *Rolling Stone* (27 January 1994), pp. 34–8
Frisby, Rupert, 'Apathy in the UK', *Lime Lizard* (April 1991), pp. 36–8
Frith, Simon, *Sound Effects: Youth, Leisure, and the Politics of Rock 'n' Roll*
 (London, 1983)
—, *Performing Rites: Evaluating Popular Music* (Oxford, 1996)
Gaar, Gillian G., 'Verse Chorus Verse: The Recording History of Nirvana',
 Goldmine (14 February 1997), available at www.nirvanaclub.com
—, 'Swingin' on the Flippity Flop: Sub Pop 20', *Blurt Online*, 22 July 2008
—, *World Domination: The Sub Pop Records Story* (New York, 2018)
Gitter, Mike, 'Revenge of the Nerds', *Kerrang!* (24 August 1991), pp. 16–17
Glickman, David, 'Peeled Opened and Shattered', *Impose Magazine* (2015),
 https://imposemagazine.com
Goddard, Simon, *Simply Thrilled: The Preposterous Story of Postcard Records*
 (London, 2014)
Goldberg, Michael, 'Rock 'n' Roll Fanzines: A New Underground Press
 Flourishes', *Rolling Stone* (29 March 1984), p. 57
Gordon, Kim, *Girl in a Band: A Memoir* (New York, 2015)
Guardian Music, 'Think You're a Loser? Sub Pop Wants to Send You to
 College', *The Guardian*, 19 February 2016
Hafitz, Michael, 'Tape Reporter', *Boston Rock*, 26 (February 1982), p. 31
Hebdige, Dick, *Subculture: The Meaning of Style* (London, 1979)
Heijting, Gutter, 'De bloem van Sub Pop: Nirvana and Tad', *Opscene*
 (February 1990), available at www.livenirvana.com [Dutch text]
Henderson, Justin, *Grunge: Seattle*, rev. edn (Berkeley, CA, 2016)
Hepworth, David, *A Fabulous Creation: How the LP Saved Our Lives*
 (London, 2019)
Heylin, Clinton, *Babylon's Burning: From Punk to Grunge* (London, 2007)
Higgins, J. R., 'Hell Bent for Litter', *Backlash* (November 1988), p. 1.
—, 'Mudhoney: No Nonsense Seattle Supergrunge', *Backlash* (December
 1988), p. 1
—, 'The Posies at the Attic, May 20', *Backlash* (June 1989), p. 11
Hornby, Nick, *High Fidelity* (London, 2000)
Humphrey, Clark, *Loser: The Real Seattle Music Story* [1995] (Seattle,
 WA, 2016)

Huq, Rupa, *Beyond Subculture: Pop, Youth and Identity in a Postcolonial World* (Abingdon, 2006)

Jenkins, Mark, 'L7, Love Battery's Metallic Movement', *Washington Post*, 19 June 1992, p. N18

Jones, Brian, 'The Power of a Production Myth: PJ Harvey, Steve Albini, and Gendered Notions of Recording Fidelity', *Popular Music and Society*, XXXIX/3 (2019), pp. 348–62

Jones, Nick, 'Smashing Pumpkins: Fuck Off . . . We're from CHICAGO!', *Spiral Scratch*, 9–23 January 1992, p. 2

Jovanovic, Rob, *Nirvana: The Recording Sessions* (London, 2012)

Kalmar, Veronika, 'Blood Circus: My Riff's Bigger', *Backlash* (June–July 1988), p. 5

—, '*Sub Pop 200* (Sub Pop)', *Backlash* (December 1988), p. 7

—, 'TAD: God's Balls (Sub Pop)', *Backlash* (April 1989), p. 9

Kearney, Mary Celeste, *Gender and Rock* (Oxford, 2017)

Keightley, Keir, 'The Historical Consciousness of Sunshine Pop', *Journal of Popular Music Studies*, XXIII/3 (2011), pp. 343–61

—, 'Reconsidering Rock', in *The Cambridge Companion to Pop and Rock*, ed. Simon Frith, Will Straw and John Street (Cambridge, 2001), pp. 109–42

Kelly, Christina, 'Kim Gordon', in *Trouble Girls: The Rolling Stone Book of Women in Rock*, ed. Barbara O'Dair (New York, 1997), pp. 449–52

Kimmel, Michael S., *Manhood in America: A Cultural History* (New York, 1996)

King, Richard, *How Soon Is Now? The Madmen and Mavericks Who Made Independent Music, 1975–2005* (London, 2012)

King, Sam, 'Down on the Bleach', *Sounds*, 9 June 1990, pp. 20–21

Klein, Naomi, *No Logo* (London, 2005)

Korvette, Matt, 'Deaf Wish', *Sub Pop* (n.d.), www.subpop.com

Kruse, Holly, *Site and Sound: Understanding Independent Music Scenes* (New York, 2003)

—, 'Local Identity and Independent Music Scenes, Online and Off', *Popular Music and Society*, XXXIII/5 (2010), pp. 625–39

Laing, Dave, *One Chord Wonders: Power and Meaning in Punk Rock* (Milton Keynes, 1985)

'Lamefest '89 Showcases Three Sub Pop Bands', *Seattle Times*, 9 June 1989, p. 8.

Lashua, Brett, and Sara Cohen, '"A Fanzine of Record": Merseysound and Mapping Liverpool's Post-Punk Popular Musicscapes', *Punk and Post-Punk*, I/1 (2011), pp. 87–104

Lavine, Michael, and Pat Blashill, *Noise from the Underground: A Secret History of Alternative Rock* (New York, 1996)

Lipez, Zachary, 'Jensen Ward on Iron Lung: Band, Label, and Worldview', *Bandcamp Daily*, 22 November 2016, https://daily.bandcamp.com

MacDonald, Patrick, 'Heavy Metal in the Suburbs', *Seattle Times*, 12 June 1983, pp. E1 and E6
—, 'The Dead Kennedys Stay Alive Musically', *Seattle Times*, 19 October 1984, p. 12
—, 'Spotlight Aims at Sub Pop Artists', *Seattle Times*, 23 December 1988, p. 8
—, 'Mudhoney (Who?) Leapfrogs from Obscurity to Fame', *Seattle Times*, 24 March 1989, p. 8
—, 'Acts at Backstage to Preview Upcoming Albums', *Seattle Times*, 16 June 1989, p. 8
—, 'Mudhoney's Latest: Grunge Band Gets Better', *Seattle Times*, 10 November 1989, p. 6
—, 'Local Rock Group Comes Home to Play a Show', *Seattle Times*, 26 January 1990, p. 8
—, '"Ultimate Garage Band" Gets to Play in Just that Setting', *Seattle Times*, 13 July 1990, p. 10
McGonigal, Mike, 'Colored Vinyl Is for Big, Spoiled Record Babies', *Detroit Metro Times*, 3 February 2015
McLeod, Kembrew, '*1/2: A Critique of Rock Criticism in North America', *Popular Music*, xx/1 (2001), pp. 47–60.
Maerz, Jennifer, 'Fly off the Wall', *The Stranger*, 23 October 2003, www.thestranger.com
Marcus, Greil, *Lipstick Traces: A Secret History of the Twentieth Century* (Cambridge, MA, 1990)
Marin, Rick, 'Grunge: A Success Story', *New York Times*, 15 November 1992, p. 9
Masco, Maire M., *Desperate Times: The Summer of 1981: The Complete Reprint of the Seattle Underground Newspaper 'Desperate Times' with Commentary and Indexes* (Tacoma, WA, 2015)
Mawdsley, Jim, 'The Fat Man Talks', *Boiling Point* (November 1989), available at www.livenirvana.com
Middles, Mick, *Factory: The Story of the Record Label* (London, 2009)
Moores, JR, *Electric Wizards: A Tapestry of Heavy Music, 1968 to the Present* (London, 2021)
Murphy, Gareth, *Cowboys and Indies: The Epic History of the Record Industry* (London, 2015)
Novoselic, Krist, 'Bleach: Krist Novoselic Interviews Chad Channing', *Seattle Weekly*, 27 October 2009
Paphides, Pete, 'Seven Inches of Heaven', *The Guardian*, 16 November 2002, Weekend Supplement, p. 54
Pareles, Jon, 'Nirvana, the Band that Hates to Be Loved', *New York Times*, 14 November 1993, Section 2, p. 32
Pavitt, Bruce, *Sub Pop USA: The Subterranean Pop Music Anthology, 1980–1988* (Brooklyn, NY, 2015)

Peel, John, 'Pop', *The Observer*, 29 January 1989, p. 48

Pelly, Jenn, 'Review: Total Control – Typical System', *Pitchfork*, 26 June 2014, https://pitchfork.com

Perlich, Tim, 'Guitar Onslaught Nirvana's Promise', *Now*, 12 April 1990, p. 25

Pessaro, Fred, 'Don't Waste My Time: An Interview with Daniel Stewart of Total Control', *Vice Magazine*, 19 June 2016

Peterson, Charles, *Screaming Life: A Chronicle of the Seattle Music Scene* (New York, 1995)

—, *Touch Me I'm Sick* (New York, 2003)

Piepmeier, Alison, 'Why Zines Matter: Materiality and the Creation of Embodied Community', *American Periodicals*, XVIII/2 (2008), pp. 213–38

Poneman, Jonathan, liner notes to Blood Circus, *Primal Rock Therapy: Sub Pop Recordings: '88–'89* (CD release, SP177B; November 1992)

—, booklet note to *Sub Pop 1000* (SP1000, 2013)

Porter, Dave, 'Count Them, Please', *Seattle Times*, 8 January 1989, p. L2

Pouncey, Edwin, 'Put Mud in the Music', *New Musical Express*, 27 May 1989, pp. 22–3

—, 'Balling with God', *New Musical Express*, 2 September 1989, p. 8

Powers, Ann, 'Sub Pop's Silver Jubilee Celebrates 25 Years of Artisanal Music in Seattle', *The Record: Music News from NPR*, 15 July 2013, www.npr.org

Prato, Greg, *Grunge Is Dead: The Oral History of Seattle Rock Music* (Toronto, 2009)

Pregill, Medwin, 'Pus Free Pop', *Columbia Spectator*, 26 September 1991, p. 9

Price, Simon, 'Opening Time', *Melody Maker*, 9 December 1989, p. 27

Puccio, Jim, 'Seattle Syndrome Two', *Boston Rock*, 38 (March 1983), p. 37

Push, 'Mudhoney/Soundgarden: School of African and Oriental Studies, London', *Melody Maker*, 20 May 1989, p. 28

—, 'Nirvana: *Bleach* (Tupelo)', *Melody Maker*, 19 August 1989, p. 35

—, 'Nirvana: Heaven Can't Wait', *Melody Maker*, 15 December 1990, p. 39

Rees, Susan, 'This Is Bliss?', *Alternative Press*, 44 (January/February 1992), available at www.altpress.com

Reynolds, Simon, 'Various Artists: *Sub Pop 200*', *Melody Maker*, 25 February 1989, p. 29

—, *Rip It Up and Start Again: Post-Punk, 1978–1984* (London, 2005)

Robb, John, 'On the Subs Bench', *Sounds*, 22 April 1989, p. 19

—, 'White Noise White Heat', *Sounds*, 21 October 1989, pp. 18–19

Rockwell, John, 'Berlin Rocks as Musical Walls Come Down', *New York Times*, 17 November 1993, p. C9

Rose, Cynthia, 'Sub Pop: See Label for Details – An Interview with Bruce Pavitt', *Dazed and Confused* (1994), available at www.rocksbackpages.com.

Rotondi, James, 'Steve Turner Turns on the Fuzz Gun', *Guitar Player*
(February 1992), pp. 98–100

Sandford, Christopher, *Kurt Cobain* (London, 1996)

Scanlon, Ann, 'Heaven Can Wait: Nirvana', *Melody Maker*, 14 September
1991, pp. 36–7

Schultze, Tomasso, 'Nirvana', *Trust*, 19 (September 1989), available at www.
livenirvana.com [German text]

Shaw, Greg, 'Iron Butterfly: *Scorching Beauty*', *Phonograph Record* (February
1975), available at www.rocksbackpages.com

Siegel, Alan, 'When Grunge was Fake News', *The Ringer*, 8 November 2017,
www.theringer.com

Snow, Mat, 'You, My Son, Are *Weird*', *Q* (November 1993), pp. 33–6

Soulsby, Nick, *Dark Slivers: Seeing Nirvana in the Shards of Incesticide*
(London, 2012)

—, ed., *Cobain on Cobain: Interviews and Encounters* (London, 2016)

Straw, Will, 'Sizing Up Record Collections', in *Sexing the Groove: Popular
Music and Gender*, ed. Sheila Whiteley (London, 1997), pp. 3–16

Strong, Catherine, 'Grunge, Riot Grrrl and the Forgetting of Women in
Popular Culture', *Journal of Popular Culture*, XLIV/2 (2011), pp. 398–416

—, *Grunge: Music and Memory* (Abingdon, 2011)

Sullivan, Ed, 'Nirvana – *Nevermind*', *Ugly American*, 4 (Winter 1989),
available at www.uglyamericanzine.com

—, and Rob B., 'Tad/Nirvana/Mudhoney/Subpop', *Ugly American*, 4
(Winter 1989), available at www.uglyamericanzine.com

Sutton, Terri, 'The Soft Boys: The New Man in Rock', in *Trouble Girls: The
Rolling Stone Book of Women in Rock*, ed. Barbara O'Dair (New York,
1997), pp. 527–35

Tow, Stephen, *The Strangest Tribe: How a Group of Seattle Rock Bands
Invented Grunge* (Seattle, WA, 2011)

True, Everett, 'The Damenbusters', *Melody Maker*, 7 January 1989, pp. 30–31

—, 'Sub Pop, Sub Normal, Subversion: Mudhoney', *Melody Maker*,
11 March 1989, pp. 28–9

—, 'Sub Pop. Seattle: Rock City', *Melody Maker*, 18 March 1989, pp. 26–7

—, 'Soundgarden: The Mutate Gallery', *Melody Maker*, 10 June 1989, p. 10.

—, 'Nirvana: Bleached Wails', *Melody Maker*, 21 October 1989, p. 47

—, 'Screaming Trees/TAD/Nirvana: Pine Street Theatre, Portland, USA',
Melody Maker, 3 March 1990, p. 20

—, 'The Larder They Come: TAD and Nirvana', *Melody Maker*, 17 March
1990, pp. 12–13

—, 'In My Head I'm So Ugly', *Melody Maker*, 18 July 1992, pp. 24–6

—, (as 'The Reverend True'), booklet essay for *Sub Pop Employee of the
Month: Lutz R. Mastmeyer* (SP111/287, 1993).

—, *Live through This: American Rock Music in the Nineties* (London, 2001)

—, 'Nirvana: The Betrayal of Olympia', *Plan B* (May 2005), pp. 54–7

—, 'Ten Myths about Grunge, Nirvana and Kurt Cobain', *The Guardian*, 24 August 2011, p. 22

Ulrich, John M., and Andrea L. Harris, eds, *GenXegesis: Essays on Alternative Youth (Sub)Culture* (Madison, WI, 2003)

Vee, Tesco, and Dave Stimson, *Touch and Go: The Complete Hardcore Punk Zine '79–'83* (Brooklyn, NY, 2010)

Waksman, Steve, *Instruments of Desire: The Electric Guitar and the Shaping of Musical Experience* (Cambridge, MA, 2001)

—, *This Ain't the Summer of Love: Conflict and Crossover in Heavy Metal and Punk* (Berkeley and Los Angeles, CA, 2009)

Wells, Steven, 'Dweeb Will, Dweeb Will Rock You!', *New Musical Express*, 7 July 1990, pp. 28–9

—, 'Espresso Way to Your Skull', *New Musical Express*, 18 July 1992, pp. 46–7

West, Phil, 'Hair Swinging Neanderthals', *The Daily* [University of Washington], 5 May 1989, available at www.livenirvana.com

—, 'The Heaviest HUB Show in History', *The Daily* [University of Washington], 5 January 1990, pp. 7A and 7C.

—, 'TAD: *Salt Lick* (SubPop)', *Backlash* (February 1990), p. 8

White, Timothy, 'What Do Joey Ramone's Mum and Dad Think of Their Little Boy? . . .', *Sounds*, 3 February 1979, pp. 25–7

Wilkinson, Roy, 'Soundgarden: Sonic Bloom Boys', *Sounds*, 11 February 1989, p. 18

—, 'Snap, Crackle and Sub Pop', *Sounds*, 22 April 1989, p. 18

—, 'Tad: *God's Balls* (Sub Pop SP27)', *Sounds*, 6 May 1989, p. 32

—, 'Nirvana/TAD/The Cateran: London SOAS', *Sounds*, 4 November 1989, pp. 40–41

—, 'A Load of Tony Baloney', *Sounds*, 1 September 1990, p. 16

Wurtzel, Elizabeth, 'Mudhoney Can't Sell Out', *Musician* (January 1991), available at www.ocf.berkeley.edu

Yarm, Mark, *Everybody Loves Our Town: A History of Grunge* (London, 2011)

Zabel, Sebastian, 'Sweet wie Hönig: Nirvana', *Spex* (December 1989), available at www.livenirvana.com [German text]

The items listed above inevitably represent only part of the resources on which I have drawn in writing this book. There are numerous other kinds of media that have also proven important, in addition to the original records, tapes, CDs and the many inserts that came with them. Documentary films about Seattle rock in the 1980s and early '90s, for example, were invaluable. Doug Pray's *Hype!* (1996) is only the most famous. The band retrospectives *TAD: Busted Circuits and Ringing Ears* (dir. Adam Pease and Ryan Short, 2008), *I'm Now: The Story of Mudhoney* (dir. Pease and Short, 2012), and *L7: Pretend We're Dead* (dir. Sarah Price, 2016) also provided useful quotations and information, as did Alan Zweig's *Vinyl* (2000) on the subject of record collecting. As its title suggests, the PBS documentary *Remarkable People Making a Difference in the Northwest: At Home with Sub Pop* (prod. Jean Walkinshaw, 1993) comes out somewhere between documentary and mockumentary, driven largely by the performances of Pavitt and Poneman. Cameron Crowe's feature film *Singles* (1992) is worth watching again for its musical parodies of grunge.

The official Sub Pop website (www.subpop.com) incorporates unique copy on bands and releases past and present, and a complete back catalogue of sorts. Detailed information on numbers and colours of records in a pressing, though once available, has now been removed, presumably to streamline the site in the interests of the majority of consumers (or perhaps, as I say in the main text, to preserve some of the mystique that excites Sub Pop collectors). The official podcast (http://subpop.fm) also has one or two episodes that look back over the label's work in the 1980s and '90s. Other useful podcasts include *Music-Life-Radio* (www.musicliferadio.com), most of all the episodes that treat more obscure Sub Pop artists: the long two-part interview with the Blood Circus guitarist Geoff Robinson (April 2012), for example, and the interview with Dwarves' guitarist He Who Cannot Be Named (October 2016). The You Don't Know Mojack podcast (https://soundcloud.com/mojackpod) is working steadily through every release by SST, catalogue number by catalogue number, and often sheds light on the late 1980s context for Sub Pop. Bruce Pavitt's own website (https://brucepavitt.com) has links to several recent interviews in which he has taken part.

For information on Sub Pop record collecting, and records released by comparable indie labels, there is always the crowdsourced Discogs (www. discogs.com). But John Pette's detailed discographies (www.pettediscographies. com) have proven just as essential, bringing together Pette's personal research, statistics now absent from the Sub Pop website, and knowledge, myths and rumours from within the 'collectors' community'. Marketplaces like eBay (and, again, Discogs), as well as auction-report sites like Worthpoint and Popsike, have also provided a few ideas, although certain claims – the current value of a particular record, for example – are inevitably dubious and subject to all kinds of inflationary pressures. Other claims made on these kinds of sites – the specific promotional materials and inserts, for instance, that a vendor received with their record when they bought it 'in Seattle in 1989' – are often very difficult to verify and so only of limited use in building up a historical account.

The Berkeley Mudhoney site (www.ocf.berkeley.edu/~ptn/mudhoney) is essential for information about that particular band, and includes transcriptions of magazine articles and interviews that would be difficult to access anywhere else. Livenirvana! (www.livenirvana.com) is even more extensive for Nirvana. Nothing similar currently exists for TAD, though there is Thomas A. Doyle's impressive website, which does have numerous write-ups of his place in grunge history (www.taddoyle.com). Rock's Backpages (www. rocksbackpages.com) provides access to transcriptions of selected articles from the major music press (*Rolling Stone, Mojo, Melody Maker, Sounds, NME*), all of which can also be found easily in hard copy in libraries. Full runs of smaller-scale periodicals, like Seattle's *Rocket*, are held in one or two regional library collections. Detailed sleeve notes, sometimes including artist interviews, are common in remasterings and re-releases, not least Sub Pop's recent Loser Editions.

Finally, throughout the book I refer to numerous fanzines and small music magazines, such as *Ugly American, Matter, Lime Lizard, Spiral Scratch, Spex, Backlash* and *Backfire*. Of these I have seen a few issues, or parts of issues, but never a complete run. In many cases I am not convinced that a complete set of issues still exists, except perhaps in private hands. Fanzines have simply not been collected and preserved and fetishized in the same way that records have been, even by those who created them in the first place; following, in some cases, their own aesthetic and rhetoric, they have been treated as disposable cultural ephemera, which runs counter to their importance in the discourse of grunge and alternative rock and frustrates academic and broader public interest in them. There are, of course, exceptions, and gaps may be filled in one day soon. Bruce Pavitt's *Subterranean Pop* fanzine and *Sub Pop USA* column, thanks in part to scans provided by the Museum of Pop Culture in Seattle, are now available in full in the glossy print volume cited above. So is *Desperate Times*, most famous for Mark Arm's July 1981 letter with the phrase 'Pure grunge!' in it. And so is the *Touch and Go* fanzine that preceded the label of the same name. The project to digitize the important Californian fanzine *Maximumrocknroll* in its entirety appears to have stopped for the time being due to legal wrangles and staffing issues, though some issues are available (https://maximumrocknroll.com/archive). More successfully, the Circulation Zero project (https://circulationzero.com) currently provides full electronic access to five punk zines of the late 1970s and early '80s from both coasts, some of them complete.

One response to these problems of access has been provided by various forums and online groups, where users who own copies of these fanzines (as well as all kinds of other paraphernalia from the era) can post images of them, sometimes including articles in their entirety. The Facebook Pacific Northwest Music Archives group, and Dawn Anderson's Backlash/Backfire group, are particularly good for this, even if dates and issue/page numbers of articles are sometimes missing from posts, making the materials difficult to place. I have also found that, wherever possible, it is worth tracing quotations in the secondary literature back to their apparent sources. There is at least one common quotation about grunge that, though transmitted between authors and found in almost every piece of writing on the subject, leads back to nothing at all; it is not clear whom it came from, or where, or when. It is that kind of world.

ACKNOWLEDGEMENTS

First, my thanks to Dave Watkins, David Hayden, Phoebe Colley, Emma Devlin and their colleagues at Reaktion for liking the idea for the book and for supporting the research and writing process. My thanks also to Jacob McMurray, Katherine Hughes and staff at MOPOP (Museum of Pop Culture; formerly the Experience Music Project) in Seattle for assisting with sources and other vital information.

Adam Lyon and colleagues at the Seattle Museum of History and Industry (Sophie Frye Bass Library) went above and beyond to find me obscure things I needed, as did John LaMont and staff in the Special Collections Department at the Seattle Public Library. My special thanks to them, and to staff at the Rubenstein Library at Duke University and the British Library (especially Humanities and Music and Rare Books) in London.

Finally, I am very grateful to the draft's readers, and to Kat Hyde, Mike Sadd and Tom McTague for their help and advice; also to Steve Double, Alice Wheeler, Anthony McAndrew at Camera Press, and especially to Bruce Pavitt and Michael Lavine.

Parts of Chapter One appeared previously under the title 'From Punk into Pop (via Hardcore): Re-Reading the *Sub Pop* Manifesto' in the Intellect journal *Punk and Post-Punk*, x/3 (October 2021), pp. 355–71.

PHOTO ACKNOWLEDGEMENTS

The author and publishers wish to express their thanks to the sources listed below for illustrative material and/or permission to reproduce it:

© Steve Double/Camera Press: p. 26; © Michael Lavine: pp. 70, 83, 113, 116, 142, 171, 185, 231; © Bruce Pavitt, from *Sub Pop USA: The Subterranean Pop Music Anthology, 1980–1988* (New York: Bazillion Points, 2014): p. 45; © Ed Sirrs/Camera Press: pp. 180, 209.

INDEX